The Letters of
Nunnally Johnson

The Letters of
NUNNALLY JOHNSON

Selected and edited by
Dorris Johnson
and Ellen Leventhal

Foreword by
Alistair Cooke

ALFRED A. KNOPF   NEW YORK   1981

THIS IS A BORZOI BOOK
PUBLISHED BY ALFRED A. KNOPF, INC.

Copyright © 1981 by Dorris Johnson
Foreword © 1981 by Alistair Cooke
Introduction © 1981 by Ellen Leventhal

All rights reserved under International
and Pan-American Copyright Conventions.
Published in the United States by Alfred A. Knopf, Inc.,
New York, and simultaneously in Canada
by Random House of Canada Limited, Toronto.
Distributed by Random House, Inc., New York.

Library of Congress Cataloging in Publication Data
Johnson, Nunnally.
The letters of Nunnally Johnson.
1. Johnson, Nunnally—Correspondence.
2. Screen writers—United States—Correspondence.
3. Moving-picture producers and directors—
United States—Correspondence. I. Johnson, Dorris.
II. Leventhal, Ellen. III. Title.
PS3519.O2834Z48 1981 812'.52 [B] 81–2479
ISBN 0–394–50672–3 AACR2

Manufactured in the United States of America
First Edition

As your dad frequently said:
Dorris sends love to
Christie, Roxie, and Scott

Contents

Acknowledgments

Early in our marriage Nunnally found an occasion to say to me, "When a man is sitting staring out of a window, no wife will believe he is hard at work." I learned that he could be hard at work while staring into space or shrouding himself in silence for days at a time, and also when he was talking to his typewriter. He did that when he wrote dialogue for the benefit of his discerning ear. If it failed the hearing test, a new start was made. Dialogue had to sound as if you were overhearing people talk. He never let the written word try to outsmart his ear. Story and characters had to advance with every word and line without ignoring brevity and clarity.

Frustrations usually developed when the script left his type-writer. The realities of casting and production frequently dismayed and disappointed him, but if a director, actor, or editor added something that improved the story, he became excited and stimulated by it.

Commercial success or failure of a film seemed to interest him very little. Once he had told a story in an acceptable script he felt the marketing was up to those who understood that field. There was a kind of childlike surprise and pleasure when he had a box-office success—and he had many—but he only felt responsible for the script. He liked to hear that a film he had written made money, but money making was another profession distinctly apart from his own, which was writing. Joe Schenck once said of him, "All Nunnally knows about money is that he wants more of it."

This book of letters is intended to preserve and share something of Nunnally's wit and personality. It documents many of the frustrations and triumphs of almost forty years of film making.

Letter writing, a once flourishing literary form, now all but lost, reveals the writer more sharply than it does those people and matters written about. So it is here: an unintentional self-portrait.

I would like to express thanks to our friend and editor Sylvia

Dudley for her hard work in sorting out thousands of letters and doing it with occasional peals of reassuring laughter; to Betty Stewart for twenty-five years of devoted service as Nunnally's secretary and my indispensable guide through the letter files; to Marvin Josephson, head of International Creative Management, John Sterling, a sensitive and decisive man, and his able successor, Maggie Curran, for helpful counsel.

Victoria Wilson of Knopf supervised the results of Ellen Leventhal's disciplined work. Tom Stempel's *Oral Biography of Nunnally Johnson* was a source of help and reference covering most of Nunnally's professional life.

When I read Alistair Cooke's foreword to this book, I was relieved of a nagging uncertainty about my decision to publish these letters. Only a long-standing friend possessed of insight and having a gift for expression could have written this tribute. The book is enriched by his understanding of Nunnally. My appreciation to this treasured friend is deep and genuine.

To each of these people I am deeply indebted and genuinely grateful.

Dorris Johnson

Foreword

Mr. Pepys in Hollywood

Early in 1957 I had a letter from Nunnally Johnson, asking me to do the narration for his movie *The Three Faces of Eve*. My wife and I went out to Hollywood in the spring, and that was the beginning of a friendship, and a correspondence between the parties of the first part, that never flagged till the day Nunnally died.

His letters were so sprightly and tender at the same time that I began to file them away—along with a collection of playful or confessional letters from the great and near-great—in a manila folder labeled TEARS AND WHIMSY. Pretty soon, however, the man's pawky originality confirmed somebody's description of him as "Robert Benchley with a Georgia accent" and I started a file for him alone. As the years went by and the letters came bubbling out of Hollywood, various European way-stations, then London, then Hollywood again, the notion dawned on me, not without a flash of guilt, that they might one day make a charming book.

However, one time, when Nunnally was already semi-housebound with the "nuisance" of his emphysema, we were talking about the provision in W. H. Auden's will that all his private correspondence be destroyed. I thought this reasonable but odd. Nunnally defended it with some heat. "A man's letters," he said, "belong to only two people: himself and the person on the receiving end." Mentally, I abandoned my project for the Johnson book and buried the fat file of his humor in some forgotten place from which, unfortunately, I have never managed to exhume it.

When Dorris Johnson, his widow, announced she was going to make a collection of his letters, I was at once startled and relieved. Startled out of my conceit that I was the lone beneficiary of his passing thoughts (without ever saying it, Nunnally could make any one of his correspondents believe he or she was his sole confidant). And relieved to discover that he had evidently made and kept copies of most of his letters, whether formal or intimate. If a man has no thought of later publication, this is something he will not do. I have to believe that he had recanted his original devotion to the privacy principle, and that his defense of Auden's request was a simple conviction that a dying man's wishes ought to be respected. No such request was made in Nunnally's will. And by now I am convinced he would not only have approved this collection. In his modest way, he would have been proud of it.

He would have cause. For, beyond the record of a gifted man's joys, troubles, escapades, and affections, what this has turned into also is an insider's diary of the fun, the guile, the allegiances and enmities, the social habits and pretensions of the movie colony for thirty years or more in the middle of the twentieth century. As such, it is—I now realize—a large slice of social history more dependable and revealing than the shelf of books I happen to house on the history of Hollywood during those years, just as Harold Nicolson's diaries and letters surpass the official memoirs in their capacity to make the reader feel what it was like to be a Londoner during the grandeurs and miseries of the Second World War. Nunnally would be astonished to hear that three centuries after Pepys, and more than two after the Defoe of the *Plague Year* journal, he is at one with them as a social historian of the first cut.

What sort of unpretentious man could stumble into this sort of eminence? In his splendid taped memoir of Nunnally, Tom Stempel makes the shrewd point that a small-town boy from Georgia who had lived through a Norman Rockwell childhood ("that is why Norman Rockwell is my favorite painter") took away with him "the values he was escaping from. Throughout his life, there was a tension between the desire for the order and stability represented by the idea of home and the excitement and adventure represented by the idea of escape." This is a conflict familiar enough in the lives of small-town boys who intend not so much to move into the big city as to invade and conquer it. Many of them who make it resolve the conflict—or mask it—in uneasy comfort or fussy spending (what the food and fashion editors call "sophistication"). Few of them resolve it, as Nunnally did, in engaging self-mockery. He was too intelligent to pretend to a cosmopolitanism he was uncomfortable with: he was suspicious of what he called "highbrow" literature, and on the plane of day-to-day living he never quite got over the riches and the big house. And his observation was too ruthless to let him fall back on sentimental comparisons between the old fish-fry and the Holly-wood bash.

Like many another Southerner, he maintained a surface courtesy and tact behind which glowed an owl-like skepticism about human motives, whether in Columbus, Georgia, or Beverly Hills, California. With a slight shift in his genes, he could have been a bitter man. But he had the luck of his inheritance and his gifts: a wry, uninhibited humor from his father, and a prose style of great clarity he developed on his own. He relaxed Stempel's "tension" by the highly successful device of adopting, in a flashy and cynical society, a pose not very different from that with which two other small-town boys, Mark Twain and James Thurber, were able to cope with rich and com-plicated people and also to earn their applause. Nunnally rendered himself no threat to anybody by adopting, as a second nature, the air of a bewildered mouse in a world of tigers and jaguars. I believe this book will reveal him, to an audience much larger than that of his fortunate cronies, as a remarkable American humorist.

Alistair Cooke

The Letters of
Nunnally Johnson

Introduction

Nunnally Johnson, in an oral history recorded for UCLA's film department, described himself and his work: "What I am doing, and have done—I have developed . . . 'facility' is too much of a word, but an ability to convert a piece of property . . . from its original form into a moving-picture form. I generally say when I do well I am like a first-rate cabinetmaker. . . . I have been able to work [the material] into an acceptable form. Sometimes it turns out good, sometimes I was mistaken and it didn't turn out so good."

During his more than thirty years in Hollywood, Nunnally Johnson wrote over fifty screenplays, and produced and directed both his own works and the works of others. He was a master stylist, a man whose screenplays were almost always acceptable to both the studio executives for whom he worked and the audiences for whom he wrote. In 1959 Johnson received the Laurel Award from the Writers Guild of America West for his lasting contributions to the literature of the screen.

For much of his career, Johnson commanded one of the highest salaries paid to a screenwriter, and was one of the few writers who consistently received solo screen credit: "I couldn't understand being dependent on anybody any more than I could stand a collaboration on a short story or a collaboration in a book. You do it yourself. I thought it should be done that way, and I managed to make it stick. I got the money, but the triumph was more that I was entrusted with the whole thing. . . . I just didn't want to be in any position where I was suddenly out because the fellow with me hadn't provided. If I failed, I'd failed by myself, and if it was successful, I wanted it my success, not somebody else's."

The letters collected here have been selected from a larger group provided by Dorris Bowdon Johnson, Nunnally's wife of thirty-seven years, and arranged and edited to reflect his life and work. Because his early letters were not saved, I have relied on the UCLA oral history conducted by Tom Stempel for much of the information concerning that part of his career in Hollywood in the 1930s and 1940s, and for the quotations used in the annotations to the letters.

Nunnally Johnson was born in Columbus, Georgia, in 1897. As a young man he worked briefly on his hometown newspaper, the Columbus *Enquirer-Sun*, failed to break into big-city journalism in Cleveland, where he eventually worked in a steel mill to support himself, and returned to Georgia for a brief stint on the Savannah *Press*.

During World War I Nunnally served in the army as a second lieutenant. There was a corporal in his outfit who knew someone on the New York *Tribune*. Nunnally persuaded the corporal to give him a letter of recommendation, and once out of the army he headed for New York and landed a job at the *Tribune*. The return of more seasoned reporters in 1919 sent him job-hunting again.

His work as a reporter on the Brooklyn *Daily Eagle* grew into a position as a columnist, and in Johnson's "One Word After Another" his skill at weaving light-hearted, highly readable copy about real people began to emerge. Johnson also met and married his first wife, Alice, a fellow reporter on the *Eagle*. Their daughter, Marjorie, was born in 1920, and shortly after, the couple separated.

In the 1920s Johnson worked and drank with a large group of bright men and women. He developed solid and long-lasting friendships with Frank Sullivan, Stanley Walker (then city editor of the *Tribune*, later managing editor of *The New Yorker*), James Thurber, Harold Ross, Herman Mankiewicz, and others.

Johnson married again in 1926. Although, like his first marriage, it was rocky and unpredictable, it lasted longer, and Johnson's second daughter, Nora, was born in 1933.

In 1926 Herman Mankiewicz, drama critic for the *New York Times*, had gone to Hollywood to join the purveyors of popular culture at Paramount Pictures. Johnson's contact with motion pictures up to that time was minimal. He had written some scenes for Frank Capra's silent movie *For the Love of Mike* when Capra was filming in New York. Mankiewicz's glowing reports of the money to be made (and the startling lack of competition) persuaded several New York writers to join him, and Johnson spent six weeks in Hollywood. He later recalled: "A fellow took me in his office and he said, 'Look, here are our stars: Richard Dix, Adolphe Menjou, Richard Arlen. Now we want you to do this: pick out one of the stars and do a story for him.' I may have tried a story. I don't know. My memory fails me as to what I did. It seemed to me the six weeks passed, and I can't even remember how much I was getting. . . ." He returned to New York to write a column for the New York *Evening Post.* (James Thurber recalled this assignment in *The Years with Ross*: "Nunnally had been brought in to do the paper's daily column 'Around the Town,' which I had wanted, but the city editor had said we need a man with a name to write that column.")

During the late 1920s Johnson also began to pursue more intensely his interest in writing short stories. Magazines were so plentiful during this period that fledgling writers could conceivably earn a respectable living by turning out appropriate pieces for a given magazine. Johnson published several stories in H. L. Mencken and George Jean Nathan's *Smart Set*, and in 1932 began a freelance career as a writer for the *Saturday Evening Post.* His short-story writing progressed so favorably, and profitably, that he eventually gave up his newspaper work entirely.

In 1969 Johnson recalled his years as a short-story writer.

> I sold my first short story about 1924 or 1925, when I was a newspaperman on the Brooklyn *Daily Eagle*. . . . I was covering an example of that wonderful nonsense that characterized the '20s in New York, the visit of a French guru named Dr. Coué, whose contribution to philosophic thought was, "Every day, in every way, I am getting better and better. . . ."
>
> Among the other reporters assigned to this story was a young woman named Catherine Brody, from the *Globe*, an afternoon paper now long gone. Through her I met another young woman from the *Globe*, Marian Spitzer. It turned out that both of these girls had sold short stories to the *Smart Set*. . . . With the exception of the *American Mercury*, which Mencken and Nathan subsequently edited, I know of no magazine that was so honored and respected by the more pretentious young writers of that day. At their suggestion I wrote my first story and one of them took it in to Nathan. A few days later I received an acceptance in the form of a most courteous note. . . .
>
> My only recollection of it is that it involved a suicide. . . . Nathan claimed that all first stories by ambitious young humorists involved a suicide. This was unhappily the *Smart Set*'s last year, but I believe I sold it five or six other stories before it expired.

For a while I made no more effort at short-story writing. Without the *Smart Set* I felt lost and hopeless. But before the year ended I had sold one to the *Saturday Evening Post*. An oddity about this sale was that I had sent it in direct [sometime earlier] and it had come back ditto. Now again I was persuaded that this was no field for me. But again at the insistence of Catherine and Marian a literary agent, Otto K. Liveright, took an interest in what I might be able to do. Had I anything to show him? Only the story that had been rejected. Let me have it, he said. Taken again to the *Saturday Evening Post*, this time it was accepted. "Johnson has submitted stuff to us before," one of the editors told Liveright, "but nothing as good as this one."

For something like ten years thereafter I sold stories quite steadily to the *Post*, some fiction, some humorous articles. In fact, I appeared so constantly there that it became a legend that I had never had a rejection, that in fact I had sold the *Post* something like a hundred stories without ever having one returned. There was never a faultier legend.

It was also a distinction to be known as a *Saturday Evening Post* writer, though not in the sense that it was a distinction to appear in the *Smart Set*. The latter had an intellectual, or perhaps more accurately a sophisticated distinction. . . .

But there was also an annoying aspect to writing for the *Post*. It was such a mighty power and it had such arrogance that a writer identified with it could not offer his stuff elsewhere even when it had been rejected. That is, not to *Collier's* or *Liberty* or any other weekly magazine. No objection was made to offering it to a monthly magazine, the *Cosmopolitan* or the *Redbook*, for examples, but the writer was given to understand that any sale to another weekly might very well result in narrowing the strike zone. A loyal *Post* writer, so he was given to understand, was often the beneficiary of a pitch that just caught the corner. One who so ignored this tacit rule would have to deliver straight down the middle every time thereafter.

As it happened, my consistency spared me more than two or three of these bad calls, and since the *Post* lifted the price from time to time I was not bothered by it. . . .

Not long ago I discussed with Paul Gallico a decision that we made at the same time. We were both working for newspapers and there are few things so attractive to anyone, even a writer, as a steady weekly salary check. Paul, who was sports editor of the *Daily News*, was getting more money than I, but the character of the decision was the same. Should we hang on to our jobs and thus have less time to write magazine stuff or should we throw caution to the wind, take a walk, and trust to God and magazine editors that we would be able to live at least as well as we had been living? And without being aware of it at the time, we made the same decision. We left our papers.

I doubt that Gallico ever had any reason to regret his venture into freelance writing, but presently along came 1932, and in 1932, as a part of the Depression, the *Saturday Evening Post* grew thinner and thinner. The big advertising contracts signed during the happy '20s were coming to an end and were not being renewed. And a magazine's content is measured by the volume of its advertising. Where at one time there were as many as twelve short stories in an issue of the *Post*, there were issues now, in 1932, that carried but three. If my calculations are correct, this cut my own personal market down as much as 75%, and at that time the short-story business was made up of some fast company. To name but a few, there were Lardner, Tarkington, Fitzgerald, J. P. Marquand, and a dozen other exceptionally able storytellers. That summer I got a feeling that more of my stories were being rejected than I had submitted. . . .

This was when I was forced to consider returning to newspaper work, assuming I could still get a job there, but before I could return to a city room I was offered a job in Hollywood.

Merritt Hulburd, a former *Saturday Evening Post* editor, was working as story editor at Paramount. His offer of a job at Paramount persuaded Johnson and his wife, Marion, to move to California. Johnson felt that his background as a short-story writer helped him develop his screenwriting skills.

The short stories were very good training because a novel doesn't have to have a form, really. . . . With short-story writing it has to be a poem. The kind of short-story writing I did was: you tell the situation, you develop it as well as you can, and then you have a solution at the end. . . . And that's the pattern of the movies, that you open up, as they say, with a long shot into the characters, set up the situation, build it up, and then at the end you have some sort of resolution. Now that's the standard way and you have to learn the standard way before you can experiment and make variations on it.

In the early 1930s Hollywood still had the air of a colony about it. Self-contained, and for the most part self-interested, its social structure was solidly based on its business structure; social strata were defined in terms of weekly paychecks. But even this self-enclosed community was not immune to the Depression. By 1933 one third of the nation's movie theaters had closed.

Under Roosevelt's National Industrial Recovery Act, the studios cut employees' salaries across the board. In order to counter demands for higher salaries, they instituted strict regulations binding their employees even closer to the individual studio: limitations were placed on what one studio could bid for the services of someone under contract at another studio, effectively discouraging employees from "looking around." It was not until 1938 that the Screen Writers Guild was certified by the National Labor Relations Board, giving the Guild full status as arbiter in screen-credit disputes and allowing it to establish minimum wages.

Out of the economic confusion of this period emerged the men who would keep Hollywood going. Many early industry leaders toppled under economic strains, and a younger group of men took over. Darryl Zanuck at Warner Bros. emerged as one of the strongest.

Zanuck began his movie career as a scriptwriter for Fox Films in 1923, moved to Warner Bros. in 1924, and became the well-paid, much-valued writer for Warner Bros.' highly successful Rin-Tin-Tin series. Within three years Zanuck was made head of his own production unit, shared in Warner Bros.' profits, and supervised the total Warner Bros. production schedule. Under his control, the studio developed an efficient formula for movie-making—a Warner Bros. movie was inexpensively made, it was fast-paced and action-filled— and Zanuck's abilities to turn out movies quickly enhanced his reputation as a producer.

In 1933, following a dispute with Harry Warner, Zanuck was approached by Joseph Schenck of United Artists about starting a production company, and readily accepted the offer. With William Goetz (then L. B. Mayer's son-in-law and a producer at RKO), they formed 20th Century Pictures to produce films for United Artists to distribute.

Zanuck was especially adept at selecting the right story; he also had the ability to get the right talent together for any given project. Perhaps because he had begun his own career as a writer, he had a respect for and understanding of writers that was unusual among Hollywood producers. When 20th Century was beginning its production schedule, Nunnally Johnson had already written *A Bedtime*

Story (1933) and *Papa Loves Mama* (1933) for Paramount. Zanuck asked him to join his company. It was the beginning of an association that would last more than thirty years. Johnson gave this evaluation of their relationship:

> Zanuck was, you might say, happy as a lark with me. He saw he had to get out thirty or forty pictures a year and he delegated authority in a way, but he kept a tight rein on everybody. . . . To be able to make thirty pictures, he must have about ninety sets of people engaged on this script or that script. So, better or worse, he liked me, because he'd hand me the stuff, and he didn't have to see me again for ten or twelve weeks. He didn't have to bother about that at all. Not that I was going to bring him a perfect script, because I wasn't. But it was easier to pick up a script which he found out from experience wouldn't be a disaster. It would have the form or shape and it may have many faults, but one session, you know, and maybe a second session later, would take care of it and so that became our way of working.

Johnson's first movie for Zanuck, *Moulin Rouge*, was released in 1934. It was a rewrite of another movie; as Johnson said in later years, "Zanuck was a nut on rewriting and redoing things." Johnson's next two films, *Bulldog Drummond Strikes Back* (1934) and *The House of Rothschild* (1934), were among the first big successes of 20th Century.

At the beginning Johnson was hesitant about working on *The House of Rothschild*. He recalled, "This is a dramatic story. All my characters are liable to fall into flour barrels and things like that. I write kind of low comedy." With Zanuck's encouragement, however, Johnson produced a remarkably moving script. It was Johnson's first dramatic picture and it was also one of the first movies to deal directly with anti-Semitism. "[Zanuck] thought it would make a dramatic picture on a subject which at that time, 1933, was the beginning of the Hitler thing. . . . It was an electric subject."

During this period Johnson wrote *Kid Millions* for Samuel Goldwyn. Again he got along well with the producer, appreciating Goldwyn's constant contact with every step of production.

He returned to historical drama with *Cardinal Richelieu* (1935), a less happy and less successful experience than *The House of Rothschild*. George Arliss—20th Century's "house impersonator"—and his coach, Maude Howell, continually rewrote the script, and although Zanuck lent his support to Johnson, Johnson eventually asked to have his name removed from the credits.

In 1935 20th Century merged with Fox Films, and Darryl Zanuck was made vice-president and chief of production. Although Fox had been one of the early sound pioneers, with good facilities and an elaborate distribution network, its films simply hadn't attracted audiences. The talent and the organization that characterized 20th Century were what Fox needed.

Zanuck and other producers in the 1930s recognized that American history and literature provided a huge source of story ideas. Re-creating history in big-budget movies with big-name stars was a surefire way of showing America's greatness while at the same time attracting big audiences.

Nunnally Johnson wrote two such historical dramas, both concerned with the Reconstruction period. *The Prisoner of Shark Island* (1936), directed by John Ford, was the story of Dr. Samuel Mudd, the man who set John Wilkes Booth's leg after the Lincoln assassination. The screenplay was inspired by a story about Mudd that Zanuck had read in *Time*. As in other movies of the period, good and evil were sharply defined. But the sympathetic attitude toward a man vilified by history was unusual.

Johnson's other foray into American history was *Jesse James* (1939). Again dealing with a curious choice of hero, Johnson was able to establish audience sympathy by stressing the injustices the James brothers suffered before becoming outlaws. And with Tyrone Power in the title role, it was not difficult for audiences to decide where their support should lie. The rather negative depiction of the "establishment" was an unusual emphasis for the time. But by portraying Jesse James as a heroic individual fighting the indifference and cruelty of big business (in this case, the railroads), Johnson hit upon a theme to which Depression audiences could readily relate.

Johnson also wrote and produced *Wife, Husband and Friend* (1939) and *Rose of Washington Square* (1939), and devoted some of his time to producing films by other screenwriters. He produced Shirley Temple's *Dimples* (1936) and nursed William Faulkner through the script for *The Road to Glory* (1936) ("I don't suppose that there were forty lines Bill wrote that we could use, and I don't think he cared much. [Joel] Sayre wrote a good deal of it, and I think I rewrote most of it").

Although Johnson continued to produce his own screenplays, he soon stopped producing the works of other writers.

> In addition to a picture that I was writing, I became responsible for other pictures. I would look for stories and Zanuck would look for stories, and I'd have two or three or four pictures going and writers working. . . . This was a complete fiasco because I cannot tell people how to write. I could tell them that I was unsatisfied with it, but I was an incurable writer. I wanted to do it myself. . . . Then Darryl called me and he said, "Look, would it be all right if you just produce pictures you write yourself?" . . . After that I never tried to produce pictures with anybody else. I was just incapable, that's all. I was a writer, not only primarily, but solely.

When Zanuck bought the movie rights to John Steinbeck's *The Grapes of Wrath*, Johnson was his natural choice for screenwriter. John Ford directed.

Johnson discussed the adaptation with Steinbeck, who said, "You can make a good picture out of [it] and I hope you do, but my statement remains right here, in the book, that's all." The screenplay is a faithful adaptation of the novel; although parts were transposed to make a smoother screenplay, the only striking departure from the original was the "upbeat" ending of the movie. Steinbeck's rather pessimistic conclusion of the novel was replaced with an earlier passage, Ma Joad's stirring tribute to the American people and their ability to persevere.

The loose structure of Steinbeck's book could not be transferred intact to the movie screen. Johnson worked with what he considered the "skeleton" of the novel: "To me it was a wonderful story of people driven out by an act of nature, you might say, in the Middle West and out here [California]. I have very little to do with politics, so there was never any feeling of a picture which was aiming to do more than show the plight of some very ordinary people." He followed his cardinal rule of adaptation: "A screenwriter's duty, his loyalty, is not to the book. Whenever I work on these things, my eye is on the audience, not on the author."

John Steinbeck was pleased with the screenplay. *The Grapes of Wrath* won plaudits from audiences and critics alike, and was 20th Century–Fox's biggest hit of 1940. As Frank Nugent wrote in the *New York Times*, "In the vast library where celluloid literature of the screen is stored, there is one small, uncrowded shelf devoted to the cinema's masterpieces. To that shelf of screen classics, 20th Century–Fox yesterday added *The Grapes of Wrath*."

For Johnson, *The Grapes of Wrath* brought a more personal happiness. It strengthened his relationship with Dorris Bowdon, the actress who played Rosasharn. Johnson had first met Dorris in late 1938, after his divorce from Marion. Dorris, a native of Memphis, Tennessee, was a contract player at 20th Century–Fox when they met; she was later assigned to principal roles, and appeared in five films as a principal between 1938 and 1945.

Nunnally and Dorris married in February 1940, and remained happily married until Nunnally's death. They had three children, Christie, Roxie, and Scott.

Johnson wrote and produced eight films for 20th Century–Fox during the early years of the war, beginning with *Chad Hanna* in 1940. This movie about a small traveling-circus troupe received little attention, and was to become a family joke as Johnson's children chose to introduce him as "the man who gave you *Chad Hanna*."

Johnson once again worked with John Ford on *Tobacco Road* (1941). Zanuck had paid $200,000 for the film rights to Erskine Caldwell's novel, a large sum in those days, and Johnson approached *Tobacco Road* with a great deal of enthusiasm: "I thought I knew *Tobacco Road* and *Tobacco Road* people backwards and forwards. At least I knew their reasoning, and I think it [the screenplay] was written that way. . . . It was a hell of a lot nearer the South than *Gone with the Wind*." The film itself was a great disappointment to Johnson. He felt that Ford had wielded too much power and was particularly insensitive to the regional comedy of Caldwell's novel. Ford simply could not capture the humor of the screenplay, and Johnson maintained that his tendency to "change all the characters from crackers into Irishmen" destroyed the movie.

Released in 1942, *Roxie Hart* was a funny, breezy newspaper story that starred Ginger Rogers and Adolphe Menjou. Johnson felt that the director, in this case William Wellman, turned to a broader, cornier style than the screenplay warranted. His fondness for the screenplay is reflected in the fact that he and Dorris named their second daughter Roxanna.

Life Begins at Eight-thirty (1942), adapted from a play by Emlyn

Williams, was written for a star, Monty Woolley. Johnson wrote again for Woolley in *The Pied Piper* (1942) and in *Holy Matrimony* (1943), an adaptation of Arnold Bennett's *Buried Alive*. Johnson recognized Woolley's dependence on good material, and said, "I guess I fell into a rhythm that he liked and could do."

Two of Johnson's screenplays concerned themselves with the war. In *The Pied Piper*, which Johnson co-directed with Irving Pichel, Woolley was a man leading young children out of Europe at the start of the war. Otto Preminger had a small part as a Nazi general who enlists Woolley to take his Jewish niece out of German-occupied France.

The Moon Is Down (1943), adapted from John Steinbeck's novel, is a more serious exploration of the war. Set in Nazi-held Norway, it is for the most part fairly typical of the films of the period, expressing sympathy for an occupied ally in its depiction of the Norwegian underground. But one element is fairly unusual for a film of this kind: as in Steinbeck's book, the Nazi colonel (played by Cedric Hardwicke) is a sympathetic character. Johnson explained, "He was a soldier. He did his job. But he didn't believe in what he was doing."

Producers had great power during the early 1940s, and Johnson, with his agent, Johnny Hyde, recognized both the financial and creative benefits of independent production. In 1943 Johnson joined Leo Spitz (a wealthy Hollywood lawyer) and Bill Goetz (one of the founders of 20th Century) to form International Productions. Robert Goldstein, 20th Century–Fox's New York representative, joined as head of International's New York office. Although Zanuck offered Johnson $5,000 a week and a five-year contract in hopes of retaining him at 20th Century–Fox, Johnson thought that he had gone about as far as he could at the studio, and looked forward to a more exciting career in a company in which he was a partner.

Johnson remained at International Productions for four years. It merged with Universal in 1947, and he returned to 20th Century–Fox. There he easily resumed his working relationship with Zanuck, and continued to have the same independence and authority he had enjoyed before leaving the company. Johnson produced all his own screenplays at 20th Century–Fox—usually one or two a year—and worked with Jean Negulesco, Henry Koster, and Edmund Goulding, among other 20th Century–Fox directors. His output was quite varied: he introduced American audiences to Richard Burton in *My Cousin Rachel* (1952), shepherded in the new age of CinemaScope with *How to Marry a Millionaire* (1953), and turned the best-selling novel *The Man in the Gray Flannel Suit* (1956) into a screen portrait of suburban America.

Johnson was sole director of *Night People* (1954), and although directing was not his strongest skill, he directed several more of his own screenplays. *The Three Faces of Eve* (1957) was probably his best effort in this capacity.

When Darryl Zanuck left 20th Century–Fox in 1956, Johnson lost a great deal of the support he had depended on for most of his career. Twentieth Century–Fox and the other big studios were confronting difficult times. Johnson's dissatisfaction eventually led him to try independent production.

In 1960 he and his family moved to Rome for the filming of *The Angel Wore Red*, produced by Johnson's own company, Spectator. The company never got off the ground, but Johnson remained abroad for both personal and financial reasons. He and Dorris lived in London, where he wrote several family comedies for the screen, including the adaptation of his daughter Nora's novel *The World of Henry Orient* (1964).

Nunnally and Dorris returned to the United States in 1967 and, after a brief stay in New York, went to Hollywood, where Johnson spent the last years of his life.

Nunnally Johnson considered himself first and foremost a screenwriter, a title of which he was proud. Unlike many other screenwriters, he felt no need to "prove" himself by writing novels or plays; he worked as a producer and director more as a matter of convenience than because he had any ambitions in those areas. His skepticism about the role of a director, and his indignation at the attention directors received, underscored his belief that a well-executed, literate screenplay lies at the heart of any good movie.

As a writer during the height of the studio system in Hollywood, Johnson learned to respect the skills of a producer like Zanuck while remaining firm in his ideas of what constituted good movie-making. He was willing to share his ideas with the actors and directors with whom he worked, and in later years was a willing advisor to young writers. His honesty in dealing with the studio executives added to his professional reputation; he was known to be dependable, and he was respected for his uncompromising attitudes.

In his private life, Johnson demonstrated the same sort of integrity he brought to his work. He remained loyal to his friends, encouraging them in their work, yet offering criticism when he felt it appropriate. He had little patience for the pretensions of Hollywood, and less for its rivalries and intrigues. Although he had a wide circle of friends in Hollywood and New York who were active in liberal politics, he kept himself aloof from national politics in much the same way as he remained his own man in studio politics.

Johnson's work and his letters leave an abiding impression of a man who cared a great deal about what he was doing, and how he was doing it.

Ellen Leventhal

1944–1953

As in the early days of 20th Century before it merged with Fox, International started as a company heavily dependent on its creative energy. Its material assets were negligible: movies were produced at Samuel Goldwyn's studio, and all of International's equipment was rented. Fortunately, because of William Goetz's long record at 20th Century–Fox and Leo Spitz's good reputation in Hollywood, the new company was able to get bank financing without too much difficulty.

Nunnally Johnson wrote and produced five screenplays during his years at International. The independence he had desired was a mixed blessing: although he had greater freedom in selecting materials, neither Goetz nor Spitz provided adequate supervision, and Johnson was overwhelmed with production details, which encroached on his writing time.

Two of his films for International anticipated important post-war trends in American film-making. War refugees had arrived in Hollywood, and men such as Billy Wilder, Edgar Ulmer, and Robert Siodmak brought the techniques and themes of the Austrian and German film tradition into the Hollywood studios. Johnson's *The Woman in the Window* (1945) was one of the early examples of this influence. It owes much of its artistry to Fritz Lang's direction. Johnson's screenplay meshed well with Lang's creative techniques— night scenes and the sordid urban environment were captured with threatening intensity. The story of a little man who meets his downfall as the result of sexual temptation, it is almost a textbook example of Breen Office requirements. However, the protagonist, played by Edward G. Robinson, was a sympathetic character, and Goetz insisted on a compromise: the story is presented as a dream, though the audience doesn't know this until the very end. Johnson later said, "Eddie played it so beautifully that you accepted the fact that he had had a dream and that it had embodied people that he knew.

The audience accepted the fact that they'd been taken, because it was all in such good humor by then. . . . The comedy end really saved it, because I hate dream pictures unless you let them know in the beginning. I think it's a cheat otherwise. I didn't want to do it that way, but there it was."

Johnson's *The Dark Mirror* (1946) reflected another new aspect of American films. The war had forced people to question the very nature of evil; many had become fascinated with psychopathy and violence. In *The Dark Mirror*, the story of a psychotic twin, Olivia de Havilland played both the good twin and the evil one. Film viewers could no longer depend on "white hats" or "black hats" as clues to character. The film-makers of Hollywood had begun to confront the ambiguities of reality.

William T. (Pete) Martin, a special editor on the *Saturday Evening Post*, wrote articles on movie personalities, and often consulted with Johnson for background information and informed opinion. His series for the *Post* was collected and published as *Hollywood Without Make-up*. Martin also wrote *Will Acting Spoil Marilyn Monroe?* and worked with Bob Hope, Bing Crosby, Ethel Merman, and others on their autobiographies.

TO PETE MARTIN

March 18, 1944

Dear Pete:

The series seemed to have been received with pleasure and satisfaction out here. As for Dave Chasen, he is ecstatic. He has posters all over his restaurant about it. I sent him the original manuscript that you sent me, just for his own personal pleasure, and I am sure that he will treasure it until death takes him. My favorite so far is the King Brothers.

Of course, I could argue with you about some of the stuff in the King Brothers story. You assumed that easy and familiar position that the immensely successful companies throw their dough around like drunks and it is only the dubs like the King boys who make their pictures wisely. It wouldn't have hurt you to point out that while the King Brothers are being very shrewd and thrifty they are making bad pictures which do not make much money. In contributing to this odd legend of Hollywood Idiocy you neglected to note the fact that with all of their sagacity and economy the little independents so far represent no threat to Metro-Goldwyn-Mayer, who I assume blew money out of their ears making *Mrs. Miniver* and other such oil wells. This method of doing business may be a source of great satisfaction to the King Brothers and their mother but I don't think that the stockholders in MGM would be greatly won by it. However, I suppose it will always be impossible to convince outsiders that a moving picture company, particularly a big one, teems with bookkeepers, accountants and notary publics whose commissions never expire, all bent on seeing that each buck is spent where it will buy the most. Or I might ask you this question: If you suddenly came into possession of a major studio would you hire the King Brothers to run it?

I may be seeing you in a week or two. I am finally in a position to offer myself for some kind of Government chore for a few months and I am coming East to talk to the OWI and the OSS to see if there is anything for me. *The New Yorker* asked me to go abroad as correspondent for awhile but I couldn't accept the job at that time. I have been considering the idea of seeing if it would still be interested, or if perhaps the *Post* might have some kind of an assignment for me, so that I might get a closer view of the war, but I am rather disposed to utilize my time in what might be described as a "useful" way. I don't know how much interest I might be able to arouse in an editor after so many years, so I will not resort to that idea unless I am turned down definitely by the OWI and the OSS. In any case, there is one condition attached to my employment—I am not going to occupy any beachhead with the first wave of Marines, not at my age and with my nervous disposition. I will give you a ring when I reach New York, where I will be located at the Sherry-Netherlands Hotel.

Many thanks for your kind words about *Holy Matrimony*. The new Gary Cooper picture [*Casanova Brown*], which is almost finished, looks very good. We miss you in the officers mess and all send best regards. Give my love to the Bird Woman [Mrs. Martin].

T O   J A M E S   T H U R B E R

January 12, 1945

Dear Jim:

Just to clarify this matter, I had had a clipping of "Walter Mitty" on my desk for nearly three years. It seems that one of Harold Ross's missions in life has been to get it made into a picture. Every time he saw me in New York he attacked me with such violence that it generally took five or ten minutes for me to find out that he was denouncing me for not doing this, and about every eighteen months he sent me a vituperative letter describing me as only one idiot in an industry of idiots for not making *The Secret Life of Walter Mitty* and wound up by declaring that he was giving me one more chance to prove my membership in the human race. Enclosed always was another clipping of the story.

I must say that I have studied it over and over again in order to see how it might be reasonably expanded into a full-length picture without disturbing its remarkable quality as a short story. I heard Benchley's broadcast and thought it was very good, considering Bob's limitations as an actor, and I heard that Moss Hart had mentioned it on "Information, Please." But it was neither of these broadcasts that solved the problem for me. Last Sunday afternoon a fellow named Hy Kraft* and I were talking about it and during the conversation he made some suggestions which seemed to throw open a pair of double doors for me. I could only brood over how stupid I had been not to have seen the possibilities as they were suggested to me then by Kraft. So beginning Monday I began discussing it with Leo Spitz and Bill Goetz, my partners in this business, and they also caught on fire. It was during the heat of conflagration, while [Robert] Goldstein was trying to get you on the telephone, that we learned for the first time of the Goldwyn situation. I can't tell you how disappointed I was, after all this buildup, to find the story already claimed.

Herndon [Thurber's literary agent] was very nice about it. He consulted Goldwyn yesterday, Thursday, and it was his conclusion that while Goldwyn was still skeptical about the material a writer named Everett Freeman, on Goldwyn's payroll, is so filled with enthusiasm that Goldwyn decided to give him every opportunity to do what he could with it. My sincere hope under the circumstances is that Freeman falls flat on his tokus with it. It will take ninety days from December 19th, however, for its fate with Goldwyn to be decided.†

So for the time being there is nothing for us to do but wait. If Freeman fails to satisfy Goldwyn and the option is not taken up, Herndon says he will bring it to me, since we are prepared here to meet 20th Century–Fox's offer. My original idea was that it should be for Jack Benny and if I do it that is probably who would play it. With good direction I am certain he would get exactly the right note in it. He certainly should have done it on the radio. Bob was

---

* H. L. Kraft wrote the screenplay for *Stormy Weather*.

† Goldwyn did produce *The Secret Life of Walter Mitty*. Released in 1947, it starred Danny Kaye and had a screenplay by Everett Freeman.

good, very good, but Benny has a certain facility in front of the microphone that Bob simply hasn't got.

The first of the two pictures I am going to do this year will be *Ashenden, or the British Agent,* the old Somerset Maugham book, and I still hope that something will happen that *Walter Mitty* can be my other production. I know you did what you could about it but I have no one to blame for the disappointment but my own obtuseness. My eventual recognition of the picture possibilities in this story after about three years of study must constitute the slowest literary "take" in history.

My very best to you and Helen.

Johnson wrote two films for Gary Cooper at International. His first was *Casanova Brown* (1944). Though it was based on the play *The Little Accident* by Thomas Mitchell and Floyd Dell, Johnson altered the original considerably, keeping just the basic plot line, and eliminating, to keep within the strictures of the Breen code, an out-of-wedlock pregnancy. He later wrote *Along Came Jones* (1945), using a "straight" Western story by Alan LeMay, and transforming it into a comedy of mistaken identity. Initial hesitation about using Cooper in a comedy lead proved unfounded, though from Johnson's point of view the direction by Stuart Heisler left much to be desired.

TO WALTER KERR

June 9, 1945

Dear Walter:

I might have known that you would understand what I was trying to say in *Along Came Jones*. Almost without exception, the critics took it to be simply another account of some people trying to shoot the ass off Gary Cooper. Actually, as you saw at once, I was again using the cold, unflinching eye of the camera to probe a sick Society. Never for one second did I think of Cooper as a tramp cowhand; to me he was Western Man, eternally gallant, eternally defeated, and the picture itself one long bitter laugh at life. (I think I also had something in it about all life being an illusion and Man the victim of his own whatever it was, but I don't see how that could have fitted in, do you?) But they didn't understand *Chad Hanna* either. . . . This sort of obtuseness used to anger me, but now I just laugh. What the hell!

My best to you and yours.

Jed Harris, the Broadway producer, was a good friend of the Johnsons' and godfather of their daughter Christie. Louise Platt, Harris's wife at the time of this letter, was an actress trying her hand at playwriting. There is no record of a professional production of Platt's play.

TO JED HARRIS

November 16, 1945

Dear Jed:

Miss Louise Platt is one of the most wonderful comedy writers I have ever read. I'm in bed at the moment, cold or bronchitis or pneumonia or something, and last night I lay here and just chuckled and laughed over the script. All I could think of at times was how wonderful Louis Calhern would be as Sirus.

Is it a play or not? Obviously it needs a lot of cutting, to get rid of the waste motion and get down to the wonderful little guts of the scenes, and I wondered if the line of the story, whatever it is, couldn't be made clearer. As a picture of a delightful and wonderful family, it is first rate, but I kept losing sight of the anecdote involved, like Father's got to be christened.* I kept getting a feeling too while reading it that there was a certain pertinence, possibly somewhat remote, to a rather larger issue of the day, to wit, the Navy mind. In other words, the Blue and the Gold. I got to thinking that if it were called *The Franklin Field Spirit*, the idea might be implied. I seem to be getting in Sirus some of that stubborn, bullheaded loyalty that is making the Navy such a dangerous quantity at times. It's the same kind of mentality, somehow, that clings to battleships, sneers at air power, and puts the old Annapolis ring above everything. However, that may be soaring a little high from what Louise has written. Still, it might be worth thinking about.

I think you ought to go to Louise and ring her and and kiss her with pride, and I certainly assume that you are going to do something about getting it into proper shape for production.

Yours,

Between 1941 and 1946 the size of the movie-going audience was tremendous; figures run as high as ninety-five million attending every week. At the end of the war, the movie studios had every reason to be optimistic. After all, their stars would be coming back, their au-

* A reference to the long-running Broadway comedy *Life with Father.*

diences would be bigger than ever when the troops returned, and the foreign markets, so long unavailable, would be opened again.

However, Hollywood was about to undergo its greatest crisis; politics, the growth of the television industry, and changes in studio structure would undermine the power of the American film giants.

The most devastating blow to the industry came from the United States government in the case of *The United States* v. *Paramount et al.*, which effectively eliminated the "vertical structure" (production, distribution, and exhibition of films) the major studios had enjoyed for so long. In 1938 independent theater owners had initiated a suit objecting to the policies of block booking and claiming that studio-owned theaters got the first choice of movies. In the late 1940s the United States Supreme Court found that the movie companies with vertical structures constituted monopolies and were guilty of restraint of trade. In 1949 the Court declared that production and distribution must be separated from exhibition. One by one, the great old studios were ordered to divest themselves of their theaters.

Exportation of films had always been an easy source of profit for the studios. American films were seen all over the world. Following the war, however, many European nations were not anxious to have money leaving the country. They were also interested in building up their own film industries, which had of necessity languished during the war years. Many countries instituted quotas on the importation of American films. In addition, restrictions were placed on the amount of profit that could be taken out of the country by American corporations. Independent American producers as well as divisions of the big studios would have to work abroad to have access to these "frozen" funds.

The business of Hollywood had always been production of movies, and power struggles and dissensions ordinarily confined themselves specifically to the process of making movies (and money). To the outside world, Hollywood presented a united front.

As early as 1944, however, when the Motion Picture Alliance for the Preservation of American Ideals was created, a schism began to develop. The Motion Picture Alliance was formed by important people in the industry, including John Wayne and Ward Bond, to rid the industry of "communist" influences. For the first time, people *inside* the industry were willing to testify against their co-workers. A United States Chamber of Commerce report further divided the Hollywood community with its declaration that the Screen Writers Guild was dominated by communists, while the strikes of the craft unions in the same year were attributed, by the Motion Picture Alliance, to communist infiltration.

Any pretense of a united stand disappeared completely during the hearings of the House Un-American Activities Committee in 1947. Focusing primarily on writers, the committee ruined the careers of people on all levels. Major motion-picture producers capitulated to HUAC in their Waldorf Declaration of 1947, in which they pledged that they would not employ persons known to be communists, and condemned the Hollywood Ten, stating they "had impaired their usefulness to the industry, and were suspended without compensation."

The films of the late forties and early fifties reflected considerable reactions to this unprecedented shake-up of the status quo. The political atmosphere, hardly conducive to creative work, caused the studios not only to shun controversial people, but to avoid films that seemed to contain any sort of message.

In 1946, Ilka Chase, actress and author, had just been married to Dr. Norton Brown.

TO ILKA CHASE

November 29, 1946

Dear Ilka:

Yrs of the 16th instant rec'd and con'ts noted. Welcome, Dr. Norton Brown. Welcome, Mrs. Norton Brown. Welcome, Edna Woolman Chase [Ilka's mother, and the editor of *Vogue*]. Welcome—

Dorris already had EWC on her party list,* had got the date of her arrival from the *Vogue* office here, and only awaited her arrival to issue the bid. But to our shame, we don't know EWC's husband's name. Will you supply it? The unfortunate fact is that he is a member of the Eastern branch of what is known here as HOSA—Husbands of Stars Association. Such local members as Gene Markey [husband of Myrna Loy and previously married to Joan Bennett and Hedy Lamarr], William Dozier [husband of Joan Fontaine], Marcus Aurelius Goodrich [husband of Olivia de Havilland], will sympathize with him. On second thought, I withdraw Marcus Aurelius Goodrich. He probably thinks he still has an identity of his own. He'll learn?

* The Johnsons were having a party for *Mr. Peabody and the Mermaid*.

My picture is in *Vogue* this month. Is yours? And you with your pull!

Lawrence Schwab was a Broadway producer.

TO LAWRENCE SCHWAB

December 24, 1946

Dear Larry:

. . . This is Xmas Eve and I have no doubt that within the next hour three drunks will walk into my office and begin their conversations with, "Johnson, you've never really liked me." This will be true.

Did you hear anything about Stanley Walker in that town that I can spell but can't pronounce, Ciudad Trujillo? The last I heard of him, two or three months ago, he was bound for there, for what reason I don't know. However, I can tell you now that you are not a reporter yet. You don't write like one. You write like a trained seal. Look at your lead. "I arrived here from Miami, etc." That's the way Fannie Hurst covers a story. Who the hell cares about your arrival? Tell us about that political disturbance. Get some names. The way your story should have started was, "This tropical capital today seethed with rumors and counter-rumors of violence while the guard was doubled around the presidential palace."

Make the story stand up, or somebody's going to question your expense account. . . .

We are all sick and I hope you are not the same. A very Merry Xmas to you, Mildred and Junior.

R. G. Harrop, a bombardier in World War II, wrote Johnson that during tense moments on bombing raids over enemy territory his incantation of the name "Nunnally Johnson, Nunnally Johnson, Nunnally Johnson" created a vocal pattern that distracted him and therefore lessened his tension and fright.

TO R. G. HARROP

January 23, 1947

Dear Mr. Harrop:

Yes, I had heard the story of your use of my name and because it seemed to be about the only use I was in the war, you can imagine how amused and pleased I was. I have been trying to remember who told it to me. All I can recall is that I did not know the man very well and that he came into my office with some other friend. But I remembered the story itself in exact detail.

For your idle interest, my odd first name was also my father's. It's a fairly well known family name in Georgia, where we lived, and my father's father named his son after a business partner, one James Nunnally. Even in Georgia it was still a source of embarrassment to me. New teachers were unable to understand it at first and I was constantly having to repeat it, whereas boys named Tom, Dick, and Harry were not rendered so conspicuous.

When I began writing I became grateful for it. Johnson is no name to be remembered but having Nunnally in front of it arrested the eye and aided the memory, which is a matter of commercial importance among writers. Now I am used to it but am never long permitted to forget that it's a queer one. Many people mispronounce it and others are unable to distinguish its sex. Over the telephone I am quite often Natalie Johnson. I get letters addressed to Miss Nunnally Johnson. Once the late Ray Long, then editor of *Cosmopolitan* magazine, sent for me in the belief that I was probably a very gay, fetching young woman, which he liked, and was obviously dismayed and disappointed to find that I didn't answer to that description. Our little conference was brief.

But never, of course, has it served any useful purpose comparable to the use you made of it. I am grateful for the wild chance that flicked it into your mind at the particular moment. From now on I have some documented reason for a little pride in it.

With best regards.

The Senator Was Indiscreet was released in 1947. A collaboration by Charles MacArthur and Johnson, and directed by George S. Kaufman, it was a political parody about, as Johnson put it, "a fellow who figured he had no talent for doing anything else but be president of the United States." *Life*, which had run a favorable spread on the movie, recanted after Clare Boothe Luce saw it and declared that it was hardly "100% American." Several organizations condemned it before it opened. "It had a curious experience. It came at a time when everybody that didn't wrap the flag around himself was a commie," Johnson later said.

Herb Graffis was a columnist at the Chicago *Sun-Times*.

October 21, 1947

Dear Mr. Graffis:

May I take exception to the enclosed column on two counts, (a) prejudice and (b) ignorance.

Obviously you have no knowledge whatever about the picture called *The Senator Was Indiscreet* beyond some idle remark or newspaper comment which has come to your attention. This picture does not present "congressmen" as subjects of scorn, suspicion and ridicule; through one senator it lampoons cheap political chicanery.

While you yourself clearly feel qualified to indict Hollywood, the entire industry, for some individual project to which you object, I, as the producer of this picture, am inclined to be a little more cautious. I simply haven't that fearless confidence in my judgment and information.

For instance, I would not make a generalization about newspaper columnists based on my distaste for Westbrook Pegler. Neither the code under which moving pictures are made nor my personal inclination would permit me to indict the entire legal profession because I disapproved of the behavior of some lawyers. Nor would I, either as a reasonably cautious producer or as a citizen of this country, make any such declaration or charge against the United States Congress. It may not be a perfect thing but I know of no better form of government.

I see no reason, however, why this loyalty should stop me from making a pictorial comment on certain practices and methods of politicians any more than yours stops you from making similar comments in print. Only in totalitarian countries is it forbidden to think incorrectly about individuals, in or out of Congress. I know of no interpretation of our right to free speech which confines its aplication to writers for newspapers.

And only through ignorance or thoughtlessness could you have made your statement that Hollywood is careful not to kid itself. It has done so to the point where the whole subject has become even more tiresome than a number of others that we use. Offhand I can call your attention to *Boy Meets Girl*, *Once in a Lifetime*, made three times, *Merton of the Movies*, made two or three times, *What Price Hollywood?*, *Hollywood Cavalcade*, many parts of *A Star Is Born*, and probably a dozen others the names of which I could dig up if I thought it were necessary to prove the point. *Merton of the Movies*, doing its level best to burlesque Hollywood people and Hollywood practices, is probably playing at your neighborhood theatre this week.

The truth is that I imagine you would, and perhaps will, enjoy *The Senator Was Indiscreet,* as you might enjoy an amusing cartoon in a newspaper. I make this objection to you at this time because the matter of free speech for the movies is greatly in jeopardy, and I have read enough of your columns to be positive that you would not knowingly and willingly add to any movement which threatened to limit free speech in any medium, yours or mine. I believe that if this present effort succeeds in imposing any form of censorship on the movies its next target will be the radio and eventually the press.

Very truly yours,

In a letter to the *New York Times,* Johnson further defined his political position. Entitled "Confessions of a Confederate," it was published on December 28, 1947.

My name is Nunnally Johnson. N-u-n-n-a-l-l-y, Nunnally. I was born December 5, 1897, in Columbus, Ga., of white Methodist parents. I am married to another white Methodist and have, all told, four children, all of them white Methodists, too.

I am not a member of the Screen Writers Guild.

I am not a Communist.

I am not a Republican.

The only organization that I belong to is the Limited Editions Club, which I am assured is as clean as a hound's tooth.

I have not attended a meeting or gathering of any sort where anyone was scheduled to rise and speak on any subject whatever, political, educational, or just entertaining, for twenty-five years, or since I was a cub reporter and had to cover such enlightening exhibitions nightly.

As for contributing money to causes, once in Dave Chasen's restaurant I slipped ten bucks to a girl in a low-cut blouse who turned out to be collecting for the Abraham Lincoln Brigade (and me a Confederate!), but the accepted view about town is that politically I am a tightwad from way back and would not give 85 cents to see Henry Wallace walk on water. I bat and throw right-handed. . . .

Nobody seems to want to know what frats a book publisher

belongs to, to make sure he isn't running around with the Wrong Crowd. Nobody hauls a radio producer up on the carpet and says, "You did a bad thing in one of your broadcasts, but if you think we're going to tell you which one it was you're crazy." Nobody subpoenas a stage producer and warns him to watch his step if he doesn't want to get a horn on the next play. And nobody, but nobody, drags a newspaper or magazine publisher down to Washington and pokes around in his political background and associations by way of seeing to it that he isn't sneaking a subversive line or two across in his How-to-Cook-a-Pot-Roast column.

But with a moving picture producer it's different. Either he unbosoms himself at once these days, to be measured by the New Standards, or the next thing he knows the Man is around from the Committee. Or worse still, he becomes subject to the attentions of the Committee's volunteer field workers. . . .

If he fails even one of the ghostly tests set by these unofficial agents, the air is suddenly full of yells and screams and charges of treason and the whole pack is off for Washington with a bale of shorthand notes showing that a bit player in the third reel said, "Well, my goodness, that is some mighty red blood on Bickerstaff's left hand." And sure enough, even before breakfast the Man is around to git him.

Recently, to give some semblance of form and definition to this high-minded hobby, certain members of the group descended from the mount with two tablets of stone tersely graven: Screen Guide for Americans—A List of the More Common Devices Used to Turn Non-Political Pictures Into Carriers of Political Propaganda, including thirteen flat orders to the rest of Hollywood on how pictures are to be made from now on.

This development has made it doubly necessary for me to open the books but immediately on myself and everyone else connected with . . . *The Senator Was Indiscreet,* for what have we done, first crack out of the box, but busted wide open the very first of these commandments, the one forbidding any light treatment of politics! I couldn't be more embarrassed.

And yet none of us should have been altogether surprised by this particular fiat. In the whole history of our country nobody had ever before treated politics lightly. Nobody had ever used politics and politicians as material for comedy. Oh well, a few perhaps, yes, if you want to count Reds like Mark Twain, Will Rogers and Irvin Cobb. But I mean real Americans, true blue and loyal to their country.

Who today ever speaks lightly of politics and politicians with the sole exception of newspaper cartoonists, editorial writers and radio comedians?

It was an absolutely fresh subject that we had hit on, a virgin field for comedy, and we should have expected some totalitarian objection to its use in a picture.

As a matter of fact, we were not altogether negligent in our preparations for this courageous venture into the unknown. We took certain precautions.

For one thing, it was agreed among us at the studio that it might be a wise move for me to drop my subscription to *PM* temporarily and take a whack at reading a column by George Sokolsky, whoever he is. For another, it was suggested that I should stop going around telling people that an expression like "We disaffiliate" clearly indicated that John L. Lewis must have studied English under Amos and Andy. Too frivolous. And for still another, it was thought just as well to begin softpedaling the fact that I once produced a poorfolks picture called *The Grapes of Wrath* and to concentrate instead on my sponsorship of *Dimples*, an early Shirley Temple masterpiece.

The same carefulness went also into the casting of the picture. But since in those days we didn't know it was okay to inquire into a player's beliefs, we were forced to resort to a secret process of testing William Powell, Ella Raines, Peter Lind Hayes and the others for Americanization, and all, I am happy to report, came through with flying colors. For example, when we suddenly played "O Chichornia" on the set to note involuntary reactions of joy and homesickness, they hissed it, the whole company.

But our most masterly stroke, really a matter of sheer inspiration, was in the selection of a writer. Since George S. Kaufman, the director, and I were not only Democrats, but Roosevelt Democrats at that, the smartest move we figured we could possibly make would be to suck a Republican in on the deal. In any business at all these days and in particular the movie business, it does a Democrat no harm whatever to be seen as much as possible in public with a certified GOPster, and if necessary, give him a piece of the business itself, just as a few years ago the crafty Republican contemplating negotiations in Washington quickly provided himself with an old line Democrat to stand up front.

The Republican pillar of respectability we took in was named Charles MacArthur and while he didn't look the part and God knows didn't act it, he had the papers to prove himself a registered paid-up GOP card-toter and so we wasted no time in tying him up. When presently it turned out that he could also write and was, in fact, the possessor of a distinguished record of achievement both in the movies and on stage, one can imagine our pleasure and satisfaction. Personally, I hadn't even known there was such a thing as a witty Republican. Live and learn, live and learn.

It is still possible, of course, that the Man will be around anyway, in spite of all our precautions, but somehow I doubt it. I put a lot of faith in old Charlie's presence in our line-up. Because the way I figure it, a 1947 or 1948 Congressional committee will think a long, long time before finding anything questionable in a picture written by a good, solid, substantial, high-tariff Republican. MacArthur, I mean.

TO GEORGE S. KAUFMAN

1947

Dear George:

Yesterday the American Society of Interior Decorators awarded their 1947 first prize to the interior decorating of *The Senator Was Indiscreet*. Honestly, George, I have to laugh when I think how some people shook their heads over that picture. You'd think we didn't know what we were doing! Even when it didn't win the Oscar I kept right on smiling—because I already had a tip on that big ASID award. Nothing but the big stuff for us, eh boy?

Bill Dozier, the Hitch-hiker to Fame, has finished his first picture with his wife. It's called *Letter from an Unknown Woman* and Joan Fontaine plays the part of Julie Haydon, shy-type gazelle, eyes roll when she's talking to her lover. Well, sir, I've already written the sequel to it in case it's a hit. Dozier's picture is about a girl who falls in love with another of those God damned pianists (CLOSE UP of fingers on keyboard sort of fellow) and nuzzles around him until, finally, what the hell, he gives her a bang. Next week he goes to Milano to play a concert and that's the last she sees of him—for ten years. By then she has a nine-year-old boy that looks like the pianist and she is married to another fellow, no musician, but what does she do now but go for this piano player again. And to her horror, what do you think? He doesn't remember her! Right in the middle of this nuzzling, it dawns on her that he doesn't know who the hell she is and, frankly, doesn't seem to care so long as she gets those clothes off in a hurry. So out into the snow she runs and that's the way the thing straggles off to its tragic conclusion.

Well, my picture is a bigger affair than that. It's called *Collected Correspondence of an Unknown Woman* and instead of one incident I have something like a dozen. In other words, the piano player knocks her up regularly every five years and never DOES recognize her. Every semi-decade around she comes again, with another new kid tagging on behind, and every time he throws her on the bed and marks up another score. Once or twice he says, "Your face certainly does look familiar to me," but that's all. Of course she does everything she can think of to get out of him some further recognition than that, but nothing doing. Even when she lines up eight children behind her, every one of them the spitting image of him, all he says is, "Jesus Christ, have we got to have that mob around while we're doing it?" Finally, and this is the fade out, he's a real old bastard, can't hardly play Chopsticks, much less cross-handed stuff, and around comes this old bag again, a dozen little illegitimates trailing along behind, and nuzzles up feebly, still hopeful but much too proud to tip him off who she is, and after some heavy preliminary work, he manages to ring the bell again, possibly for the last time in his life, and as he is leaving the house and putting his hat on, we go to a CLOSE SHOT of him and he shakes his head and quavers, "I don't care what ANYBODY says, I've seen that broad somewhere before!" FADE OUT.

Dorris is doing fine. She goes to a psychiatrist too. Every day. Gives her somebody to tell her dreams to. About three years ago she told me one she had and it was all about Lord Mountbatten, so I refused to listen to any more stuff like that.

My best to three generations of Kaufmans.

TO GEORGE S. KAUFMAN

January 17, 1948

Dear George:

Because I don't know where to write Anne and Bruce [Kaufman's daughter and son-in-law], please give them our warmest congratulations, and my guess is that you will get as much happiness out of this as anyone. The child will unfortunately smell for a year or two but once you get past that, you've got the whole situation licked. Also on those rare occasions when she is polished and powdered for public presentation, there is no sweeter fragrance this side of Lana Turner.

I rather feel sorry for Moss [Hart] because I feel quite sure that by now his son has a valet and he will never experience the odd pleasure of selecting a diaper for him, to be pinned of course with platinum safety pins. Without doubt father and son will bump into each other at the cocktail hour and unquestionably will find a number of things in common. I find that the role of grandfather is just about perfect. Drop in on the child when you feel like it, give her a few formal tweaks, and get the hell out before you are called on for any of the domestic attentions.

Whatever the fate of *The Senator Was Indiscreet*, never think for one second that I regret any part of it. In fact, foolish though it may sound, I would do it all over again. If there was any major error committed, it was in the original decision to do a political comedy, and I still do not regard that decision as unreasonable. The times may have been wrong for it and the level of comedy, satire, too strong for popular approval, but once that decision was taken, everything else seems to me to have worked out very successfully. People who like it are often fanatical about it. I find them quoting the jokes and describing the situations with such delight that it is impossible to regret any part of the project. The reviews in Chicago were even better than those in New York, unanimous in all four papers. The same is true of the San Francisco reviews.

I do not like to lose money any more than the next one, in fact not as much, but the picture is one that I am immensely pleased to have made and I will still get a genuine satisfaction out of it even if it sends me to the poorhouse, which is very unlikely. Without you it would be impossible for me to have this satisfaction, so I still remain beholden to you.

I have little further accurate knowledge about its ultimate financial fate. In most small towns, oddly enough, it is doing quite well, better than in the cities. All I know now, all that anyone seems to be able to guess about it, is that it has a chance of breaking even. I'll settle for that and feel fine about it.

My best to you all.

Playwright and screenwriter Charles MacArthur most often wrote with Ben Hecht. They collaborated on *The Front Page, Twentieth Century, Gunga Din,* and *Wuthering Heights.* Nunnally and Dorris Johnson had been married at the MacArthur home in 1940, and Charles had been best man.

TO CHARLES MACARTHUR

February 10, 1948

Dear Charlie:

I have sent your letter to our decoding department. There is one sentence in it which, no matter how I read it, indicates that you are becoming an editor. This is so flagrantly a misprint of some kind that I am setting the cryptographers to work on it.

It's good news that you are coming out, and Dave Chasen and Mike Romanoff are strengthening all the furniture, securing all the tables and chairs to the floor and placing the movable crockery on higher shelves. Their feeling is that you are going to have to work to get hold of some of the stuff. I wouldn't at first glance say that *Trilby* was the most promising work I ever heard of for a picture but with you and Ben working on it I am prepared to go down to El Capitan Theatre a year from next month and witness your acceptance of an Oscar for it. After that, of course, you will probably take up *The Five Little Peppers.*

Speaking of which, it will be three little Johnsons sometime in the fall. Now stop screaming. Dorris wants a boy and if Dorris wants a boy, even if it means a postponement of my retiring until I'm 95, Dorris shall have a boy. Or a girl. I was hoping that by the time we got around to this one my grandson would be old enough to take care of him, but Marjorie was a little dilatory. Apparently there will never be a time within the foreseeable future when I will not be on the floor smirking at an infant. Bobby Dolan* thinks we should go on the wagon.

I want you to forget the ice skates for your fiancée [Helen Hayes MacArthur]. Where the hell she ever got the idea that she might use them I can't understand unless she figures she can still skate on cubes in highballs. Give her something useful, like a couple of Countess Mara ties, or a case of champagne. And let me know about

---

* Robert Emmett Dolan was a musical director at MGM in 1941 and served in that capacity on many Broadway productions. He was the producer of *White Christmas* and wrote the scores for *The Bells of St. Mary's, The Perils of Pauline, The Road to Rio,* and three of Johnson's movies: *Mr. Peabody and the Mermaid, The Three Faces of Eve,* and *The Man Who Understood Women.*

Mary's [the MacArthurs' daughter] party. I'm very interested in that. Nora celebrated her fifteenth at school the other day and, I think, is planning to make her next her twenty-second. She's impatient and figures on skipping a few. But I want to know what you do for an eighteenth birthday. The information will obviously come in handy for me time and time and time again.

I look forward to seeing you and, we hope, Helen too. Bea Lillie was around for a few days and almost played a bit in *Mr. Peabody and the Mermaid*, a very good bit in fact, but other thespians argued her out of it. Their arguments, I thought, were pretty unflattering to her. They argued that people would think she was so desperate she was accepting small parts in pictures. It all seemed to me very insulting to her but there was nothing I could do but stand on the side lines and suck on my thumb. Eventually she left for a week in what sounded to me like Elizabeth Arden's Beauty Ranch. Could that be right? It presents something of an odd picture in my mind but that's what she said, anyway.

After *The Senator Was Indiscreet*, Johnson returned to less controversial material with *Mr. Peabody and the Mermaid* (1948), also for International. Johnson then found himself "available" once again, and returned to 20th Century–Fox and Darryl Zanuck. During his years as an independent producer he had missed Zanuck's support, both as a producer willing to give financial backing to a movie he believed in, and as a good judge of screenwriting. When asked by Louis B. Mayer, during a job-offer conference, why he was returning to 20th Century–Fox, Johnson replied simply, "They got Zanuck. . . . When I am working on a picture, he's part of me, he's part of it."

Cecelia Ager, an old friend of Johnson's, was film critic on *PM*, a New York City daily newspaper.

TO CECELIA AGER

July 30, 1948

Dear Mrs. Ager:

In a couple of weeks or so you may be called up by a young man, age twenty-four, named Allen Hirshfeld, son of my late doctor.

He is invading the city, object journalism, and I hope you will be able to introduce him to the city editor of the *Star*, nothing more. The odds are that he will ask the city editor for a job, but that you need not concern yourself with which. He seems a little callow to me to have served in the war and afterward to have been graduated from UCLA, but thinking of my own sophistication at that age I feel I am in no position to cast stones.

I have terminated my connection with Universal-International, and while I suppose I should make the customary dignified announcement that I am going to Palm Springs for a brief rest, after which I will return with an announcement of my future plans (I believe the usual translation of this), that I am looking for a job will go without saying. Johnny Hyde [Johnson's agent] is now rapping at doors, hat in hand, waiting for the verdict. Meanwhile I am staying at home renewing my acquaintanceship with the children, because it is wrong to lose touch with them during these formative years, and it is also pretty horrible. Why should Christie keep jumping in the pool with her clothes on? Why shouldn't Nora hang up her pajamas? Why shouldn't Roxie stop announcing to guests that she now makes coo-coo on the big toilet?

What the hell has become of Duffy?* I am now an Old Subscriber of the *Star*, reading Ager and Meany and Malden, but where is Duffy?

I am taking a subscription to *Life* in order to cancel it.

Always yours,

Wesley Stout was associate editor at the *Saturday Evening Post* from 1922 to 1936, and editor-in-chief from 1937 to 1942.

TO WESLEY STOUT

October 23, 1948

Dear Wes:

You oughtn't to done it. But even before we opened the box, we knew little Satchel Foot wouldn't get whatever was in it. The smart money was on Christie, who outweighs Roxie by a good twenty-five pounds. Nobody in the family guessed that it would be daddy himself who got into this one.

* Edmund Duffy was a political cartoonist.

We have a softball team here at Twentieth Century–Fox and we have a very stiff but simple schedule. We play MGM every Saturday. Both teams remind old-timers of that old Minneapolis team when Cantillion ran it. Every game is interrupted periodically for the players to get their children and grandchildren off the diamond. Every close play results in a hospital case. We have a doctor in each dugout.

To give you an idea, Buster Keaton pitches for MGM. We have a kid of forty-five named George Seaton pitching for us. Anybody who can catch a ball is automatically charged with being a ringer. Any new man who comes to bat unassisted has got to prove that he is over thirty-seven, which is our minimum age. Now and then we relax the rules to admit somebody like Gene Kelly, who is the most graceful second baseman since Napoleon Lajoie. He hops about so pretty out there that we couldn't bear to lose him. Our center fielder is Ben Lyon, who was a leading man for Clara Kimball Young. In right field we have George Jessel, who remains out there throughout the game because it's too much for him to walk back and forth to the dugout nine times in an afternoon. The ground rules provide that if a batter hits a long enough ball he is conceded a home run and does not have to make the circuit. Otherwise we'd never get through the third inning.

Last Saturday, to give you an idea of the hazards of this game, we had three severe injuries. On the first ball pitched, Dore Schary for MGM hit an infield fly and pulled a muscle so badly that he collapsed before reaching first base. The doctor that we provide is unfortunately a G.U. man and his first automatic move is to open the patient's fly. This did no good for Schary, for he was okay in that respect, but that was the end of his game for the day. Philip Dunne, a writing son of the immortal Mr. Dooley*, stood perfectly still at shortstop and threw his shoulder out of joint. Bill Perlberg, a Fox producer, broke a thumb taking one with his meat hand.

So far I have not got into this shambles. I made one proposal, that all grounders would be considered foul, but this was rejected, which let me out. I would have no difficulty whatever getting down to ground balls. The trouble would come when I started to straighten

---

* Philip Dunne, screenwriter and director, was the son of Finley Peter Dunne, who wrote satirical political pieces featuring the outspoken, commonsensical Mr. Dooley. Johnson and Dunne senior had been friends in New York in the twenties.

up again. But now, with Scott's [Johnson's two-month-old son] glove, I may be out there next Saturday. God knows things could be no worse. After all, we are still better than the Paramount writers' team, which threw a big victory celebration in Oblatt's saloon the other day at the end of a very successful season—eleven defeats, one tie.

Satchel Foot's straight monicker is Scott. We are already dickering with the Cleveland Indians and the Dodgers. Again, many thanks on behalf of my son and myself.

Harold Ross was editor of *The New Yorker*.

TO HAROLD ROSS

November 23, 1948

Dear Harold:

I was just talking to a man named Charles Bonner, novelist. He was telling me that he had the biggest ulcer ever turned up on the Atlantic coast between the Virginia tidewater and Moosehead Lake, Me., and cured it completely in five weeks. He says he did this by learning to dance at Arthur Murray's. He says it had completely disappeared by the time he got into the samba, and now he has no more ulcer than my baby, in addition to which he is one of the Goddamndest dancers that ever hit the floor since that memorable night when L. B. Mayer made his debut at the old Trocadero. . . .

If I hear anything else I'll let you know.

Norman Corwin, a distinguished writer for movies, radio, and television, was compiling an anthology.

TO NORMAN CORWIN

January 13, 1949

Dear Norman:

. . . I am enclosing the list of office fees. . . . It goes without saying, you understand, that any or all three of these items from me can be consigned to the waste basket without the slightest danger of my being wounded. I am an old hand at rejections.

OFFICE FEES

For reading a story, with one word comment	$5 a page
For same, without comment	$10 a page
For listening to a story while dozing	$500
For same, wide awake	$1,000
For listening to a story described jovially as "just a springboard"	$10,000
For reading stories, plays or scripts written by actors or actresses to star themselves	$25,000
For looking at talented children	$500
For talking to same	$50,000
For meeting "new faces," male	$100
For same, female	$1
For same, female, door closed	No charge

In cases of friends or warm acquaintances acquired late the night before in saloons, fees are double.

TO PETE MARTIN

April 19, 1949

Dear Pete:

I called you but you'd gone. For one thing I wanted to say goodbye and see if there was anything else I could do for you, and for another I remembered a nice sample of [Gary] Cooper's rather nice dry humor that might interest you.

When we were making *Along Came Jones* on location, there was a quickie outfit working in the neighborhood. One day the star of this outfit, a western hero named Wild Bill Elliott, rode over to pay his respects to us. Like all quickie western heroes, Elliott was a brilliant spectacle. He rode a magnificent horse, his saddle and bridle were one hundred percent silver, and he himself was decked out in a $150 Stetson, a fine tailor-made western hero suit with white piping around the pockets and shoulders and his initials on his chest. He was really a sight to behold. Cooper was wearing a worn cowhand's outfit and was really a dilapidated looking fellow as he talked to Elliott and inspected his paraphernalia. Presently Elliott galloped off handsomely and Cooper came back to me and stood with his eyes on the ground for a moment. Then he said sadly, "They give him *two* guns."

TO BUDDY EBSEN

May 9, 1949

Dear Buddy:

I have no doubt that a remake of some of the Rogers pictures would be a profitable enterprise but good God, what a courageous man you are! In case you didn't know it, Will Rogers has been canonized on this lot. Proposing a remake of his pictures with a new actor might be like going into Richmond, Virginia and announcing I had a new man to take General Robert E. Lee's place. I will fumble around to see how the suggestion might be taken but I have an idea, due to his deification, that they might have Cardinal Spellman chase me out of town with a loaded crucifix.

I like to hear from you for several reasons but one that impresses me is that you are the only man I ever knew who actually served on a frigate.

Ben Hibbs was the editor of the *Saturday Evening Post.*

TO BEN HIBBS

May 20, 1949

Dear Ben:

Many thanks for the *Post* stories. They make me nostalgic. They make me dream back over the days when Mr. Lorimer* and Mr. Stout were driving me insane with worry. However, ten years from now, if God has still spared me, I will be able to dream back over those dear dead days of 1949 when Mr. Zanuck was driving me insane with worry. There's no use crying over spilt worry; another one will be along presently.

I started the W. C. Fields story this week. It's wonderful.

The best from my family to your family.

* George Horace Lorimer, editor at the *Saturday Evening Post* from 1898 to 1935, was credited with making the *Post* the leading market for short fiction during that period.

Dean Barton, a childhood friend of Johnson's, kept him abreast of happenings in his home state.

TO DEAN BARTON

June 8, 1949

Dear Dean:

It was good to hear from you. Last night I wired Liz [Barton Dean's sister] to ask her if she would care to come out here with papa for a visit with us. I haven't received an answer yet but I do hope she can make it. It's not only that it would enable papa to make a trip with greater ease of mind but Dorris and I both thought she might like to do a little loafing with us for a couple of weeks.

Your adventures among the scholars at college are amazing. To tell the truth, I've always thought that that's what I'd like to do, go to college as an older type man. Obviously a college education is wasted on three quarters of the young people who get it. When I'm in charge of this country, I intend to do something about this. Throw out the bums, set aside special colleges for football, daisy chains, and fraternity initiations . . . and save the actual higher education for deserving oldsters, like me.

The trouble is I no longer have time for anything but work. You should see the state of my stamp collection! I finished one picture, a comedy named *Everybody Does It*,* which in spite of its title has a very good funny idea. I laughed out loud at it several times. Today, though, I cried at the rushes. The one I'm doing now [*Three Came Home*] is what is known as a four-handkerchief affair. Nothing but separations and reunions. I cry when they're torn apart and I cry when they get back together again. I'm a real textbook manic depressive these days, laughing like a loon at some of the stuff and sobbing like a wronged maiden at some of the other scenes.

In another month or so my whole life will take another turn. I will be shooting a western.† My blood will be like ice water. I'll be jumpy. If I ever get Jimmie Ringo out of this fix I've got him in now, boy, will I be relieved!

---

* Johnson's first film back at 20th Century–Fox (1949). It was a rewrite of his *Wife, Husband and Friend* (1939), and though a favorite of Johnson's in both its incarnations, neither time did it win audience approval.

† *The Gunfighter* (1950). Johnson served as producer and, although he did not get screen credit, did much of the writing. Not terribly successful at the time of its release, *The Gunfighter* is now considered a classic Western. Spyros Skouras, president of 20th Century–Fox, attributed its lack of success to the fact that Gregory Peck appeared with a mustache: "That mustache cost us a million dollars."

Christie is approaching that critical day when promotions from the second to the third grade will be decided and I take it that it's touch and go with her, for she's been carrying an awful lot of flowers to her teacher for the past three weeks. She's a Brownie now. That's a kind of junior Girl Scout. Dorris and I went to an entertainment of some kind staged by these little wood elves the other night and it was like a baby snake pit. Christie and her troupe favored us with a Mexican hat dance. There's a sort of choppy rhythm to this dance with some of the eccentric beat that you get in "Deep in the Heart of Texas." But to hell with all that nonsense for Christie. She went into a fast shuffle the minute she hit the stage and continued to do it until they dragged her off. Let the laggards pause and loaf along with the musical accompaniment; my daughter gives them their dollar's worth of dancing. . . .

The truth of the matter is that we haven't hit on Christie's talent yet. She likes to make up but she can't do anything after she gets made up. She can't even sing "School Days" in tune. She's taking piano lessons but it is more or less like the violin lessons that Monsieur Le Blanc gives Jack Benny. I expect the piano teacher to leave town any night. She made a fairly acceptable ballet dancer with two pipe cleaners the other night, using some spit and toilet paper to dress it up, and I may look around in that field and see if there's any opening for her there. Or perhaps we could send her to India and steam up one of those Hindu child marriages. That's beginning to look like our only out.

I enjoyed your letter very much. The best to you from all of us.

TO LAWRENCE SCHWAB

June 29, 1949

Dear Larry:

I liked Mary [Martin] all the time but when I saw her in Chicago in *Annie Get Your Gun* she was really great. Not just wonderful but great. Nobody can question my devotion to Ethel Merman as a comedienne but it seemed to me that Mary had everything that Merman had and was appetizing too, which I'm afraid I can't say for Ethel, not for me.

I don't know what I can add to your recollection of the historic event in Beverly Hills but what happened was that Joel Sayre and I drove up to your house in the hills to splash in your pool one warm afternoon. As I remember it, you were working on that Gilbert and Sullivan show and Miss Martin was one of a line of applicants for spots in that production. You had heard about her singing one Sunday night at the Trocadero. In those days there was a free-for-all every Sunday night at the Troc and all manner of entertainers showed up on the floor, sometimes simultaneously. Apparently Mary had distinguished herself on one of these occasions and had been recommended to you, probably by herself. Anyway, she showed up in a dark suit and a large hat and, with your permission, Sayre and I were allowed to come in and sit at one end of your ballroom while she sang for you on a platform at the other end. What you wanted was a girl who could sing clean and dirty, so she gave first a Victor Red Seal selection and then something lowdown, with equal success, as I remember it. Sayre had one outstanding recollection of the occasion. After the audition, while you were giving her one of those noncommittal routines about hearing from you later, Sayre says she winked at him. Not a dirty wink, he admits. Just a good-humored friendly wink, intimating that she'd heard this sort of thing before and was scarcely to be taken in by it.

Neither Sayre nor I can remember that you had anything much to say about her afterward, whether you liked her very much or not. I suppose we assumed that this was just another one of a number of hopeful young women you'd listened to and that that was the end of it. I must say that I thought she was rather a plain-looking girl, which I don't now.

I remember you told me later how you'd run into some producer in New York who was having trouble with a girl named June something. I can't recall her last name, but I think she was in the Bobby Clark show last year, *Sweethearts*. She was behaving during rehearsals as if she were indispensable, whereupon you proposed Mary as a possible replacement if the situation got too tough. The result was that Mary went into that show and sang while she was taking off her clothes publicly.

Do you expect to write any of this article yourself? Or are you simply going to be an editor and collect all the dough anyway?

We are all well and I am employed. Best to you both.

Mary Healy and Dorris Bowdon Johnson were brought to Hollywood in January 1938 by 20th Century–Fox, who gave them screen tests and then signed them. They shared an apartment, worked together, and became close friends. Mary married Peter Lind Hayes, and the Hayeses and Johnsons remained close friends. At the time of this letter, Mary Healy and Peter Lind Hayes were just beginning their television career.

October 14, 1949

Dear Peter:

Dorris and Nan and Bobby Dolan and I saw the program last night but I must say on a very inadequate set, with a screen so small and a reception so uncertain that it wasn't too good an opportunity to study it. Today at lunch Bill Perlberg was bubblingly enthusiastic about it. He saw it on a better screen. He and Jessel were full of praise and admiration for you and Bill sounded off splendidly about how beautiful Mary was and how well she sang and how much she added to the program last night. . . .

Just thinking out loud, as we boys say, one or two other things occurred to me about the production. I think it is an utter waste of time to design costumes for chorus girls on television. They may look fine on the stage but on such a small screen as there is in almost all television sets, even the largest, they mean nothing. Moreover, it occurred to me, you can easily have too many chorus girls in a television number. They are all scrambled together and if they wear long dresses you would be better off putting a drape behind you, because at least the drape would stand still and not confuse the background. My belief is that if girls are to be used they should be used as undressed as the law allows. Because you can't see their faces well, because the color of their garments means nothing, because they are crowded in that small stage, they seem to me a complete irritation as Arthur [Schwartz]* used them in the show last night. There is only one excuse for production girls in a show like that and that is for legs. In one situation where you had some business and were surrounded in a kind of half circle by girls, as would be okay on a stage, you were almost lost in the background. We remained to see the Ed Wynn show which followed yours and this thought of mine seemed to be confirmed. They were very stingy in that show about crowding the stage with people. It was obvious that Wynn and Dinah Shore were three times as effective by being alone in front of the camera. It ought to always be kept in mind that the show is going to be seen on a panel not much larger than a school kid's slate and that the more you put into that little space the less any one individual is going to stand out. Still again, close shots, or waist shots, pick up the action tremendously. The long shots seem to be dull. You may say that this is all based on the fact that I saw the show on a small screen but

* Arthur Schwartz was producer of the Hayes's television program.

actually it was about the standard size, not the very largest, but the most popular size next below the largest. Also, my guess is that most sets have this size screen.

You spoke of bad reviews by some of the trade publications. I think they were wrong. I think the cameras on your show were used about five times as well as those on the Wynn show. Your show seemed to me to move fast, looked slick and professional, and in that sense was extraordinarily well produced. Like Perlberg, I had the feeling that this was a wonderfully promising start. I'm sure Arthur will find things to be corrected in subsequent shows. I'm sure he'll see to it that the people don't crowd the screen too much, for one thing. It stands to reason that television people will presently find a way of using a chorus that will be effective in their medium. Obviously the stage method means nothing. You managed individually to get something out of the [Margaret] O'Brien sketch but I would hope to God I had something a bit better next time. Television plays to a few people in a small room. You could reach out and touch your audience. Comedy writers ought to keep this in mind. Working in television would seem to be almost exactly like getting up and doing something at a party, it's that intimate.

You asked me about establishing a continuity of character for yourself, whether I thought it would be good or not. I thought when I talked to you that obviously it would be better, as I've always said and thought about you in radio. But after seeing the show last night I'm not so sure. Since you are in different sketches and have different characterizations, I really don't see how that could be done. You're a football coach, you're Margaret O'Brien's father, you're doing a calypso number, all different characterizations, and I think you would only confuse things by trying to carry on a character of your own in addition to these. As a matter of fact, I don't see how it could be done without a long lot of explanation which would be of no point to me. So if I got your question right, I'm afraid I don't agree with you. . . .

We are all well and Roxie was dazzled by her birthday gift. It was really wonderful of you and Mary to come through so handsomely and don't think for one moment that we would hesitate to hock it if things get tough. After all, it's all for one and one for all, isn't it? Give Mary a kiss for me and for yourself and a firm manly shake of the hand.

Johnson was a devoted admirer of H. L. Mencken and what he stood for as journalist, author, editor, Baltimore *Sun* war correspondent and political correspondent, and contributing editor of the *Nation*. He wrote this letter to August, H. L. Mencken's brother, who lived in Baltimore.

TO AUGUST MENCKEN

November 8, 1949

Dear Mr. Mencken:

I can't think of anything that could make me happier than to hear that H. L. Mencken got some pleasure out of *Everybody Does It*. As well as I could, I have kept track of his illness through Ann Duffy [Edmund Duffy's wife] and I have wished many times that there was something I could do to convey to him first my sympathy and then my relief to hear that he was recovering. I take great pride in the news that I was in some way able to give him some amusement for an hour or so.

As for protecting the dialogue in a comedy, none but the most outrageous optimist would try to allow for laughter in a picture. Living, breathing actors in a stage play can pause and time their jokes so as not to lose that precious response. If the response isn't there he [they] can proceed to the next matter at once. But in a picture it would be pretty embarrassing to allow for laughter that didn't come. The only solution I can think of is to make comedies that aren't funny, and we do that so often anyway that it could scarcely be called an innovation. In fact, this problem arises so rarely I'm not sure it would be worth anyone's while to work on it.

Please give my best regards to your brother and my hopes for an early complete recovery. It was thoughtful of him, as ever, to send me this message and nice of you to write it.

With best regards.

TO HAROLD ROSS

November 17, 1949

Dear Harold:

I think the movie code would make a first-rate story for you. As much as it's discussed, I can't remember a really thorough examination of its operations. There is constant argument that it should be revised, after something like twenty years, and rewritten in the light of whatever progress we've made during this passage of time, but if there is any actual move in that direction I haven't heard about it. It was particularly awkward during the war, when millions of people were killing each other without being arrested and tried for it, a clear violation of the code. Herman Shumlin told me he had quite an argument with the Breen office over Paul Lukas's killing of the fascist in *Watch on the Rhine*. The code didn't seem to like the way he got away with it. I had one with them when I did Steinbeck's *The Moon Is Down*, in which a Norwegian widow, played beautifully by my wife, Dorris Bowdon Johnson, lured one of the Nazi soldiers to her bedroom and dispatched him with a pair of shears. The Breen office wanted to know about that! The delicate question raised in both of these incidents was whether the assassinations were in [the] line of military necessity. There must be scores of particular incidents like these that would be useful in such an article.

But I must admit I'm a pro-code man. I believe we have our choice between such a code and innumerable city, county, and state censors, to say nothing of church, chamber of commerce, and Loyal Order of Moose censors. It was Deacon Hays who instituted this device and, like it or not, it stopped this local form of censorship dead in its tracks.

As for that Thurber story, I can't believe you thought that idea over before proposing it. You couldn't have. But let's say anyway that I grabbed it up. Say we paid Thurber a lot of money for it and made from it a picture that pleased the critics and delighted our audiences. It opened, say, in fifteen cities the same day and all over the country people were just laughing and chuckling and enjoying themselves at it.

But meanwhile, away up there in an office in a building on West 43rd Street, a gloomy, humorless man sits at his typewriter, occasionally dreaming of getting in with nice people, occasionally wondering if it'll be noticed if he uses another of [Wolcott] Gibbs's distinctive expressions or should he fall back again on his own modest vocabulary.

So what happens! Out comes *The New Yorker*, everybody in the United States turns instantly to the movie department, and this is what they find: "At the Roxy this week, through some hellish mystique, is a doomed comedy from a story by James Thurber. I doubt if you'll find much here."

As a result of this shrewd, penetrating mystique critique, the other critics rush frantically to reverse themselves in their Sunday pieces, the Roxy is suddenly empty, hoodlums egged on by sophisticated hotheads spit on the advertisements of the picture and throw rocks at Spyros Skouras, and the entire project is doomed, costing 20th Century–Fox a hellish million and a half. Unable to stand this latest blow, the company falls into receivership and thousands and thousands of employees are thrown out of work, many of whom are driven by their bitterness into the Communist Party. . . .

And so the next time you came on a story you'd like to see made into a picture, you'd be writing to me about it on some old *PM* stationery, where you'd be barely hanging onto the rim of the copy desk, and your letter would be forwarded to me at the local poorhouse.

So think it over again, will you?

Margaret Cousins was an editor at *Good Housekeeping* as well as an author.

TO MARGARET COUSINS

August 23, 1950

Dear Maggie:

When I spoke to you on the phone Monday, and I was terribly disappointed that you weren't still there when I got to the hospital, I had no conception of the harm that had been done to me by *Cosmopolitan*'s reference to me as dead. As you very well know, I am fairly devoid of personal vanity, and if some people prefer to think of me in that state I would not dream of disputing the point. But upon my return to California information has reached me that throws an entirely new light on the whole situation.

In brief, this mistake by your much too impatient writer may have cost me a fortune of money. As of noon today, seven extremely wealthy men who had set me down in their wills for varying sums of money, in appreciation of certain qualities which I see no need to call attention to at this writing, have called in their solicitors and revised their final testaments, in the not unreasonable theory that there was not much sense in leaving dough to a corpse. I am naturally making every possible effort to correct this genuinely embarrassing misunderstanding, but at least three of them have so far remained unconvinced. I shall of course continue to press the matter, for very frankly I am simply crazy about money, but what if I am unsuccessful? Or what if they give in grudgingly, slicing their bequests out of resentment at being compelled to pay further lawyers' bills? What, may I ask, does *Cosmopolitan* intend to do in that case?

Maggie, this is just the sort of thing that makes me sore. Do not answer me directly in this matter. My attorneys, as shady a group as you are liable to meet outside your own staff, will call upon you presently with an empty suitcase. Do not, I pray you, send them away disappointed.

The Mudlark (1950) was the first film Johnson produced abroad, working in England. In this story of a young boy's encounter with Disraeli and Queen Victoria, Alec Guinness played Disraeli, a great part for any actor, Johnson thought: "It's such a showy part. Just think of it: half Satan, half Don Juan, a man of so many talents he would write novels, flatter a queen, dig the Suez Canal, present her with India. You can't beat that. That's better than Wyatt Earp." Working with Guinness was a great pleasure for Johnson, and they continued to see each other from time to time afterward.

TO ALEC GUINNESS

August 25, 1950

Dear Alec:

You were away fishing and I wasn't able to tell you goodbye before I left. I wanted to tell you also what a pleasure and a satisfaction it was to have worked with you. That's quite aside from the fact that your performance in the picture is something that I am extremely proud to have had anything to do with.

We ran the picture with Zanuck last Thursday night, the 17th, and he and everybody else was pleased with it. Your scenes with Irene [Dunne, as Queen Victoria] were little masterpieces, and after several experiments, we settled unanimously on the House of Commons speech in the one long take, the one in which the camera picks you up as you rise to speak and remains on you, moving in slowly, straight through to your exit. I can't remember a longer single cut in pictures and I can think of no such single speech to compare with it in dramatic fascination. Just as in the rushes and on the set, the audience that night was spellbound. We never even experimented with the script notions of cutting away to people reading the speech in the *Times*. That device was stuck into the speech by way of protection against any ordinary delivery. But from the time I saw you deliver it with such mastery on the set, that idea was out. The experimentation consisted simply of cutting away two or three times to groups of MP's listening. That turned out to be not only unnecessary but definitely an irritation. We also experimented with different camera angles on you. But in the end, the one clearly great satisfaction was to be had only in this one long uninterrupted cut. To me it is definitely the highlight of the picture, and I know very well that it will impress everyone who sees it in the same way.

The only other cut affecting your performance was a short but, in my opinion, very wise one by Zanuck. In your final scene with the Queen, after you say, "Most understanding of all sovereigns," and kiss her hand, we dissolve straight to the embankment procession for the finale. The long walk arm-in-arm with Irene to the door was dramatic but, as Zanuck pointed out, was a lowering of the curtain on the end of the show. If we wanted to preserve the brief spectacle of the Queen in her carriage with the military escort, we had to get to it promptly. I am sure that this was a very beneficial alteration.

In fact, the only large cut, the only one of any consequence at all, was the complete elimination of Irene's scene with her grandchildren, the one in which she examines their dentures. While the scene had its points, we found in running the picture as a whole that it was a useless interruption of the dramatic movement of the story. With that exception, the picture remains very close to what it was in the script.

I'm sorry I didn't get the chance to tell you this in London, to see what you thought about it. But Maggie Furse [costume designer for *The Mudlark*] had seen you equipping yourself for angling. Again, my most genuine thanks to you for a beautiful and impressive performance. I hope that I will have the good fortune to work with you another time, or in any case, to see you again before long. Please give my kindest regards to Mrs. Guinness.

Nunnally Johnson was always a bit skeptical about the role of the movie director, perhaps because his own screenplays incorporated much directorial guidance. He was once told by John Ford that he was the inspiration for the Screen Directors' Guild "because once when I wrote a picture at International . . . both *Time* and *Life*, saluting the new company, which was rarer than it is now, had some stuff about me, and they quoted a line I'd said about one director. I said his principal use is to see that the actors don't go home before six. Well, both magazines put it down that I said it as a generality about directors, which put me in a bad spot. . . ."

Lindsay Anderson was an editor of *Sequence*, a British film magazine, from 1946 to 1952. He began his own career as a director in 1948, working on documentary films. His first feature film was *This Sporting Life*, released in 1963.

August 26, 1950

Dear Lindsay:

It looks like a draw. My view of directors sounds to you blatantly practical and insensitive, while yours sounds to me like the reflections of a particularly moony fan magazine writer languishing over Tyrone Power.

Far from objecting to your use of these parts of my letter in your story, I am pleased that you took enough notice of them to discuss the situation again. As always, you do this with great grace and eloquence. Indeed, you honor me with your attention to what I say. But again I must caution you against using my name in connection with the quotations. Different from you, I am not a crusader, and the more practical fact remains that it would be both impolitic and foolish of me to make my own life and work uncomfortable by sounding off against men with whom I work.

I offer only one suggestion: Evidently I worded one of my sentences badly. What I meant to say was that I wondered what you would have had to say about *She Wore a Yellow Ribbon* if you had not *known* it was directed by Ford. Perhaps you might consider that suggestion and revise that paragraph accordingly.

It was a pleasure and a stimulation to meet you and to argue this point with you, and you are far from right in thinking that I regret one epithet in it. Not that I can see that I have made much progress with you. You are clearly a religious soul who contemplates my agnosticism with horror. If you should weaken for a moment, what would there be left for you! Obviously you could never lay your adoration at the feet of the writer, for you know his craft, it has no mysteries for you, and therefore no supernal powers. Not the actor, God knows! That would debase your soul too meanly. There is no question about it, it's got to be the director. He has all the qualities necessary for cultism. He has a lordly position in the picture, his powers are ghostly and not subject to worldly analysis, and his magic is visible only to his initiates. Religions have been started on far less.

Meanwhile I shall remain in the outer darkness, reading the Sacred Words of the director's disciples, and marvelling that such things should be.

My best to you.

Manuscript returned air mail.

September 14, 1950

Dear Bobby:

While at Yosemite Park for the equitation, I ran into an extremely interesting character who described himself as Honest Bob Dolan.* To others he was known as Square Deal Robert Dolan. His manner was oily and his approach obsequious and disgusting, and to put it bluntly, your son is not only a common gambler but a crook as well. I might very well have been taken in by his seductive manner, as many innocent people were, but it happened that I rembered him from the old *Cotton Blossom*, plying between Natchez and New Orleans, when he went under the name of Cameo Dolan.

At Yosemite he would sidle up to me with a deck of 50 cards so marked that they could be read easily from either side. In addition, he was equipped with a pair of dice so loaded with mercury that they wobbled constantly on a flat table and a roulette wheel so magnetized and electrified that it spat sparks constantly. None but a fool would have engaged him in a game of chance and I regret to say that he now holds my I.O.U.'s for a cool 75¢

He was accompanied on his forays into civilized gatherings by two women he described as his mother and his aunt and two gun molls named Hannah and Bebe, lush creatures not a day over 12. I happened to be accompanied by my innocent daughter Christie,† as sweet and pure a flower as has ever blossomed west of Needles, Calif., and you can imagine my feelings when I tell you that she left her heart in his hands. She loves crooks. In fact, she herself now has a deck of 32 cards and is rigging up a roulette wheel of such voltage that it takes two hands to force the ball into certain slots. In the course of time, unless they both land in the sneezer, they'll make a fine pair.

But I must say he was a winning rascal, with a merry twinkle in his eye and a way with a lass. I have to chuckle at the charm with which he picked my pockets. In fact, once I had identified him and taken the proper precautions against his wiles, we got along capitally. But if his mother sends you a collection of snapshots showing this mob each with a whacking big trout, you must understand that it was all the same fish, passed from hand to hand and photographed

---

* Dolan's son, Bob, was twelve years old at the time.
† Christie Johnson was ten.

from so many angles that it came to look like that catch that the disciples once pulled in for our Lord to feed the multitudes. This is only another sample of the duplicity of this bunch.

It was good to be back again in Hollywood, among clean-living people again, and to find a normal way of living, with Joyce Matthews still undecided whether to remarry Milton Berle again or not. Jerry Wald and Norman Krasna, or Potash and Perlmutter, have got so much publicity that Dore Schary is wondering whether being awarded plaques by the B'nai B'rith every day is as effective a device as it might be. Wald says that he and Krasna have more autonomy than Zanuck, but Bill Perlberg tells me that at Paramount he will have more autonomy than Wald and Krasna, which puts Perlberg really way out in autonomy. His first picture at Paramount was to be a story by that fellow Smith about a cat that inherited a baseball team ["Rhubarb" by H. Allen Smith]. Sounds promising, because for one thing they'll have that big cat public tied up at once. We have other horrors here too. Somebody is making a picture called *The Adventures of Skipalong Maxie Rosenbloom*. I'll let you know when this one is ready for release. I haven't been very active except I took a brief nap this afternoon.

We are reasonably well at home and your godchild is getting real loquacious. The other afternoon on the terrace he looked up with interest at the sound of an ambulance or police car siren passing down Sunset Boulevard. I said, "Do you know what that is, Scottie?" He said, "Yes, a siren." Where on earth do they pick it up!

Our love to you and that girl you are shacked up with. We miss you both.

Robert Goldstein was head of the London office of 20th Century–Fox.

TO ROBERT GOLDSTEIN

November 8, 1950

Dear Bob:

I'm sure you'll be happy to know that Jeann Blossom is Miss Hydroplane this year while Frances Campbell has just been named Miss Runabout. Both are from Long Beach. Home girls.

I should have written long before this (don't ask me why) but most of my time has been taken up with hating our new television set.

The truth is we got it only as self-defense. When the word gets around this town that you have no television set in your home you are really in trouble. From then on your home is full of people getting away from their sets, drinking up your liquor, and never leaving until after midnight. I got tired of this. And what is more, just as soon as I can dig up another house without a set I'm going to get out of mine.

Television is the only medium of entertainment in the history of the world in which you can get about a hundred times more fun when it is broken than when it's operating okay. I have already turned this idea over to Devlin, Ltd., which is what Marjie and Gene Fowler [Johnson's daughter and son-in-law, son of screenwriter Gene Fowler] call their furniture-making business, and pretty soon they are going to turn out a line of television cabinets with no television set inside. No matter what you do with this cabinet you can't get anything. A child can operate it. This may turn out to be such a profitable venture that Matty Fox [an entrepreneur] will try to get it away from us. . . .

Bye now.

Thornton Delehanty was the Hollywood representative for *Redbook*.

TO THORNTON DELEHANTY

November 20, 1950

Dear Thorny:

. . . Every time I read a quote from myself in any of these columns I become more and more convinced that Herman Mankiewicz is right about that sort of thing. He claims that Leonard Lyons has been quoting him, either correctly or incorrectly, for years and that the end is obvious. One day the men in white will walk in, throw a net over him, and take him off to the laughing academy. The charge will be flagrant idiocy, based entirely on what Lyons has said he said.

Dorris came home from the hospital yesterday and by six o'clock the bedroom was chaos. Marjie and Gene brought my grandson over to welcome grandma home, and Betty [Lauren Bacall] and Bogey were there. You heard one nurse screaming at the children and one screaming at Dorris and the children shooting pistols at Bogart and you can understand why Dorris began to get homesick for good old room 301 at St. John's. Apparently she weathered it, though, and as soon as the room thinned out she seemed to be okay.

And don't think I wasn't pleased when Dorris came out of the hospital alone. It's the first time that's happened.

Maurice Costello [early film actor] died last week. His end proved again the old rule of three, as Jimmy Starr so aptly puts it. It never fails. If one big shot passes away, you can always look for two more, just like this time—Julia Marlowe [stage actress], Maurice Costello, and President McKinley. It's really weird, isn't it?

I'm afraid we won't be able to accept your kind invitation for Christmas but we may ship the children to you.

Love and so forth.

While in England for the filming of *The Mudlark*, Johnson had begun writing the screenplay for *The Desert Fox* (1951), the story of German General Erwin Rommel. The script required much research. Johnson spoke with Rommel's family and with Englishmen who had known or fought against Rommel. "The main difficulty with *The Desert Fox*," Johnson asserted, "was how to tell this story, how to use this material in some kind of coherent fashion without seeming to even subconsciously favor one of our enemies such a short time after the war."

Although the New York office objected to casting James Mason as Rommel, Johnson and Zanuck insisted. The role revitalized Mason's career.

TO JED HARRIS

December 27, 1950

Dear Jed:

We were disappointed that you didn't show up. Since you operate like an unscheduled airline, we looked for you at any moment. When we went out in the afternoon we left word where you could reach us.

Your gifts were immense successes. All three kids pounced on the Hopalong Cassidy suit and I think Scottie came out with the pants. Rox got the hat, while Christie added the guns to her arsenal. We have more guns around our house than the Dillingers. We finally got the stuff back together and tried it out on Scottie and in the course of time I am going to take a picture of him in the outfit and send it to you. No matter how tough things may be when you receive it, you'll be cheered up.

Rox and Christie were pretty impressed by genuine solid gold jewelry, nor was your godfathership lost on Christie. She felt quite distinguished by this special attention. I'm afraid the drawing of the choir boys was lost on them but they both smiled in recognition of your flattering sketch of yourself on Roxie's card. What a vain fellow you are indeed!

I am sending you a copy of the Rommel script to look over when you have the time. I confess at the outset that the character and scope of this story are beyond my talent. It's really a pity that the story couldn't be done on the scale that it deserves. But Shakespeare was tied up with the new Wald-Krasna outfit. Congreve is doing a quick polish job for Howard Hughes, and Shaw, I hear, is dead. I will be grateful for any comments you have to make on what may be known in future as the Johnson version.

TO ROBERT EMMETT DOLAN

January 13, 1951

Dear Bobby:

If you asked any questions in your letter that was addressed to Dorris, I'm afraid I can't answer them at this writing. In her usual orderly fashion, Dorris filed the communication on her desk in a mile-high stack of Christmas cards, school reports, telephone bills, drawings of horses by Christie, and telegrams of congratulation on our marriage (February 4, 1940). I couldn't find it this morning. Anyway, it'll have to take its turn in the correspondence, and when you realize that we have still not finished acknowledging the telegrams on our marriage, many of them from people now cold in Forest Lawn, you can figure for yourself when that'll be.

The big excitement of the New Year, which you may not have heard about, was the blood-curdling fight between Oscar Levant and Walter Wanger at Mike Romanoff's New Year's Eve Party. Walter has had the blackest of years. First he was presented as a stupid stuffed shirt in Budd Schulberg's book, a widely circulated best seller, and then he popped up in the papers in connection with this unseemly affair. On top of that he was forced into involuntary bankruptcy and the bailiffs have been trying to snatch the rings off Joan's [Bennett, his wife] fingers.

There was no excuse for the beast emerging from Levant. It was New Year's Eve, everybody was either high or sick from the magnums of Cook's Imperial domestic champagne dispensed by the Little Monarch [Romanoff], and every man in the place was doing his best to feel every woman in the place, excepting his wife, and so there was little excuse for Mrs. Levant, not known heretofore as a woman to set men afire, to smack poor Walter because of a small formal grope. This has particularly infuriated the ladies of my group. They resent the implication that they were not likewise insulted during the evening. I think they are also incensed at the idea that Mrs. Levant is so combustible that otherwise decorous men are driven insane by her mere proximity. Oscar happened to be shuffling about the floor with his sister-in-law, another teetotaler, at the moment of the grope and naturally stepped forward and tried to knock Walter unconscious with his elbows, his hands being much too valuable to put in such jeopardy. Dangerous George Raft, another dancer, stepped in to make peace and was struck violently in the coat lapels by Oscar's shoulder. The result of this as related to me by a rival bad man, Humphrey Bogart, was that Raft was unnerved, unmanned, and stricken almost to paralysis by this jostle and had to be fanned for an hour afterward.

At any rate, Walter sobered up instantly, saw whom he had done it to, and screamed in horror. Later he apologized to Oscar and the apology was accepted with such courtly grace that Walter ran immediately back to the dance floor and began feeling all of the dancers at random, male and female alike. You can't imagine how shocked Joan was.

This teaches us all a lesson. Never let a non-drinker into your house. They'll start a fight every time.

I look forward to your next communication.

TO ROBERT EMMETT DOLAN

January 31, 1951

Dear Bobby:

. . . *The Mudlark* opened here last night with a big hullabaloo in the shape of a benefit performance for St. John's Hospital, and we were rash enough to take Christie and Roxie, although they had already seen the picture. This idea couldn't be described as much of a success. In spite of our efforts to discourage them, the Bogarts came along with us on this family affair, and that didn't help much, for Christie immediately got the evening off to a jolly start by announcing that Dorris and Mrs. Bogart had, to her mind, particularly ugly husbands. This didn't disturb Bogart, of course, because he's an actor and such derogatory comments never disturb an actor, but I was quite put to it to conceal the wound it inflicted on me. Christie further worked her way into Bogart's heart by rebuking him for his profanity. There is no question about it, she is an uncommonly winning child with social graces far beyond her years.

The stage show was so long that finally I had to leave the theater and take Roxie home, but not before she had complained loudly that she wished they would show something else besides *The Mudlark*. Christie saved this situation by explaining to strangers that the picture was better than people said. Why was I born, why am I living? . . .

Our best to you both.

TO THORNTON DELEHANTY

February 20, 1951

Dear Thorny:

I wish you would stop writing to me.

But before you stop, will you tell me about the Howard Barnes situation. A few days before his resignation I read in some trade paper a blind item about a critic who had shown up at an opening incapable, as the phrase goes, of performing his intellectual duties. The show, I believe, was *Billy Budd*, which I would have to be similarly incapable to get me there. At the time, of course, I dismissed the item as rather a poor gag. I opened a show in New York called *Park Avenue* and everybody showed up incapable, including one of the two authors. It got fine reviews, excepting Atkinson, God damn him, and closed at once. Since when are people complaining about a critic showing up incapable? Take Robert Coleman, who shows up incapable every night and hasn't had a drink in twenty-five years. Is it possible that it's one of those situations where it was Kay who was incapable but when the crash came Howard shoved her over and got behind the wheel and took the blame? Please let go your wife and answer these questions promptly.

Then you can resume not writing to me. Liz Taylor has just turned into the stretch with a man named [Stanley] Donen, who describes himself as a director, and they are hugging and kissing and making love all over the place and I have got no time to write to you or to read what you write to me. The way they say it out here, this Taylor kid is the greatest thing since hash.

The climax of Johnson's film *The Mudlark*, an impassioned speech performed by Alec Guinness, was based on a speech Disraeli had actually presented in Parliament. Johnson later recalled the filming:

"It was a wonderful shot, because Jean [Negulesco] put his camera way at the back of the House of Commons and moved up slowly. I think that speech ran about seven or eight minutes. He [Guinness] did it perfectly in rehearsal, and the whole stage crew burst into applause, because it was such a magnificent performance. Then I think there was only one take, only one necessary, and it was done exactly the same way, except that at one point Guinness paused, looked right and left, as if he was so emotionally moved by what he was having to say that for a moment he was silent. I was telling him when we saw the rushes how wonderful it was, and I said, 'What suggested to you that emotional pause there?' He said, 'I forgot my lines.' Whereas another actor would have every reason to say, 'I'm sorry, start over again,' or 'flub,' or something, he turned it into an additional advantage of the speech."

Monty Woolley, apparently quite impressed with Guinness's performance, wrote to Johnson with questions about the filming of *The Mudlark.*

TO MONTY WOOLLEY

February 21, 1951

Dear Monty:

The Statler Hotels give no better service than you can find right here in the Johnson unit.

1. None of the picture was shot inside Windsor Castle. The Lord Chamberlain refused to permit that, on the grounds that it was Their Majesties' private residence. All of the interiors were built on the set, as were the gates of the castle, with backings. The corridor set on the stage was quite long but we added a backing with perspective to it too.

2. I have to reply to this question, for I have your health very much in my heart. Alec Guinness's speech in the House of Commons was not only done in one shot, running around 7 minutes, but he did it repeatedly in other angles, without a fluff. Are you still listening?

3. The final shot was actually made on the embankment opposite the Houses of Parliament, along a strip connected with the County Hall. The War Office cooperated handsomely. They gave us 50 of the Horse Guards and about 150 of, I believe, the Coldstream Guards,

foot soldiers. Their rewards were, in addition to the fun they had applying their period moustaches, compulsory in Victoria's day, a pound apiece, a box lunch, and beer. We offered to serve them hot lunches but the colonel in command said, "Good God no! They'll get it all over themselves!" Since they were wearing their beautiful scarlet outfits, his horror was understandable. We did the stuff one Sunday with about 600 extras and managed to block off the modern buildings on the opposite bank with those banners fluttering over the crowd.

4. There is no question in the world but that I could have taught little Andrew Ray [the English child actor who played the mudlark] how to speak cockney but fortunately it wasn't necessary. His father is quite a well-known radio comic on BBC and Andy now goes to a public school, but the whole family is up from the streets, through vaudeville, and cockney was no foreign tongue to the boy. He's an extremely smart kid. During the first week or so of shooting he was little better than a robot but he learned fast and before the picture was over he was conscious of everything he was doing, in a professional sense, and was entering the realm of acting. In another picture or two, if he continues, he will really do something good.

Thank you so much for your kind letter. Your comment on the picture was so beautiful that I promise never again to mention the name of Alec Guinness in your presence.

Always my best.

TO ROBERT EMMETT DOLAN

March 3, 1951

Dear Bobby:

I'm sorry you and Nan aren't going to be here Sunday night. Dorris and I are being At Home at Romanoff's to celebrate our eleventh wedding anniversary. We decided to stage it at Romanoff's because we wouldn't care to have that type of people in our home. A few of them we like but for the most part you can imagine. . . .

McElway's name is McKelway. . . .

I haven't read Thurber's "The Thirteen Clocks." I have some kind of psychic block against reading stories in which animals or clocks are liable to talk. I think it's a professional fretfulness. I begin to worry about having to write dialogue for a heifer or a bureau or something like that. It seems to me I've got all I can do to turn out stuff for Paul Douglas. However, I will turn this story over to Christie, who reads anything. I'll get you a report on it from her. Or if you make a record of it and it's people singing, not bridge tables, I will be very happy to listen to it.

Dorris and I hit our second night club last Saturday night. About a month ago we caught Kay Thompson and didn't like her a bit more than when we saw her about three years ago. Saturday night we caught Lili St. Cyr, one of the most elegant strippers ever to take on the G-string. She was at Ciro's, which was jammed. I never saw a bigger flop in my life. The people were so stunned with no excitement that they practically forgot to applaud when she oozed off. . . .

I was told that her art had undergone a slight alteration between Main Street and Ciro's, the explanation being that she would now be exposed to a much more cultivated audience. This was not easy to believe. I took a look around the room, and aside from myself, it looked a good deal like that same crowd from Main Street with their neckties on. In fact, I think it was. They all had that same fine stalwart American look, their salivary glands prepared to drool at the first square inch of privileged epidermis. Miss St. Cyr (can she be one of the Boston St. Cyrs?) took 'em off with such icy gentility that it apparently intimidated these sturdy pioneers. She wouldn't even look in our direction. Her thoughts seemed to be far away, on some gathering of characters out of *Harper's Bazaar*, and the general feeling was that she could have gone about this divestment in a motel room with just as little danger to her honor. . . .

Bob [Dolan's son] told me yesterday he had got a letter from Nan but no love, just a letter about wanting to work in a picture with Siodmak.* I spent a good part of an evening with old Robert Siodmak the other night. He was so cute I thought he was going to leap on my shoulder. . . . When we parting, he did a fig-bar and asked me if I would come see his picture.† I told him no, because I knew I wouldn't be able to see anything on the screen. It's a waterfront picture, and if there's anything one of these European geniuses like it's an opportunity to shoot everything in the dark, with people appearing in silhouette behind piles of stuff on the dock. But if Nan is in it

---

* Robert Siodmak directed Johnson's *The Dark Mirror*. His other credits include *The Suspect*, *The Spiral Staircase*, and *The Killers*. Nan Dolan, Robert's wife, was the actress Nan Martin.

† Probably *Deported*. Nan Martin apparently never appeared in a Siodmak movie.

I'll go anyway. I can already see her in a glistening raincoat, because these foreigners like rain too, standing under a street light looking for her man, who has been knifed by Richard Conte. Poor Nan.

Love to you both from all of us.

Harry Brand was the head of the publicity department at 20th Century–Fox.

TO HARRY BRAND

April 3, 1951

Dear Harry:

I have been so preoccupied with my own health, or lack of it, that I haven't devoted the proper amount of time to yours. Gee, you're lucky. My doctor wouldn't order me anywhere outside of the city limits. "Just stay right here in bed," he said, "and the bill will be along presently."

Naturally I was present at the annual spring dance of the Studio Club at the Coconut Grove last night. I sat between Gloria de Haven and Pamela Mason and directly across from Andre Hakim [Turkish-born film producer, married to Susan Zanuck, Darryl's daughter]. You can't beat a position like that. As it turned out, there was a slight coolness at our table before the evening was over. I wouldn't dance with Hakim.

If I wanted to, I could tell you a million things that would either interest or convulse you, but Darryl is back now and Al Lichtman [the executive at Fox responsible for distribution] has explained to him that the failure of certain pictures is 1000% the fault of the studio. The distribution department, he has informed us, will not acknowledge responsibility for any picture that is not a smash success. They simply cannot afford to do a thing like that and still keep their pride. So you go on back to the golf course, or hammock, as I believe you call it in Arizona, and rest well with the reflection that little is happening here beyond the production of excellent pictures that nobody cares to see. As Spyros Skouras said to me the other day, "VshciehtuA&Bsjchejchgch." And he's right, Harry.

My best to you.

April 19, 1951

Dear Baby and Baby:

Between Zanuck and General MacArthur, I can hardly hear myself think. The situation between MacArthur and Truman is causing more excitement than Arlene Dahl and Lex Barker. This morning MacArthur made one of the greatest speeches ever heard of and at lunch today, which I will be at, Zanuck will quote it twenty-five decibels louder. You're missing a lot, and I doubt if a view of the Colosseum by moonlight will make up for it.

Things are moving very fast indeed. Right after you left everybody in the country but moving picture people wanted to make Kefauver President. Just as he was sitting down to write his speech of acceptance, Sterling Hayden got up before the Un-American Activities Committee and said he'd been a Communist, but in a cell with a lot of grips and back-lot people. That was the end of the Kefauver boom.

Truman fired MacArthur and we all switched over to MacArthur for President. It is an odd thing in this situation that nobody has come out so far for Truman for President. MacArthur flew in ahead of his plane and was given a reception in San Francisco that made C. B. DeMille hang his head in shame. It's a good thing Bogey hasn't got a picture running now, for it would be the only one in the whole country which would be packing them in. The rest of the nation is in front of their television sets listening to television reporters interviewing jerks on what they think of the global situation.

Your son is visiting my son today. At least that's what I figure. My secretary spoke to Scotty on the phone this morning and when she asked who is this, he replied, "This is Stevie." The only explanation for this is that Stevie is there and the two children have become confused with each other and don't know which is which.

I could tell you a million other things, every one of which would make you gasp with astonishment, but I'm sure you are anxious to get out to the Colosseum and see Mervyn LeRoy thrown to the lions.* No, that can't be right, unless he was an undercover man mixed up with the Christians. However, that's an occupational risk of undercover men. We miss you, especially your wife.

Our best to you both.

* LeRoy had just finished filming *Quo Vadis*.

Johnson became part owner of a race horse, sharing ownership of Saucy with Don Ameche, Frank Capra, Bing Crosby, Howard Hawks, Bob Hope, Winthrop Rockefeller, and others. Dick Andrade, a Texas horse-breeder, kept the group informed of Saucy's progress.

TO DICK ANDRADE

April 24, 1951

Dear Dick:

[Dave] Chasen has just flashed me the word about Saucy. You probably won't believe it but I have never owned 1/256th of a horse before. Needless to say, I am 1/256th thrilled.

I need a little further information but doubt that Dave will be able to give it to me. I do not like to say this about a distinguished restaurant but if he has ever had any previous experience with a horse it has been in a kitchen. Who, for instance, is feeding this steed? And under what colors will she skim around the track? In the event that I travelled to a track where she is racing, would I be shown my 1/256 of her to pat? Would I be entitled to 1/256 of a seat in a box?

Already I love this noble animal, at least my part of her, and am subscribing to *Racing Form*. Dorris has found a perfume called New Mown Hay and hereafter will use it to the exclusion of all others. Let us not go further into any jokes that occur to you in connection with this reference to hay. I myself intend to pal around with Bill Goetz as much as possible. We will discuss our stables.

Your generosity is unprecedented in my experience and I assure you I intend to do everything possible to make you and Saucy 1/256 proud of me.

See you at Churchill Downs.

P.S. Please give my very best to Saucy's father.

TO FRANK SULLIVAN

April 30, 1951

Dear Frank:

Chasen tells me that Ross's [Harold] condition is pretty serious. Do you know anything about it?

I liked your piece in the *New York Times* about Saratoga Springs. I love that town. I stopped at the United States Hotel once, a few years ago, and that was all right too except that I had to sleep with my head at the foot of the bed so I could get some light to read by. All they had in the room was a chandelier. Charlie Butterworth stopped there once. He told me it was the only hotel he was ever in where they could slide the breakfast under the door.

I sit next to Charlie Brackett* at lunch nearly every day and after he talked about Saratoga Springs for some time I had a kind of hankering to live there when I retired. But that of course was before I learned of the gambling there. Naturally I wouldn't want to be in a town that closes its eyes to sin like that. Out here we have an odd but, I suppose, satisfactory arrangement for those things. Draw poker is legal but stud poker is Goddamned near as illegal as murder. I don't quite follow this, but then I don't quite follow a number of things these days.

I'd like to write more but I'm so wrapped up in what Arthur MacArthur is doing all the time that I can't keep my mind on anything else. I'll certainly be glad when he gets all those baseball caps and settles down to a normal life again. Because if he keeps on, all those baseball teams are liable to be playing bareheaded.

Brackett has a new car, a Jaguar. We're buying him a foxtail for his radio aerial.

My best to you.

TO LAUREN BACALL

August 21, 1951

Dear Betty:

We started the picture yesterday, to my great regret, without you.† Miss Shelley Winters will do what she can to fill your dainty shoes. My heart of course remains with you.

This casting has one rather important advantage over using Lauren Bacall. I am now in position to keep very close track of the romance which is holding all America enthralled. I know now every

---

* Producer and screenwriter; president of the Academy of Motion Picture Arts and Sciences 1949–55.

† Bacall had been Johnson's first choice for a part in *Phone Call from a Stranger* (1952) but had turned down the role in order to accompany Bogart to Africa for the filming of *The African Queen*. Shelley Winters was given the part. *Phone Call from a Stranger* was Johnson's first experience of working with Bette Davis—and, not coincidentally, the first time he was officially requested not to appear on the set of a picture he was producing. A directorial suggestion from Johnson so infuriated Davis that she refused to work if Johnson were present.

move, with certain exceptions, made by Shelley and Farley [Granger]. I will be able to know what they eat, what they read, whether they intend to cling to each other until death do them part, or whatever the hell else. If they decide the whole thing has been a mistake but that each retains a deep respect for the other, professionally, I will know this ahead of even Jimmy Starr.

I don't even pretend that this altogether compensates for not having you so near. I say nothing of the close track I could keep of Bogey's financial situation, or his integrity as an artist and a man of business. I will confine myself to saying that it is pleasanter to sit around the set with you than with Miss Winters fully clothed. But we had no choice, our money was rapidly running out and it was thought best to get this picture done on any terms. In brief, our loss is America's loss.

I had intended to write you, with a full heart, of the engagement of Betty Hutton and Norman Krasna, one of the sweetest stories ever told. It was the general belief of all who knew them well that God had intended them for each other. I have never heard of two people so beatifically happy that weekend. She informed reporters that she was honored and humble to be beloved by such a brilliant man. She added, and allowed herself to be so quoted, that he was a doll. He, for his part, was no less gallant. He stated, publicly, that she was the most remarkable girl that he'd ever met. I take it that this statement included her mother, who is pretty remarkable in her own way, but I didn't have the time to check on that.

I had scarcely sat down to my kidney-shaped desk and thrust my quill pen into the inkpot to do my feeble best with this romance, one of the noblest since Tex and Jinx, when word came that not only was the engagement ended but she was thinking of withdrawing her description of him as a doll. Norman had no statement to make, which is the way of a gentleman. Betty simply said that it was all a mistake and that they parted with a deep respect for each other, professionally. The only question still remaining concerns the ring. In his exuberance Norman seems to have presented her with a ring about the size of an avocado studded with diamonds. Nothing has been said so far as to who gets custody of this bauble.

We look forward to your return. The only news we can get about you is from Radie Harris [gossip columnist in *Variety*], whose literary style is one of the most singular since Max Beerbohm. In other words, I can't tell what the hell she's trying to say. I can get out of it only that she has never met anybody yet who hasn't been crazy about her.

We send our love to you and Bogey and Stephen. Dorris is well, or rather not very well. She's had a few dizzy spells recently and they trouble us. The children are awful.

M E M O   T O   J O S E P H   M A N K I E W I C Z

September 7, 1951

Dear Joe:

I'm sorry I couldn't make it yesterday afternoon. I was tied up. I made a deal with the same man who ties up [Lew] Schreiber.

After the war, the commercial expansion of television progressed at a remarkable rate. From 1946 to 1950, motion-picture stocks had declined 40 percent, while television stocks rose 243 percent. Studios refused to supply the growing television networks with films, and refused to advertise movies on television. Exhibitors were especially adamant about television, insisting that movie stars not appear on the air, and that old movies not be sold. Film-makers had little choice; theaters seemed to be their only market, and they could not afford to offend exhibitors.

The studios eventually recognized the power of television. In 1951 Columbia Pictures started Screen Gems, a production subsidiary; Walt Disney created *Disneyland* in 1954; and by the mid-fifties MGM, United Artists, Universal, and 20th Century–Fox all had divisions producing television shows. Old movies began to appear on television, and the studios foolishly sold their films outright rather than leasing them. The studios also blundered by releasing films to television without clearance from the artists who had worked on them. The guilds reacted strongly, making demands for remuneration. An agreement was finally reached in 1951: the film companies could release all pre-1948 films without negotiation or payments because contracts up to that time gave the studios all television rights. However, the release of post-1948 films required negotiation and payment to guild members. The Screen Actors Guild members could cancel any contract with a studio if a film was released without the Guild's permission. The Screen Directors' Guild and Screen Writers Guild later adopted a similar policy.

After reading Milton MacKaye's article in the *Saturday Evening Post* in January and February 1952 about the effect of television on the movie industry, Johnson sent him the following letter.

TO MILTON MACKAYE

October 25, 1951

Dear Mac:

I think you've done a superb job. And so far as I can see, an accurate and fair one. I read it through immediately upon its arrival and marvelled at the ground you had covered and the entertaining thoroughness with which you had covered it. The only question remaining is, are we doomed or not? . . .

There is only one point of consequence that I thought might have been a little more emphasized. That is that, in the opinion of many, including me, motion picture making can't lose. I mean the actual making of stories on celluloid whether by the existing companies or by new companies or by the television people themselves. All would have to use, in effect, the same personnel. You make it clear at one point that 50% of the entertainment on one network was already filmed stuff. My guess is that in time this percentage will be greatly increased. Neither politics nor sports nor God is going to provide enough in the form of material for television journalism to occupy more than a tiny percentage of the God-awful amount of time that television will call for. Nor do I believe that there are enough comedians or puppets or even human beings with anything to say or do to take up much more of that time. When the freeze is off and there are thousands of television stations this necessity for filmed material is going to be infinitely multiplied.

Hollywood, speaking of it as a location, will have to provide this material. It may cause all kinds of revolution in the way of putting the stuff on film but it will undoubtedly have to be done, and the demand for film makers of all ranks will undoubtedly be tremendous. As you found out, there is not a good deal of improvement to be noted yet in the case of, say, writers, but employment among technical people is already very high indeed. The reason the writers have not been benefited yet is that a good deal of this stuff, like those daffy pilot films, is being made on shoelace tips. The stories are being written by the producers' wives, if I am any judge of stories, but in the course of time it will be brought home to these Gower Street [the area in Hollywood where low-budget film studios were located] impresarios that they cannot go on bedazzling children with nothing on the screen but shadows. Then they'll have to turn to the writers, such as they are. There have never been enough good writers even for one studio, much less the entire movie industry, and there is no reason to think that this small supply can be spread over the entire business of making pictures for whatever purpose. . . .

I accept your examination of the situation as you obviously intend it to be accepted. You gathered the information fairly and accurately and brought it together clearly for the reader to study first and then exercise his own judgment. I don't see what else you could intelligently do without coming right out and making a Drew Pearson prediction. It seems to me you have done the story magnificently and as reward Ben [Hibbs] should let you pad your expense account.

Nevertheless, Jed Harris is still a better director than Josh Logan will ever be, but how the hell can I tell that to you when you never saw or heard of or talked to but one director in your whole life? Jesus, MacKaye!

TO PETE MARTIN

October 26, 1951

Dear Pete:

I had expected to report to you before now but Charlie Feldman [a producer and agent], who seems to know as much about Dietrich as anybody here, has not kept his promise to come in and to see me about her. This may be because he is having some kind of tiff with Zanuck over the title of a picture I am doing. He claims it's an encroachment of a title he owns. Anyway, I talked to him last week and he insisted that he was the one that knew it all and that Dietrich's story was a great story. You can take this for what it's worth, he being her agent, in addition to which I have no reason to believe he knows what is a great story and what is not.

My view of the thing, in case you are interested, is this: a good two-thirds of Dietrich's story is printable only with the most delicate of treatments. Apparently she operates with the careless assurance of an Errol Flynn, and she is said to have contemplated an autobiography to be called *Beds I Have Slept In*. So most people, when asked who could tell about her, mention her various lovers, such as Remarque and Doug Fairbanks, Jr. I talked to a fellow who was doing a biography of Ezio Pinza not long ago and his task was a difficult one indeed, this songbird's fame being much like Miss Dietrich's, as much sexual as artistic. He had even a tougher situation than you would have, for he told me that his story had to be submitted to Mrs. Pinza. As a result of this condition, his story was getting thinner and thinner, since you can write about how well a man sings for just so long.

I suppose the most dramatic part of Dietrich's life would be that during which she was under the influence of Von Sternberg, who fished her out of Germany and brought her to this country. By all reports she worshipped him and regarded him with that same admiration that C. B. DeMille regards C. B. DeMille. Von Sternberg was out here recently but I don't know where he is now, though I could find out if your interest continues.

There is no doubt that she is one of the very top personalities that have ever been in pictures, at least within speaking distance of such magnificents as Garbo and Valentino. Also she has managed to enrich her life with such things as war work and activities, social as well as romantic, that are not common to the ordinary run of stars. But I confess I am unable to judge how much of this would be of interest to a great many readers of the *Post*. If I were you I would go through the morgue of some great newspaper like the *New York Times* or the *Herald Tribune* and see what has been written of her over the years and try to determine from that if a fuller account would justify the time and effort you would have to put into the story. As it stands, Feldman and Von Sternberg are the best sources of information that I can locate. If I can find out anything else, which I will try to do, I will let you know at once.

As always.

TO NAN DOLAN

November 6, 1951

Dear Nan:

I read *Jinx* [the autobiography of Jinx Falkenburg] in one sitting, from October 28 to November 5. It was a book that I simply could not put down. The high point, I imagine, was when she exclaimed, "I like to died!" on page 122, though I daresay many critics will prefer the scene on page 118 where she says, "He kills me!" It doesn't matter. There are riches enough here for us all.

I take it for granted that you have the moving picture rights tied up. All I wish to say is that before you talk terms with anybody else, see me. This could very well be 20th Century–Fox's Sunday punch for 1952. It has everything that *Quo Vadis* has and tennis too. But I can hardly wait to see Zanuck's face when he hears that I have read it ahead of him. Thank you ten million times, Nan. You are a true friend. Five years from now I will suggest to Bobby that he remake it as a musical.

I haven't seen much of your husband since you left. He may be (a) so lost in unhappiness that he refuses to show his face in public, or (b) out with some other girl. That's show business for you!

You may have a bit of time on your hands while waiting to hit the road, so why not take a look around and see if perhaps Faye [Emerson] and Skitch [Henderson] are writing their own story? If we could get the galley proofs on that one we might hit the country with a one-two punch. It's all nonsense that the world is waiting for the sunrise, it's waiting for the true story of Faye and Skitch. See what you can find out.

On the other hand, we have turned up out here a real novelty, a situation in which I have no interest at all. The morning papers report that George Sanders and Zsa Zsa Gabor are on the verge of a rift and I can hardly keep my mind on this long enough to tell you about it. If there was ever a couple that I don't care whether they get together, don't get together, or dive off of Mulholland Drive, it is George and Zsa Zsa. You will hear no more from me on this subject. Let Wald and Krasna have it.

That's about all except that Christmas was a bedlam and nobody invited us anywhere on New Year's Eve, much to our relief, and so we sat around the fire and got quietly fried at home.

You are missed.

TO CHARLES MACARTHUR
AND HELEN HAYES

January 2, 1952

Dear Helen and Charlie:

Things are shaping up very well. On my birthday Frank Sullivan sent me a doily set bearing the seal of the late Confederacy. Now the plates. We are almost ready to secede again. Only the other day I heard some of the fellows around Schwab's Drug Store talking about throwing some stuff at Ft. Sumter again. It's only a question of time, particulary if the North doesn't do something about Winchell.

Lovable Robert Emmett Dolan came in last night and brought us word, happy word, of both of you. We split a bottle of the bubbly three ways and lifted one glass to the MacArthurs. This was a hell of a triumph for me in particular, for none of us felt for one second that, following a modest celebration New Year's Eve, I would be able to lift an empty glass, much less a full one.

Your gifts were all successful. Chris now looks better with her scarf and binoculars bag, Roxie definitely smells better, and Scotty is more of a problem than ever with his accordion. Though neither of the girls will be altogether satisfied until they unwrap a package and find Jamie [the MacArthurs' son James] in it. We all send you our love and have no doubt we will hear next from you on that hundred-and-fifty-foot yacht as guests of the Black Comet of Broadway.

P.S. The only news I've heard is that Santa Claus got a black eye—laid the wrong doll under the Christmas tree. Tell Jamie.

TO THORNTON DELEHANTY

March 13, 1952

Dear Thorny:

I suppose you know that Bogart is as busy as Taft after this year's Oscar [nomination] for his performance in *The African Queen.* To hear Betty talk, you'd think they were headed for the White House. We are all going together to the ceremonial that night preceded by motorcycles bearing flares and followed by a delegation from the Mummers' Parade with a huge banner declaring that Bogart is for the Little Man and against entangling foreign alliances. The truth is, the man is promising anything to anybody. The ritual is at the Pantages Theatre this year and he has a seat on the aisle in the second row, with four men from the defensive platoon of the Los Angeles Rams to clear the way to the microphone in case his name is mentioned. Betty and Dorris and I are supposed to keep stamping our feet and yelling, "We want Bogart!"

His chances seem to be pretty good. His chief rival for the honor is Marlon Brando, who may lose out because few people can remember whether his name is Marlon Brando or Marlo Brandon. There is a school of thought that gives old Brandy the edge on performance but Bogey is personally more popular. They say he bathes oftener and smells better than Marly and this sort of thing influences the more esthetic members of our little colony. Others say they will never vote for Marlosky until he fixes his shoulder strap. One of Bogart's campaign claims is that he wears a whole undershirt at all

75

times. This is corroborated by Betty. It all takes place next Thursday night and I suppose it'll all be like another New Hampshire.

We are all well enough, nothing to boast of, and wish you well, Mrs. Calabash, wherever you are.

Johnson wrote and produced the film adaptation of Daphne du Maurier's *My Cousin Rachel* (1952). Henry Koster eventually replaced George Cukor as director, Olivia de Havilland was chosen to play Rachel, and Richard Burton, in his first leading role in an American film, played her husband. Johnson's first impression of Burton was that "he was wonderful in the picture, and he's the kind of man you look at and you know this is quality, this is a real fellow with passion. It was inescapable. If he opened a door, if he turned a knob, it wasn't like Conrad Nagel turning a knob. He turned the knob with his whole being."

Margaret Furse, costume designer for Johnson's *The Mudlark*, also did the costumes for *Oliver Twist*, *Becket*, *Anne of a Thousand Days*, and *The Lion in Winter*.

TO MARGARET FURSE

March 24, 1952

Dear Maggie:

I regret to inform you that we also ran. I agree with you that the voters were not only blind and stupid but crooked as well. The award in our category went to Edith Head of Paramount for those revolting rags in *A Place in the Sun*. This sort of thing will not happen when Eisenhower gets in.

We are still mumbling about the cast for *Rachel*. Once Vivien Leigh eliminated herself I've been rather at a loss. You'd think that the world would be full of thirty-five-year-old actresses able to give off a hint of mystery but none of them that I've been able to think of have been able to convince me.

As for the young man, I am at the moment debating the matter with George Cukor, who will probably direct the picture though the deal hasn't been signed yet. Cukor is a creature given to spraying clouds of dreamy words, and as nearly as I can get it he has in mind an actor who's young but old, simple but complicated, stolid but neurotic, and short but tall. He believes that this type would be perfect. Do you happen to know such a character around London?

Why do you accept jobs in London? Why don't you tell people that you can only work on location, either in Paris or Rome? The other day I saw a man named Cecil Tennant, an agent, whom I met a year or so ago when he was over here visiting the Oliviers while they were acting here. He had just arrived in this country and was lean and sinewy but hungry. When he came in to my office last week, having resided in New York since November, he was no longer hungry and obviously had no need to be. He must have put on three stone, five shillings, and sixpence. He was big enough to lick the world's champion, whoever he may be this week. In Paris or Rome, where you should be, you could probably have developed just as well.

I send you my love.

Fred Allen had written and starred in an episode in *We're Not Married* in which he and Ginger Rogers portrayed a couple who conducted a "breakfast chat" radio program from their own home.

TO FRED ALLEN

April 9, 1952

Dear Fred:

Any haggling over writing credits was news to me, but I now learn that whatever it was, it's been settled. I should still prefer to find a way to credit you on the screen with the radio broadcast, not because I am moved by any particular sense of honesty but because it is so well known that I'll only be accused of theft anyway.

The picture is now finally cut and is to be scored this week. The first rough version, and not too rough at that, failed to excite the enthusiasm I hoped for. It seems that episode pictures are tricky affairs and the way to present them is not easy. I imagine it's like the routining of a revue on the stage. A great deal of experimentation is necessary.

In addition to which, the movie audience mind has little experience in quick stopping and starting. So we devised a series of brief scenes using Victor Moore and Jane Darwell in a debate as to whether he should give a refund on each of these illicit ceremonies he performed and inserted them between the episodes. This worked out with remarkable success. They gave a kind of silly unity to the whole affair. When we ran it the other night in this form it went off very well indeed.

So far as your stuff was concerned, with Ginger, you couldn't have asked for finer, more sincere laughs. The marriage sequence got the picture off to a really wonderful start, and we used your whole episode as the opening number in the succeeding series and it too was a complete success. However the picture is received as a whole, I'm sure you can count on a first-rate reception for yourself and your stuff. I don't know how it could have been better received the other night nor do I know anyone who could have come anywhere near your comedy performance. Now all we've got to do is show it to the public and ask them for Christ's sake to give us some money for it.

My best to you and Portland.

P.S. I was terribly sorry to hear of Best Pratt's death. I had wanted to introduce him to Marilyn Monroe, who would probably have a bone to pick with him, if that's the way to put it.

TO MR. O'CONNOR

April 21, 1952

Dear Mr. O'Connor:

Faulkner's chief sponsor for movie work has been Howard Hawks, a very well known director. I believe that Hawks persuaded Faulkner to come out here first for *Today We Live*. In 1934 when we engaged Hawks to direct *The Road to Glory* he suggested that Faulkner be brought out here to work on that script too.*

The writing of a script is often a pretty disorderly business. A writer is engaged and somehow fails to turn out what the producer likes or wants. Then a new one must be engaged. It was too discouraging a business for me to continue on as a producer responsible for screenplays by other authors, and so today I have no more to do with that sort of effort. I write my own screenplays and then produce the pictures. I simply hadn't the temperament or ability to supervise the writing of other writers. It's a talent like that of editor. I doubt that writers as a rule ever make good editors. They lack an editorial detachment. They would probably want everybody to write like themselves. So it was with me as a producer.

As for screen writers, the old-timers often degenerate into hacks and have few fresh ideas, but their craftsmanship increases. This is what such writers as Faulkner usually lack. When I set to work to get a screenplay out of a novel called *The Road to Glory*, I found I had skillful constructionists but not very much in the way of good

---

* Johnson had worked with William Faulkner on *The Road to Glory*, produced for 20th Century–Fox in 1936.

emotional scenes. It was Faulkner's strange emotional drama, or something of it, that we wanted in *The Road to Glory*. That was why Hawks suggested him and that was why we employed him.

Roark Bradford's account of my meeting with Faulkner was a little elaborate. It is true that we went immediately into conviviality but it was far from as extensive as Bradford described it. Nor was it at MGM. It was at Twentieth Century–Fox. Bill arrived with a pint of bourbon in a paper sack and another inside. He's a very independent fellow with a bottle and so he managed to rip his thumb opening the bottle he carried exteriorly, but since we had a wastebasket handy, he permitted [the blood] to drip there while we carried on our discussion. In the end we went out to continue our discussion in a saloon.

The legends about Faulkner in Hollywood are many and are fine for recounting across a table but I don't believe that they need to be transcribed for posterity nor do I think you would be interested in them in the particular kind of work you are doing. As you know, he is an extremely shy and diffident man and it needed a few drinks for him to open up. This naturally interfered with his writing but never to such an extent that it jeopardized his usefulness on a script. When he did get down to writing he wrote with amazing speed, all handwritten with a pen in quite small, quite legible writing. He confined himself to specific scenes, leaving it to us to put in the technical directions. As he wrote them these scenes were always much too long, but editing them was a simple and pleasant matter, for they were always doubly dramatic when reduced to the compact form necessary for the movies.

But for all the fact that Faulkner has worked out here several times, I doubt that he could be described as a screen writer in any sense. He always seemed pleased enough to have such work offered to him and responded willingly and amiably to all advice and directions. But clearly he was not enthusiastic about the medium for himself. I don't believe that this was out of snobbishness or any feeling of superiority but rather out of the fact that his life had long been dedicated to narrative writing, short stories and novels, and it was just that he recognized the technical character of screen writing and saw no reason why he should abandon a field he loved and was trained in, to tackle a new and sometimes difficult technique for which he had no particular love. He came to Hollywood, I am sure, either for the money or out of friendship for Hawks. Not that this mattered to us. He was a fine writer, he came willingly and without apologies, and he gave the very best that was in him, as a professional, and he was not called on to add love and affection to these already sufficient qualities.

In any case, I shouldn't call him a screen writer at all, nor do I think he ever thought of himself as such. He was more or less like a specialist in certain literary qualities who was called in to do what he could to inject them into a moving picture script. Some of this he did superbly and some of it without much quality. But that happens to be true of nearly all writers in such circumstances. Only the hacks and mediocrities are consistent. Bill came out to Hollywood like a plumber with all his tools, did the very best job he could, got his pay from the man and went on back to Oxford, Mississippi.

He never had such anxiety and enthusiasm for the movies as Scott Fitzgerald had. Scott was an amateur throughout his life and in all forms of writing. This of course is not a reflection on his work but a general description of his approach to it. He was never a professional in that sense, as Faulkner was and I suppose is. This amateurism of Fitzgerald's led him into all kinds of naïve enthusiasm about his own work in pictures, which so far as I could see was never very good. He was immensely proud of a script that he did from his short story "Babylon Revisited," one of the very best he or any other American short story writer ever wrote, but I read it a few years ago and to me it is unusable. To me he managed to destroy every vestige of all the fineness in his own story. He had padded it out with junk and nonsense and corn to an unbelievable extent. The author of *The Other Side of Paradise*, that biography of Fitzgerald published a year or so ago, cited this script as evidence of Hollywood's mistreatment of Fitzgerald and quoted someone as describing that particular script as flawless. There was also in the book a scornful reference to the interference of Joseph L. Mankiewicz, then a producer at MGM, in another script that Scott wrote, and Mankiewicz was by implication set up as the man who had broken Scott's spirit here.

My respect for Fitzgerald and his work as a short story writer and for one novel is boundless, but he floundered badly as a screen writer and his failure here was no miscarriage of justice. Earlier in life, when he had fewer problems, he might very well have distinguished himself in moving picture writing as admirably as he did in magazines and books, but if I am any judge of what part of his moving picture writing I read, he was next to useless. He had wit in his conversation and he had wit in narration but what he set down for wit in his dialogue always seemed to me rather trifling wisecracks.

The Johnson family, Columbus, Georgia, c. 1904. Left to right: James Nunnally Johnson, Cecil (aged four), Johnnie Mae, and Nunnally Hunter (aged seven). Johnson's mother was the head of the Columbus Board of Education; his father was a coppersmith.

Nunnally Johnson (first row, second from right) on his first job, selling the *Saturday Evening Post* with other young hawkers, Columbus, 1905.

On the set of *The Man Who Broke the Bank at Monte Carlo*, 1935, with Nigel (Willie) Bruce (center, background) and Ronald Colman (right). Johnson had been with Fox for only a year but had already written the screenplays for *Moulin Rouge*, *The House of Rothschild*, and *Bulldog Drummond Strikes Back*.

A birthday party for Shirley Temple on the set of *Dimples*, 1936. At the head of the table, Bill "Bo Jangles" Robinson; three seats to the left of him, Nunnally Johnson, who developed the idea for the movie; the script was written by Arthur Sheekman and Nat Perrin.

A radio promotion for the as yet unreleased *The Grapes of Wrath*, 1939. Standing: director John Ford and screenwriter Johnson; seated: Henry Fonda (Tom) and Jane Darwell (Ma Joad).

With Gary Cooper on the set of *Along Came Jones*, 1945.

With Helen Hayes and Suzie, the MacArthur-Hayes donkey, Nyack, New York, 1939. Three weeks into production on *The Grapes of Wrath*, Johnson left for New York (Darryl Zanuck took over as producer) to work with Charlie MacArthur on a play based on an incident in the life of John Barrymore.

Miami, 1944. Jed Harris (left) and Johnson (right) had been friends since the early 1930s. At the time of this photograph, Johnson's play *Dark Eyes*, produced by Harris, was on Broadway.

With Ginger Rogers on the set of *Roxie Hart*, 1942.

Left: With Alec Guinness during the shooting of *The Mudlark*, 1950, which Johnson wrote and produced. (See his letter to Guinness on page 52.)

Below: Johnson, director Jean Negulesco, and Irene Dunne as Queen Victoria.

Above: February 1940. Johnson; his bride, Dorris Bowden; flower girl Mary MacArthur; and the minister who is about to perform the ceremony (for years, Johnson was sure that Charlie MacArthur, who had made all the arrangements for the wedding, had simply hired an actor from Central Casting to play the part).

Left: With his wife and children, baby Roxie and three-year-old Christie, 1945. Dorris Bowden had been an actress at Fox for six months when she and Nunnally first met. They worked together on two movies, *The Grapes of Wrath* and *The Moon Is Down*.

With his daughter Christie. Halloween, 1944.

But neither Faulkner nor Fitzgerald gave their great efforts to the movies and so it would be foolish to become too critical of them in a field which one entered only for reasons of money and friendship, and the other out of a kind of final desperation. Their glory and honors were earned in other spheres and will endure as long as they deserve to. Movies were a kind of side issue and last resort for them and they shouldn't be judged by their accomplishments, or lack of them, in a field which was not of any genuine importance to them.

To tell you the truth, I don't remember anything about Faulkner's work on *Slave Ship* and indeed was surprised to find that he had worked on it. As for his work on other pictures, I know very little about it. I trust that these rather sketchy recollections will be of some use to you.

Very truly yours

P.S. Now that I think of it, *The Road to Glory* was not an adaptation from a novel but a story contrived to make use of a French picture that we had bought, called *Wooden Crosses*. It was a fairly spectacular production, some of the film being beyond anything that we were able to do over here at that time, and our chore was to concoct a new story in which we could use some of the battle stuff. My recollection is that a good deal of the framework of this new story had already been worked out before Faulkner was called in. It turned out to be a pretty effective and impressive show, but largely because of the film we got from the French picture.

Gladwyn Hill was a reporter at the Los Angeles bureau of the *New York Times*. Johnson wrote him this letter after learning that Herman Mankiewicz's daughter had sent Albert Einstein a math question, which he obligingly answered. Unfortunately, the answer was incorrect.

TO GLADWYN HILL

May 20, 1952

Dear Glad:

To hell with Judge Crater. Ever since Dudley Nichols turned up Charlie Ross in a speakeasy back in the twenties and did a serial of three long stories in the *World*, only to discover that he had fallen for a vaudeville actor's press agent, I have been very cautious about discovering lost ones.

Herman tells me that Einstein flunked the problem. It is Herman's belief that this uncovers a gigantic hoax. According to Herman, sometime back in the thirties there was a Gestapo raid in Berlin and a bushy-haired Jewish tailor fled into a fine schloss where it turned out that the occupant, a Nobel prize winner, had just conked off of heart failure. So the tailor disposed of the body and has passed himself off ever since as the great physicist Einstein. This turned out to be a particularly easy deception because it was widely known that there were only six people in the world who could understand what Einstein was talking about. So no matter what this tailor said, no matter how nutty, everybody just laughed and said, "Well, that's the way it is with Einstein." Thus it had gone on for decades, with this fake fellow sitting around in Princeton and playing his fiddle, until a high school girl sent him an arithmetic problem. Carried away by his own deception, he tackled this little problem and immediately fell on his kisser. Within another week you will probably be able to break the story that the real Einstein has been dead for twenty years and that the world has been honoring a fellow who was not even, so I hear, a very good tailor. You take it from there.

Once their theaters had been sold in accordance with the Supreme Court decision, the heads of the studios produced far fewer pictures. Production schedules were cut back, and as a consequence, many long-term contracts were not renewed.

Actors, directors, writers, and producers, losing the security of the old studio system, looked for alternatives. The trend toward independent production accelerated; producers sometimes formed corporations for only one picture. A change in the income-tax law made it possible to earn and keep more money as an owner in a corporation than as an employee whose salary was subject to taxation. The studios provided sound stages, equipment, and services, and served as distributors (some demanded the right to approve a film's star before agreeing to distribute the film).

Presumably this letter was written to the Bogarts when they were on location in Africa for *The African Queen*.

TO HUMPHREY BOGART
AND LAUREN BACALL

May 26, 1952

Dear Sailor and Slate:

Well, it seems that Mr. and Miz George Kaufman were dinner guests at the rich Mr. and Miz William Goetz's [now a vice-president at 20th Century–Fox] the other night, the platinum plates and crystal being used for the occasion. An emerald or a ruby was dropped in each of the gentlemen's liqueurs during the Coronas afterward, while a single flawless pearl nestled in the ice of each lady's white creme de menthe. So as the evening wore on, Mr. Goetz took Mr. Kaufman for a stroll among the iridescent blossoms of the Goetz's MGM garden, and presently paused, as is Mr. Goetz's wont, to take a leak into an orchid bush. "Will you join me?" he asked Mr. Kaufman politely. "No, thank you," replied Mr. Kaufman, "not without a gold cock."

In the case of mixed company of a certain social delicacy, this tag line can be rendered in French: "Mais non, merci beaucoup—jamais sans un coq d'or," which can then be translated immediately back into English for the benefit of those ladies who don't get it for Christ's sake.

You're well out of it here at the moment. 20th–Fox has just announced a pay cut of 25% for everybody getting from $500 to $1,000 a week, 35% from $1,000 to $2,000, and 50% for all receiving more than $2,000, a week. I fall, if you'll pardon the mention of money in front of Bogey, in the 50% bracket. We all have our choice of (a) taking the cut, (b) not taking the cut and being cut dead in the officers' mess, or (c) getting the hell out. The town's sweating, and the guilds are all conferring day and night, suspecting that 20th–Fox is spearheading an industry-wide slash. Andre Hakim has announced that he will have nothing to do with anyone rejecting the company's proposal. I don't know what I'll do about it until my agents, barristers, and tax accountants make up my mind. The Warner Brothers announced a couple of weeks ago that they were selling out completely to a syndicate headed by a man named Louis Lurie, but the deal fell through. I understand the Lurie crowd wouldn't go through with it when they learned that Milton Sperling* was going to pull out with his wife's folks. Loyalty. It came out then, in fact, that that's all they were after, actually: Sperling, and once they had him lined up, they were going to get rid of the studio and theatres to whoever wanted them. Now the report is that Harry is planning to fire Jack and just call it Warner Brother.

Liz Taylor has switched from Somebody Donen to Somebody Else. José Ferrer informed the House Un-American Activities Committee that the reason he was a member of all those Commie organizations was that he was thinking about Art all the time and never noticed all those whiskers and bombs around the meetings. He said he campaigned for that colored Communist councilman in NY under the impression that he was a Republican and represented the Union League Club. I think he also assumed the fellow wasn't colored at all but just blacked up for the moment. This sterling actor is now being billed as José Snerd. Rebel Randall has her own disc jockey show now.

The Hollywood Stars are in fourth place. There were only 4,000 at the game last Sunday afternoon and Mr. Leonard Goldstein† explained it by reminding us that Tallulah Bankhead's off the air now and people can stay home Sunday afternoons. I've had a couple of nice little sessions with Miss Dorothy Something, Joe Di Maggio's ex-and-future wife, and she's just fine. Gave me a baseball. Mike Romanoff's has opened again and it's a beautiful place, except that there are three steps down from the bar into the dining room and it's only a question of time before Bogey and I and many of our friends of like tastes are going to enter la salle de manger on our kissers. Something's got to be done about that. I think Mike's pretty worried over the size of the proposition now. The waiters all wear black jackets now, with gold buttons and food spots—very smart effect.

Dorris is well. I'm well. After July 1, I suppose, I'll just be 50% well. There has been some fraternization between our sons but I'm afraid I haven't the details. Hedda Hopper tried to MC some kind of ANTA show in NY last week and was booed—repeat booed—off the stage by the audience. On account of her 188% Americanism, I suppose. I think she claims that George M. Cohan (born on the fourth of July) was a Red. You have no idea how many Commies

* Film producer; at one time married to the daughter of Harry Warner.
† Leonard Goldstein, a low-budget film-maker at Universal, produced the Ma and Pa Kettle series and several Francis the Talking Mule movies. He also produced crime movies and Westerns.

were flushed during the hearings, everybody singing on everybody else. I listened to Walter Winchell last Sunday and I'm pretty well convinced that he's broadcasting from an insane asylum. General MacArthur told Congress he was just an old soldier and wouldn't die but simply fade away, fade away, fade away, which turned out to mean that he was going to lecture in every town in the country during the next year. Some fade.

Goodnight.

Alistair Cooke was, at the time of this letter, chief of the Washington bureau of the *Manchester Guardian*. Johnson's letter of inquiry began a warm and lasting friendship.

TO ALISTAIR COOKE

May 27, 1952

Dear Mr. Cooke:

Have you found anything to support this statement?* I wrote and produced a picture about Rommel last year, *The Desert Fox*, and in my preparations I made many inquiries about the alleged visit to this country without getting any satisfactory answers. Both Frau Rommel and Manfred Rommel, to whom I talked on several occasions, denied it, and while this may not be conclusive they were truthful with me in all other respects, so far as I was able to determine, and I could think of no reason why they should have lied about this. I finally set it down as one of the several legends concocted by Goebbels to provide color for Rommel when he first came into public notice in Germany. This was certainly true of the legend that he once went to Egypt as an archeologist and examined North Africa for military information. But I have long known of you as a conscientious reporter and I am curious to know if you have finally dug up some substantiation for this old rumor.

Very truly yours,

---

* The statement Johnson refers to, which Cooke had included in an article in the *Guardian*, was made to Cooke by General Jacob, who claimed that as a young man Nazi General Erwin Rommel had visited Civil War battlegrounds in America where night raids had taken place.

Edmund Goulding was the director of Johnson's *Everybody Does It* and *We're Not Married* and many other films including *The Trespasser, Grand Hotel, Dark Victory,* and *Nightmare Alley.*

TO EDMUND GOULDING

July 24, 1952

Dear Eddie:

I too was shocked by the size of the ads in the *New York Times* and wrote about it to Zanuck. He passed it along to Skouras, who called me in to explain the situation. He said that the full-page ad in conjunction with Macy's was carried in twelve newspapers in and around New York City. The only paper that didn't carry it was the *Daily News,* which refused to accept theatrical advertising at department store rates. But such ads cost the company money too, for the cost is divided equally between Macy's and the producer of the picture.

Mr. Skouras leaned against the wall of his office and his wails could be heard as far as Stage 16 as he told me about hard times and the lack of money for advertising or anything else. I was tempted to ask him if all of the advertising dough hadn't perhaps been spent on *Viva Zapata,* but fortunately recalled that this was no time for me to make clever points. At any rate, whatever the sum appropriated for *We're Not Married,* the bulk of it had gone into the Macy ads, which I must say were tremendous and effective. I still thought that those shy little classified ads for the picture that were no larger even in the Sunday editions were not very reassuring, but after this damp session with the boss it was clear that nothing could be done about it unless you and I were prepared to finance the project out of our own pockets. I agree completely with you that we were treated with very short shrift, and I believe also with you that with something more than a half-hearted effort behind the picture it could have done a great deal better. As it was, it has done well everywhere it has opened, though I was disappointed that it didn't go a third week in New York.

But I will tell you right now, Eddie, that if you think I am going in and raise hell with anybody in authority at a time like this, you are out of your mind. Safe there in New York, you don't know the feeling here of jumping every time somebody taps you on the shoulder from behind. Why, before my session with Mr. Skouras was over I found myself drying his eyes with my own handkerchief, and in leaving, I did everything I could to assure him that he could not have done better for us and that we intended to devote the rest of our lives to supporting him for Mr. America. I tell you, Eddie, you have to walk very carefully indeed these days.

My best to you.

TO PETE MARTIN

August 29, 1952

Dear Pete:

I was talking to Leonard Goldstein last night and it was clear that he was in the race for who discovered Bing Crosby. He says he had Bing under contract for five years from the time Bing got here from Spokane in 1927. He said that Bing teamed up with a man named Rinker and the two were hired by Will Morrissey for a revue that Morrissey put on here in Los Angeles. Morrissey, if you remember, was a legend of the twenties. He was alleged to have been able to produce a show with less actual cash in hand than any man in history. Bing can probably tell you a thousand stories about Morrissey, all good.

But Bing and Rinker were not even regarded highly enough actually to be in this turkey. It seems that they did their act in the orchestra pit between acts, Rinker playing the piano, Bing singing, and both of them making peculiar lowdown sounds. That's when Leonard says he saw them and signed them to a contract for five years. That was also the time when Paul Whiteman came through California on a tour with his band, and at that time Whiteman was the biggest man in the band business, both by reputation and poundage. Leonard says he had got Bing and Rinker a couple of weeks in a picture house here and a couple in San Francisco after the Morrissey show, and it was then that he managed to persuade Whiteman to listen to them. Apparently everybody else had turned them down. Bob Goldstein, Leonard's twin brother, at that time was managing Abe Lyman, also a very big band, and on his brother's recommendation tried to get Lyman to take on Bing and Rinker, but Lyman simply said that he wouldn't touch them. Lyman is now in the restaurant business.

According to Leonard, Bing and Rinker were sensationally successful with Whiteman until Whiteman hit New York to reopen the Palais Royale, where for some unaccountable reason the two young men laid a bomb at the opening show. They were a complete flop. Somewhat bewildered by this unexpected failure, Whiteman didn't know at first what to do with Bing and Rinker but presently came up with the idea of teaming them with a third fellow, Harry Barris, and calling them the Rhythm Boys, whereupon they became as big a success as they had been originally a failure in New York.

Leonard says he got Bing and Rinker their first movie work for one week, making a short for Ray McCarey, Leo's brother, at $750. Thereafter no more movie work until Bing did his stuff for Mack Sennett. Both Leonard and Bob seem to have an immense lot of information about Bing at that period. For instance, when CBS signed on Bing for his first big network program, I think for El Cremo cigars, the whole of show business in the West just laughed and laughed because they never figured that Bing would be sober enough to reach the studio the opening night. As it turned out, Bing was cold sober but, as it will happen with singers, fear and nervousness practically paralyzed his vocal cords so that an apology had to be made on the air for his non-appearance. You can imagine how the rest of show business interpreted that apology. According to Leonard, he took on Everett Crosby (Bing's brother) to teach him the agenting business with the result that at the end of the five years Everett felt himself accomplished enough to take over Bing, apparently without any particular hard feelings on Leonard's part. Leonard has promised to dictate some notes for you on this part of Bing's life and I will do what I can to goose him to it.

Al Bennett was an editor at the Globe Publishing Company.

TO AL BENNETT

September 24, 1952

Dear Mr. Bennett:

I will look forward with the greatest interest to your 75th anniversary edition, and most particularly to that part of it about Ed Howe.* There was easily forty years difference in our ages when I met him and I am sure that there have been few men in the world who could span that gap to create the degree of admiration and affection that I had for him. It may have been because he was probably the first man of his age that I ever met who wanted me to sit down and drink with him.

* E. W. Howe (1853–1937) was an editor, critic, philosopher, essayist, novelist, and newspaperman. He was editor and owner of the Atchison (Kansas) *Daily Globe* from 1877 to 1911.

This was back in Miami around the end of the twenties. I have seen him referred to as a crusty, ill-tempered old curmudgeon but I must say these were never the words I would apply to him. With me he was salty, rowdy, and full of a kind of a wild old man's fun. During those winters we seemed to be constantly approaching, celebrating and bidding farewell to his birthday, all in the neighborhood of eighty, and since it was prohibition days, gin was our tipple. I have never known why, and never cared much at the time, but for some reason he always described a martini as an old-fashioned cocktail. Now the martini, as the whole world knows, is a powerful weapon, and even at that age I had a tremendous respect for it, but when Ed brought out a bottle of gin and began to describe the simple, classic purity of this old-fashioned cocktail that he was concocting of gin and vermouth, it began to sound like a combination of mother's milk and some magic healing potion. You would have thought, to hear him tell it, that this was what mankind needed to go back to, to regain its peace and strength. He was, as was often proved, wrong about this.

If he was pessimistic, it was with such a strange, dry humor that it seemed only a tart wisdom. The last time I saw him he told me quite cheerfully that it would be the last, and when I protested, he said, "Look, Nunnally, when you get to be as old as I am you only buy three pairs of socks at a time."

There was a circumstance about this last meeting of ours that I am sure would have amused him if he had been able to be aware of it. We were sitting around my cabana at the Roney-Plaza one morning when I remembered that I had to mail a letter. The letter contained an alimony check. He stared at me with amusement when I explained proudly that I had been paying alimony for some nine or ten years. He looked at me as Noah might have looked at an adolescent who was telling him about a drizzle. He had, he said, been paying alimony for, I think, some thirty-five years. This seemed almost incomprehensible to me, and pretty appalling, I might add, when he went on to explain that the beneficiary of this alimony was even older than he was. It was then that I took occasion to advise him that he must certainly hold out long enough to outlive this obligation.

When a few months later Miss Adelaide wired me of his death, among my first thoughts was a regret that he hadn't been able to do it. This was before I read his obituary in a Los Angeles paper. I must confess that even in that moment of sorrow I found a certain satisfaction in a line in the story to the effect that he had indeed outlived it, though by only a matter of two or three days. It was the sort of thing that would have appealed to his mordant sense of humor if only he could have been aware of it. But as Miss Adelaide wrote me later, he hadn't. He hadn't been aware of anything for those few days before the end came.

Note to Mr. Bennett: I hope that you will be able to use at least some part of this, but I realize that there is a certain kind of reminiscence that may not be quite in place at certain times and under certain circumstances. So feel quite free to cut this wherever you wish. However, I doubt if the man who wrote that story about his son being about the drunkest of the bunch would mind what I have written with that same admiration and affection that I had for him when we were together in Florida.

Very truly yours,

Frank McCarthy was a producer for 20th Century–Fox; his credits include *Decision Before Dawn, A Guide for the Married Man,* and *Patton.*

TO FRANK MCCARTHY

October 13, 1952

Dear Frank:

You're a very smart apple. You don't have to be here at luncheon when Darryl comes in with the latest political flashes, all from the most authoritative and confidential sources open only to him, and we all try not to look at the various newspapers already carrying Darryl's inside stuff in big headlines. The decibels have heightened to the point where no one careful of his hearing can sit within three chairs of that end of the table, except Mr. [Joseph] Schenck, who keeps well up in the conversation by remarking from time to time, "I hear he's no good in bed." Mr. Schenck is a consistent man, and much too old to be distracted from sex by such childish nonsense as politics.

I'm still for Ike but largely because my daughter Nora would cut me off without a cent if I jumped to Stevenson. But it's a pretty shabby spectacle to see Lodge, Hoffman, and Duff pushed over the cliff and Ike arm-in-arm with Taft, McCarthy, and all that crowd. It seems to me one of the most public and shameful betrayals I have ever witnessed in many years of witnessing betrayals. Stevenson still transfixes you with the superiority of his character and eloquence on television but he too of course has slipped here and there. Only he does it with such grace that it is not always easy to detect it. But they all do. It's a degrading business and neither of the men is the man he was when he was nominated. Ike, though, has been the most flagrant and outrageous and shameful hedger. You'd be able to explain all this, but you would be very sorry you had to.

As for Honest Dick Nixon, I'm sorry you missed his TV show. Weekly *Variety* reviewed it under the title "Just Plain Dick." It was an overwhelmingly successful proving that he was not personally dishonest, which I doubt if anybody ever charged him with, but with never a reference to the propriety of this kind of private sponsorship. In fact, if we may judge from the public response to Dickie's baring of his soul and tax returns, it is now all right for any private interest, such as General Motors, to back any member of Congress, just so long as the money doesn't actually go into the public servant's pocket. Dick is now being received everywhere like General MacArthur at San Francisco. The only real sufferer, of course, is Pat. Dick stated publicly to some fifty million people that Pat still wore a good Republican cloth coat—"but I always tell her she looks good in anything." It may have escaped some, but not Pat, that this doomed her to cloth coats forever. Even in the White House, should God will this, and on the coldest day in history in Washington, when every other woman in town is warm under her fur, poor old Pat's tail will be patriotically freezing under that honest Republican cloth coat. In the cold as well as the hot war, there are casualties among the women and children, too.

The rumors of any kind of upheaval at the studio seem to have died down, though there is one that Blaustein [Julian, executive producer at 20th Century–Fox 1951–1952] is looking for greener pastures. And Siegel tells me that Schermer [Jules, an associate producer at 20th Century–Fox] is leaving. Meanwhile, Hakim has crashed through with another smash, just as soon as they finish three weeks of retakes on a picture that was originally shot in four. Everybody just laughs. Leonard Goldstein has come aboard and is already worried because Zanuck wants to read one of his scripts. His position seems to be that his scripts won't stand reading. I think he's right. If Darryl ever tries to improve these things that Leonard cooks up, they're dead. Nothing else of any moment seems to be happening around here.

Dorris and I send you our best. I'm afraid we won't be able to make the Tenth Annual Jack o' Lantern Ball at the Jonathan Club this year but in our own quiet way, in a little circle of our friends, we manage to get along.

TO THORNTON DELEHANTY

October 20, 1952

Dear Thorny:

I'm sorry I didn't get to talk to you yesterday. I wanted to ask you the name of the little soubrette for whom you are backing *The Seven Year Itch*. Obviously you wouldn't be socking your money into a theatrical venture for anything else. But I imagine it'll be worth it, once the show is open and you and she are on your way to Reisenweber's for lobster and champagne. Then home through the park in a hansom. It's the only life.

I'm told that the Bogarts will be whistle-stopping to New York next week but you expose yourself to them only at your own risk. All of Betty's friends, including her husband, are hoping it will all be over after November 4th and she will be herself again. At the moment she is somebody else, I don't know who, unless it's Frankie Spitz [Leo Spitz's wife]. The only sign of the old Betty that I've detected recently was her report to Dorris that the Gov let his hand fall carelessly on her knee and left it there for some hours. No politics there that I can see. Bogart, though a little feverishly Stevensonian himself, has taken rather a noble position. He points out that while it may be possible for one divorced person to reach the White House, it hardly stands to reason that the country will accept two, so the only decent thing he can do is, naturally, the Dutch act. Among historians this is referred to as the Nathan Hale position.

I may be in your vicinity around the end of November. The announced purpose is business but you will guess immediately that the real reason is to attend Ed Sullivan's Harvest Moon Ball. We don't have things like that out here. Marion Davies had a little get-together the other evening, but I wasn't invited. Hardly anybody, in fact, was invited. Just the newspaper people, everybody on the papers from gossip columnists to cooking editors, and photographers. I didn't mind in particular until I heard that her husband, Captain Brown, skipper of a sea sled, had sneaked three dozen dribble glasses onto the tables. That I was sorry I missed. The rest of the crowd was made up of guests of the Beverly Hills Hotel who heard the noise and went over to see what was up. It wasn't Marion.

My best to George Axelrod.

Claudette Colbert starred in *Three Came Home*, written and produced by Johnson in 1950. It was based on a true story of a woman and her husband who were reunited after being held in separate Japanese prisoner-of-war camps.

TO CLAUDETTE COLBERT

December 31, 1952

Claudette dear:

I promised myself that I'd answer your hello, via Bob Goldstein, before 1952 was out, now here it is New Year's Eve. Mr. and Mrs. Lederer* are the hosts of the year, tonight. I'm told that this is a step up from Sam Spiegel, but as I grow older I face this annual ritual with greater and greater trepidation. We will set out for the revels with the Bogarts, which may complicate matters still further. Betty would go to parties three times a day if they were available. She has an appalling energy. Tonight, I'm sure, she will see herself as the Toast of New Orleans and I will be carrying the roses that she will clutch between her teeth. Bogey of course will be busy working on his own legend as Quite a Character, setting fire to people, et cetera. Don't you wish you were here?

The Negulescos had everybody dress up and come to their house last Sunday night, my last time out. It was a cross section of Hollywood society, and I could hardly bear it. I never saw so many people that I detested in one room. I had hardly sat down behind the woodbox before Virginia Zanuck [wife of Darryl], whom I don't dislike, came over and complained that someone had poured a martini on her foot. For one of those mysterious reasons that nobody will ever be able to understand, other things got poured on her all during the evening. Just seemed to be hexed. The minute somebody got really tight they either threw their drinks on her or put out their cigarettes on her back. She began to look like an old spittoon.

I left even before dinner was announced. The mere thought that I might be seated next to someone I loathed and would have to chat with affably was too much for me. Dorris remained. My spies tell me that she did very well with the gin and tonics and early in the evening denounced several guests by name and with particulars. I won't attempt to describe Dusty's [Mrs. Negulesco] hostess outfit. I can only say that if I were French I would describe it as outré. That

* Charles Lederer was a screenwriter who often collaborated with Ben Hecht and worked a great deal with director Howard Hawks. His credits include *His Girl Friday, I Was a Male War Bride, Monkey Business*, and *The Spirit of St. Louis*.

means that it was the God-damndest thing you ever saw. There are times, you know, when Dusty outdresses Jean. I went home and read *The Hound of the Baskervilles*. Very good book.

We miss you here but I don't know why you should miss much of Hollywood. I met Jane Wyman's new husband and that's all there is to that. John Huston is back and I think Olivia's [de Havilland] got him. After seeing *Moulin Rouge* she was quoted as saying: "At last John has come of age." Unquote. This statement rang through the town. Nothing has been heard like it since the Gettysburg Address. Later in the evening John went to sleep sitting up on a sofa and snored at the ceiling while Olivia tried to force black coffee down him while she stroked his brow. Now what do you make of that?

Hedda managed to stir up some pickets for the opening of the picture and later the American Legion stepped in to guard the Republic against John and Ferrer. Ferrer is as innocent as a child of any Communist taint. He whooped it up for thirty front organizations, none of which he suspected, and travelled for over two years in a show with Paul Robeson without knowing he was a Communist. In fact, I don't think he even knew he was colored. The American Legion, on hearing this, exonerated him immediately, but he hasn't cleared himself yet with Hedda. This is the kind of thing that keeps the pot boiling here.

I don't know any more dirt or would certainly tell it to you. We miss you very much but are somewhat consoled by the fact that when you come back we will know a very rich woman. We both send you our love and wish we were with you, either here or there.

TO ROBERT GOLDSTEIN

January 10, 1953

Dear Robin:

I trust you will note who is lighting whose cigar in the enclosed photograph.* All I can tell you about its effect on Leonard is that he summoned me to his office this morning to give it to me. He asked me to send it to you (he felt too shy to do it himself) but for a while I was tempted to send it to Zanuck instead and tell him that

---

* The photograph showed Darryl Zanuck lighting the cigar of Leonard Goldstein, Robert's brother.

Leonard had had five thousand prints made and was distributing them through the town.

All I know otherwise is that I got a letter from Frank Sullivan telling me that Miss [Beatrice] Lillie got shikker at a party the other night and bit Mrs. Gilbert Miller. No explanation. Just grabbed her and bit her. Quite a character, Lady Peel.

Why don't you get in touch with Maggie Furse, now Mrs. Stephen Watts, while you're doing nothing around there? Stephen, I believe, is in Africa on some kind of mission, probably looking for Dr. Livingstone. They live at 1 South Terrace, S.W. 7.

1953–1956

Milton MacKaye had written in the *Saturday Evening Post* in January 1952, "Life in the shade of Beverly Hills palm trees today is lived dangerously and in an atmosphere of civil war." Cooperation between the movies and television was slow in developing. When the FCC questioned the studios about holding back films and stories to which they had rights, the studios reacted sharply and defensively: it was a purely competitive situation, and television networks, like every studio, would be required to bid for what they wanted.

Television had created some jobs, but not as many as one might suppose. B movies, which had kept many crafts people, actors, directors, and writers employed, were no longer being made. Crime and cowboy movies had been the mainstay of movie "cheapies," and it was evident that television was an excellent and prolific master of both these forms.

Moviegoers were getting fussy; they could see all the most ordinary fare on television. They wanted something special at the movie theaters. The idea that "better pictures" would reverse the box-office slump was a short-lived one. Hollywood followed a much more basic show-business conviction: *novelty* was the key.

Cinerama was an attempt to show off the advantages of movie-theater viewing. Another multi-lens process, 3-D, also enjoyed a brief period of popularity. However, once the gimmick was experienced, people showed little interest in returning to the theaters.

Hollywood needed a less technically complex, more versatile system. And Spyros Skouras, in the middle of a desperate fight for control of 20th Century–Fox, found the answer: CinemaScope. Skouras bet his future, and that of the studio, on this wide-screen process.

The camera lens for CinemaScope compressed wide-angle shots onto a narrow strip of film; a compensating lens on the projector expanded the image against a wide, curved screen; three speakers were used for the soundtrack and seemed to project voices precisely from their points of origin. The great advantage of CinemaScope was that the compensating lens could be attached to any projector. Conversion to CinemaScope in the theaters was easier and less expensive than any preceding big-screen effort.

In the spring of 1952, 20th Century–Fox announced that all its features would be filmed in CinemaScope.

February 7, 1953

Dear Thorny:

Mrs. Bogart tells me that you deny that you are rich. If this is true, there's naturally not much point in any further correspondence with you. I already know enough poor people.

And so in conclusion, I am enclosing an ad calculated to burn you up because you won't be able to get here in time for the revelations. Out here in the West, we don't mess around with science any more. We go straight to the Shrine Auditorium for our stuff. What I'm going to try to do is get one of those little one-inch-high men and send him to you for your birthday. Don't lose him.

I don't know whether I can write to you any more anyway. This business is a mess. Every day it's something new—3-dimension, 2-dimension, 1-dimension, round screens with no dimension. The producers here at Fox haven't any time to make pictures. They're buying Fox stock and sitting around in brokers' offices.

My next picture, in which Mrs. Bogart will be one third of the stars, in 7-dimensions, is to be made in our version of Cinerama, which means that everything, even close-ups, will look like it's taking place on the old Hippodrome stage. . . .

TO HUMPHREY BOGART

February 14, 1953

Dear Bogey:

The word here is that as a result of your unfortunate accident, you had to cancel five interviews, which your wife described as, for you, a fate worse than death. Every [illegible] would undoubtedly be able to make it up, possibly by receiving the reporters two at a time. Incidentally, a fellow showed up at Romanoff's the other day with the statement that he was writing an autobiography of you. Had you forgotten that? He was there to question Mike [Romanoff] about you, but Mike denied knowing you. He said that he knew two or three different characters that you had assumed, but as for Bogart the Man, the True Bogart, the Inner Bogart, that he didn't know. We now describe you as Mr. X, the Human Sphinx. Won't talk. Can't get a word out of him. Wild horses couldn't drag the truth from him.

Betty called on us the other night, with Irving Lazar. I suppose Rock Hudson was busy. She was as pretty as a picture, told me what a magnificent actress she was, and then we all had a drink together. Dorris and I had invited her for dinner, but then remembered that we had Olivia de Havilland coming, and remembered that Betty has no patience with a flighty person like Olivia, who won't take her art seriously. So we did a fast shuffle to enjoy the double pleasure of seeing these two young women the same evening. We sent Olivia home early.

I suppose you know that what you are making is now described here as a flat picture. Somebody invents a new method of 3-dimension every day and sometimes twice a day. Also variations of Cinerama. Anybody making a picture with nothing but a good story and two dimensions is put in the same class with David Wark Griffith. . . .

Please tell John [Huston] that I saw *Moulin Rouge* the other night and thought it wonderful. The truth is, I hated every actor in it, but the accumulation of story and beauty made up for this personal prejudice. But perhaps I should except Zsa Zsa. I simply cannot hate any woman that pretty. And when added to such beauty is a talent that literally takes one's breath away, you can well imagine that I could not possibly dismiss her lightly.

As I told Betty, I write this letter only on condition that you do not answer it. If you replied, out of some elemental sense of courtesy, I would feel compelled to reply to your reply. Not to be outdone by my savoir faire, you would reply to my reply to your reply. In no time at all, we would be so busy writing to each other that you would have no time to act and I would have none to hug your wife. I am convinced that this would be a far better world if people stopped writing letters like this to each other. Verbum sapiens. French.

We expect to see Betty tonight. The little sovereign [Mike

Romanoff] is giving a Valentine Day ball, and I don't have to tell you how eager I am to get there and have another go at the Lindy Hop. We will miss you, I suppose.

    Yours in Christ,

Zanuck and Skouras chose *The Robe* as their first CinemaScope release. It was made in fifty-two days at a cost of $4 million and, released in September 1953, was an immediate success with the public. By 1955 it had grossed $20 million.

    Although *The Robe* was released first, Nunnally Johnson's CinemaScopic *How to Marry a Millionaire* was completed earlier. Johnson made no special effort to tailor his screenplay to a new technological process (he once said that he "put the paper in the typewriter sideways when writing for CinemaScope"). By his own recollection, the cameraman and Negulesco, the director, were responsible for any of the special effects in *How to Marry a Millionaire*. This letter was written when filming was about to begin.

TO JEAN NEGULESCO

                                       March 9, 1953

Dear Jean:

    At last the great day has come. You alone know how they have fought to keep us from making this picture. You alone know the jealousy, the bitterness, the lack of faith in this project that you and I have dreamed of doing for years now.

    They said we were fools! They said we were dreamers! They said we were too artistic! But you and I, we have always had faith in this story!

    So now that the great day has come at last, and we have overcome all opposition, let us go forward and make this the finest picture that was ever turned out in the entire history of CinemaScope. Let's make them eat their words.

    Give my warmest, deepest, most emotional felicitations to every single member of the cast! And to yourself, God speed on this great crusade!

    Gottfried Johnson

TO CHARLES LEDERER

                                       March 11, 1953

Dear Charlie:

    You're a shrewd operator but I see through you immediately. You are trying to get in on the ground floor of this cockateel caper.

Well, you'll have to get up a little earlier, my friend, to get anything past Johnson & Johnson & Johnson, for I have muscled my way into the firm as business adviser.

You know as well as I do that five dollars is not going to cover the kind of cockateel our outfit is going to turn out. That's laughable even to think about. You can't keep a thing like this quiet in the cockateel world and it's already the talk of the caper that a Johnson & Johnson & Johnson cockateel will be a bird strictly from Tiffany's. Already we have on file applications, well in advance, from the American Association of Cockateel and Parakeet Associates, the Cockateel Institute, and the Cockateel Branch of the British Bird Watchers Club, and our males haven't even made the first pass at the females!

I have an immense respect for all three of my children when it comes to cadging a fin off a guest. Only last night Scotty got something like a dollar and sixty-five cents from Sol Siegel, purely through wheedling, and sixty cents from Richard Burton, which is even more remarkable, because Burton is Welsh. Apparently much the same sort of thing goes on when the girls manage to sequester a solvent guest, but frankly, I can't permit it. Especially when the guest is obviously trying to swindle the children.

So permit me to return your five dollars. Your name will go down on the list in its proper order, first come first served, and you'll get your bird in time. This system is ironbound, steel-clad and inflexible except that a little oil in papa's hand might run your name up the list a couple of notches. The books, of course, are rigged.

Caught you that time, eh, boy?

TO HUMPHREY BOGART

March 14, 1953

Dear Bogey:

Your wife is doing a very excellent job in the picture and I think you will be pleased with her performance, as we are.

Please do not waste my time by acknowledging this flash. I am too busy a man to read letters that do not enclose checks. For in addition to producing a picture for which there are only three projection machines in existence that can show it, one in projection room 5, one in Darryl's projection room, and one on an empty stage at Western Avenue, I am writing a script for a picture which I see in the papers has been removed from the schedule. So, since the

picture is not to be produced anyway, a good deal of my time is occupied in settling on a director who will not direct it and actors who
will not play in it. This leaves me time only to read my fan mail.

Henry Ginsberg [production head of Paramount] and Scarlett
O'Hara Ginsberg [Ginsberg's wife, Mildred] are divorcing after
something like a quarter of a century of marriage. Don't understand
that either. On the other hand, Marilyn Monroe shows no professional improvement. Yesterday on the set she ran up to me, breathless
as usual, and gasped, "Which way to the men's room?" I offered to
take her there but she said she only wanted the direction. Neither do
I understand that.

So much for you.

Johnson worked closely with the cast on *How to Marry a Millionaire*. He
explained:

I made a deal with him [Negulesco]. I never heard of anybody making a deal
like this, and I don't know if anybody else would have permitted it. I said,
"Hey Jean, would you let me rehearse the actors and their lines before each
scene?" He said, "I'd be delighted." So that's the way we did the picture. . . .
Although I am not an actor, at least I knew where the emphasis went, and I
could give them something of the tempo. The actors were pleased as hell, Jean
was pleased, and the picture turned out about five times as good. . . . Betty
Grable was quite capable of delivering a line very well. She's a very good
comedienne. I didn't know what Bacall could do because I'd never seen her
play comedy, but she could play it first rate. And Marilyn, I didn't know what
to look for there.

TO THORNTON DELEHANTY

April 9, 1953

Dear Thorny:

I had just sat down to write you last week when I got word about
Einstein's revisions on his theory of relativity and of course the fat
was in the fire. It was only the week before that I had finally got the
hang of the original version, and was naturally looking forward to a
few weeks of rest, when bang, along comes this new arrangement.
Since then Dorris and I have had time for little else. Forgive me,
will you?

The three girls are a good story. Everybody went around with
their fingers in their ears blabbering about what temperament there
would be on the set, and needless to say, the gossip columnists, those

lice, have done everything possible to foment trouble for us. They've printed all kinds of mischievous rumors, quoting one against the other, and pointing out fictitious privileges given to one above the other two, in the most desperate effort you ever saw to create feuds. But it hasn't worked in the least.

I don't think Betty Bacall and Betty Grable had ever met before. I don't know who's met Marilyn Monroe but Joe Di Maggio. But Betty Bacall fell in love with Grable and now thinks she's the funniest clown she ever had the pleasure of knowing. Which is not far from true. Miss Grable is a real hooligan, and is a fine salty, bawdy girl, without an ounce of pretense about her. In addition, she's giving a better performance than anything she ever did before.

The two Betty's have gone out of their way to help, and make friends with Marilyn, but Miss Monroe is generally something of a zombie. Talking to her is like talking to somebody underwater. She's very honest and ambitious and is either studying her lines or her face during all of her working hours, and there is nothing whatever to be said against her, but she's not material for warm friendship. Except, of course, for DiMag.

We'll be through with the picture early next week and what I've seen of it looks pretty good in this new CinemaScope. It's a larkish story, the girls look very beautiful, and its purpose is to see if something indoors and with just two or three people can look good on this new wide screen. . . .

The news that you might come out here is very good news. I'm sure we can cook up some new salad recipes for the *Woman's Home Companion*. Miss Bacall, or Miss Bagel, as Miss Grable calls her, will be leaving here in a few weeks for a month in the fashionable French capital with her fashionable husband. This will give her just time enough to bail him out and flee across the border to catch the steamer from Barcelona. I'll tell her you called.

My wife sends you her affection. I send you a manly shake of the hand.

In 1953 Johnson assumed for the first time total directorial responsibilities on a movie. The film, *Night People*, was a Cold War story, filmed in Berlin and Munich and starring Gregory Peck. Although film critic Pauline Kael objected to Johnson's approach to a complex political situation, claiming that the political attitudes were not derived from a historical understanding, Johnson defended the film as a valid reflection of men's characters and as a good adventure story. He felt he had made every effort to be fair-minded in his screenplay:

There are so many bastards, and there are so many cowards, and there are so many brutes, and there are so many decent guys. Any time I've done a picture, I've tried to make that the basis of my using the enemy. . . . You have to accept that there are decent people here and they believe as much in what they're doing as we believe in what we're doing.

TO ROBERT GOLDSTEIN

April 21, 1953

Dear Bertie:

Everything has stopped here. . . . The last of the stages closed down this afternoon and not a wheel is turning on the whole lot. I don't expect to get back into action myself until Friday morning. Whatever became of Eidophor? Whatever became of CinemaScope? Whatever became, in fact, of pictures?

I'll have the first draft of the Peck script in another week or so. I think it's a very exciting story. Except that I will hate to have to live in the Hotel of the Four Seasons in Munich for more than a week or so. I don't speak Munich and they probably don't speak Georgia, so it looks to me like an impasse already. Meanwhile, we finished *How to Marry a Millionaire* and are now trying to figure out how to put it together so it'll make some sense. If we are unsuccessful in this, I intend to turn it over to Leonard [Goldstein] and let him put it out as a Ma and Pa Kettle picture, in which a thing like that wouldn't matter. . . .

Winchell has been infesting the studio for the past week, which means that I haven't been able to eat in the executive dining room. As you know yourself, Winchell is a perfectly splendid fellow with but one wee weakness—he thinks people are glad to see him. At last reports, the executive dining room had been reduced to him and Darryl and Ray Klune. Not that Ray wants to be there. He simply can't figure out how to walk out on Winchell and yet not walk out on Darryl at the same time. Very baffling situation.

If you want to know the whole story about Olivier and Lady Olivier, ask Pam Mason. Oh boy!

Why don't you send me a lot of money?

May 20, 1953

Dear Robert:

I expect to be arriving there on BOAC flight 510 at 9:45 a.m. Friday the 29th, this month. If your brand new Rolls Royce were there to meet me I would be one of the happiest little producers you ever saw. I shall be pigging it at the De Vere Hotel, which is in Kensington, on the way to Chelsea, and that was all that Freddie Fox could find for me. Suits me.

Negulesco has passed the crisis but is still a very worried boy. Last Sunday while playing croquet he lost his temper over some error on the court and flung his mallet to the turf. It hit on the handle and leaped up again like Charlie Chaplin's cane and bludgeoned, oh God, Mr. Zanuck right between the eyes, drawing blood, or plasma, whichever he is equipped with. Three stitches had to be taken in Mr. Zanuck's skin, which was wide open with ideas pouring out like a leak in a bag of grain. I scarcely need tell you what this did to Mr. Negulesco's emotions. Nevertheless, there seemed to be no need for him to take strychnine, cut his throat, hang himself, and shoot himself too. For the truth of the matter was that Mr. Zanuck took it very well, contenting himself with putting Mr. Negulesco on layoff. That's why Dusty is now using old cigar butts and things like that to paint with instead of brushes.

Leonard seems to regard this as very funny. Leonard has no kindness in him. Leonard's idea seems to be that Negulesco had it coming to him. "All the little man wants to do is hit a stick in the ground with a little black ball," Leonard says, "so why the hell should Negulesco try to stop him?" Leonard's idea is that so far as he is concerned, Mr. Zanuck can hit this little stick with this little black ball day and night and see how much he cares.

I am leaving Dorris home this trip. . . . I will be in London for perhaps a week, just for a look-see. Ring me up at the DeVere.

Clifton Fadiman was an essayist and literary critic on *The New Yorker*.

December 16, 1953

Dear Kip:

If you take up the subject of puns again, you might consider the Circumstantial Pun, which calls for a very special and often highly complex set of circumstances for its use.

For example, our Mr. Kaufman once had one in mind which he confessed he doubted he would ever be able to use. The locale would have to be somewhere in the Orient during a war with the Japanese. The season should be late autumn, and on a particular morning our forces would have hanged a small Japanese spy. If such were the case and Mr. Kaufman were there, he felt that he could not unreasonably remark, "There's a little Nip in the air this morning."

Bennett Cerf had one calling for even more difficult circumstances. Suppose, though, that Syngman Rhee had a son who came to this country and obtained employment with one of the Luce magazines. Suppose, then, too, that he disappeared mysteriously and a city-wide search was instituted for him. Then in the course of time he would have to be discovered, perhaps in a Third Avenue saloon. Then the detective could walk up to him and say, "Ah, sweet Mr. Rhee of *Life*, at last I've found thee!"

The arrangements for the use of one by the late great Herman Mankiewicz had even greater ramifications. Only an idealist could hope for such an assemblage of people and places but Mr. Mankiewicz felt that it would be worth the wait, however long. In this one, Congressman Emanuel Celler would be aboard a train bound from New York to Chicago with a group of friends. Likewise aboard would be members of the New York Giants and the Chicago National League team. Now we'll say Representative Celler strays away from his friends and they go in search of him. They find him in the club car dozing in a chair between Stanley Hack [of the Chicago Cubs] and Leo ["the Lip"] Durocher. Now if everything is exactly in order and one of Mr. Celler's friends has a slight accent, he could very well say, "There's Manny asleep between the Cub and the Lip."

All very unlikely, of course. But you can see I've enjoyed your examination of puns.

TO RICHARD BURTON

December 28, 1953

Dear Dick:

I saw Marlon Brando as Mark Antony last night and you can stop worrying about him anyway. This is my Christmas gift to you.

I am now at work on the script of *How to Marry a Wandering Jew*, a bit of *The Robe*, a bit of *Ivanhoe*, and samples of other period pictures that have been successful.

I also got around to seeing *The Robe* a couple of weeks ago and I thought you were superb. This is my Christmas gift to Sybil [Burton's wife]. Mason was the only one in *Julius Caesar* that I thought I could apply superb to, though of course Greer Garson's performance is not to be lightly dismissed. Gielgud I thought stately, traditional, and excessively histrionic. There's a man who apparently won't give an inch to humanity.

My best to you both for the New Year, and I hope we see you before much more time has passed.

Harry Evans was presumably a literary agent.

TO HARRY EVANS

January 22, 1954

Dear Harry:

To my great disappointment I have been unable to share your feeling about "Bachelor's Baby Sitter." A year ago, I might very well have. But with Zanuck unable to find anything of interest for Cinema-Scope in anybody wearing a collar and necktie, it would be, I'm sure, a waste of time to approach him with this story. For another thing, we have got to continue making Biblical stories until we use up all those garments we bought for *The Robe*. A year from now you may be able to see an actor in CinemaScope wearing Boston garters and a Tattersall vest, but not much before then.

As for reminding Darryl of his hock dancing in a Paris saloon, again your timing couldn't be worse. Four nights ago at Ciro's in the presence of about three hundred of the gentry, the latent Tarzan in him came out and he stripped to the waist and performed a few antics on a trapeze. Among other things, he made three gallant efforts to chin himself with one hand, a feat which he said only five men in the world could do. A few minutes later, as every newspaper in town announced, it turned out that there were only four who could do it. (The other four, Harry Brand told the United Press, were Dore Schary, Y. Frank Freeman, Harry Cohn, and either Jack or Harry Warner, take your pick). As a result of all this jocular publicity, Mr. Zanuck is being treated with particular respect and solemnity these days. So don't ask me to remind him of any other hi-jinks, not for a month or so anyway.

I'm sorry about this story but I really don't think it has the punch to compete in the heavyweight market these days. I hope you don't mind if I read the rest of the magazine. I thank you very much indeed for thinking of me when you got the story and I hope to God this won't exclude me from future consideration when you come across something that sounds good to you.

My best to you.

TO THORNTON DELEHANTY

January 26, 1954

Dear Thorny:

Will you be good enough not to answer my letters promptly? You answer quickly, I answer quickly, you answer quickly, I answer quickly. Pretty soon I've got time for nothing else, just answering your letter quickly. Then one day I'd get mad and drop the whole correspondence. Otherwise, if I tried to keep at it, my work would fall off, Zanuck would speak sharply to me two or three times, and next year they wouldn't pick up my option. This wouldn't bother me at first, but presently I'd learn that the word had got about that all I did was correspond with you. I suppose we could sell the house but we'd have to take a pretty big loss on it. I'm sure the studio would give Dorris some kind of stock job, like Mae Marsh's, and at least the children wouldn't starve, but I can't pretend that they would be able to have much of a childhood. So for God's sake, cut it out, will you?

The clipping I enclose shows me on a typical evening out.* Sometimes I'll have Marjorie Main too, or maybe Martha Raye, but all in all, this is about as fair a picture of the way I step out in the evening as any other. Dorris? God only knows.

---

* Nunnally in evening clothes escorting Marilyn Monroe and Lauren Bacall to the premiere of *How to Marry a Millionaire* while Dorris is being pushed aside by photographers.

You may want to hear what happened to my friend Zsa Zsa the other evening. Christmas Eve, in fact. George Sanders, who tells the story, said that his lawyers and Zsa Zsa's had come to a property settlement agreeable to both parties until it came to the point of Zsa Zsa's signing the paper. Then she refused and began to ask for more and more and more. This irked George. But he figured it wouldn't be difficult to get something on her.

So on Christmas Eve, that holy day, he prepared to raid her home to catch [Porfirio] Rubirosa in the hay with her. He planned to lean a ladder against a second-floor balcony and enter her bedroom through the French doors there, but he couldn't remember whether the doors opened in or out, so, being a careful fellow, he sent a gift over to Zsa Zsa that afternoon by his butler, who was also instructed to nip upstairs and get information on the door situation. They opened out.

Around two-thirty that night, while every son-of-a-bitch and his brother in town was singing "Silent Night," George got in a car with four Sam Spades and set out for the house in Bel-Air. His operatives were such horrible looking fellows that he thought it best to take along something in the shape of a gift for Mrs. Sanders by way of alibi if the Bel-Air cops stopped him. So he wrapped up a brick in some holly paper. They found Rubirosa's car parked outside and the Sam Spades all went through a "Dragnet" routine of jotting numbers and photographing fingerprints and then George and his friends sneaked around the house and set up the ladder.

The rules, it seems, call for the husband to enter first. Otherwise, charges of breaking and entering can be lodged against outsiders. The ladder turned out to be a little shaky and George got quite nervous. As he explained, "I felt it would be most embarrassing if I fell and broke my leg and Rubirosa had to take me to the hospital." But he made it to the balcony all right and found the windows open. Zsa Zsa likes fresh air. So he dashed in bravely and found himself in a scramble with a Venetian blind. Through them he saw two naked forms break the record for the dash to the bathroom, where the light was on. As soon as he could untangle himself from the blinds, George rallied at the head of his operatives and all made a dash for the privileged sanctuary. Rubi and Zsa Zsa had slammed the door shut but in their excitement they forgot that it could also be locked. The door opened inward and it then became a head-on push between George and Rubi, Rubi trying to hold the door shut, George trying to bull it open. Now according to George, he was hitting low, just like Knute Rockne always said, and with a powerful lunge he managed to get the door open about a foot, which to his astonishment brought him face to face with Rubirosa's organ, whereupon, in a moment of whimsy, he shook it heartily and called Merry Christmas to them both. This mortified Rubirosa. It was then that Zsa Zsa called out, "Now, George, really! Please be seated and I'll be out in just a moment." She emerged in a diaphanous negligee, leaving the shy Mr. Rubirosa skulking in the can.

George says her conduct then was above and beyond reproach. In the most elegant fashion, like a veritable Clare Luce, she greeted her husband and his four thugs and invited them to sit down and talk it over. While the thugs stared, George mentioned the lateness of the hour and that he felt that they should be pushing on. But when they started to exit by way of the balcony and the ladder, Zsa Zsa was shocked that they should believe she would not show them to the front door as she would any guest in her home. So she led them downstairs and was reminded on the way of the Christmas tree. "You haven't seen it, George! You must! It's perfectly beautiful!" So she led them all into the living room and they all admired it. "Did you get your gift?" she asked. George said he hadn't, but the evening could be taken as an entirely adequate gift so far as he was concerned. "Never mind, it'll be there bright and early in the morning," she assured him. Then she opened the front door for them, shook hands all around, and they all exchanged God bless you's.

TO LAUREN BACALL

February 19, 1954

Dear Betty:

. . . I have dropped work on *The Wandering Jew* (I am always dropping work on *The Wandering Jew*) and am now on something called *The Man Who Never Was*,* about a stiff being dropped overboard off the Spanish coast during the war to fool the Germans with some false information planted in his pockets, and this may take me to England this summer.

Ava Gardner's shipwreck in the storm was front page news here. But it just goes to show what happens when you go out with a

---

* Johnson stopped work on *The Man Who Never Was*, explaining that it "was a first-rate story, but when I got to it I found I could tell it all in about thirty minutes. I didn't know any way of padding it. . . ." The movie was made and released in 1956, with Nigel Balchin as screenwriter and Ronald Neame as director.

glamourous star. There were 750 words describing Ava's dishevelled hair and bravery and a final paragraph, like the tail end of an obituary, giving the names of other survivors, which said that also present in the boat was Joseph Mankiewicz, director, and two other people. What about Joe's hair?

Dorris, who has one of the filthiest minds in town, and I don't say that just because she's my wife either, jumped to the immediate conclusion that the incident was stolen directly from the one in *How to Marry a Millionaire* when Fred Clark wound up his holiday with Betty Grable on the George Washington Bridge. If I've told Dorris once, I've told her twice not to say things like that.

Jed Harris came in for a drink last Sunday afternoon and is still with us. I can't figure out what he wants here unless it's the rest. He came in so full of vituperation against Hollywood last night that I figured he had been turned down by somebody on something. It's worth Jed's using my underwear and putting out his cigarettes on the floor just to hear him sound off against Hollywood when the town isn't proving hospitable. Such choice of words! Such brilliance! It's discouraging to listen to him.

Fred MacMurray's in love with June Haver and I have done everything in my power to try to get excited about this fact, but it's no use. Pamela Mason says Nicky Hilton is crazy. While dancing with her at the Zsa Zsa party the other night he made all kinds of erotic proposals to her. God damned if I can see what's crazy about that. Pam, who is the most interesting and inaccurate reporter, said that Zsa Zsa invited a hundred, prepared food for seventy, and forty came. However, the press was there from as far away as Pomona and they all got excellent pictures of Brian Aherne as Renoir and Eleanor [Mrs. Aherne] as his favorite model. By the rarest stroke of luck imaginable, Dorris had a cold and I had to stay home too, to take care of her. We played Scrabble.

Scotty and Stevie [Bogart] both seem to be in excellent health and unbearable. Christie [age eleven] now dresses like a Barbary Coast tart, and Roxie [age nine] now claims to have the first case in history of total bursitis, one solid ache from head to toe. I cured it with fifty cents. Now why the hell can't doctors think up something practical like that?

Tell Bogey I got his view of Orson Welles in the nude and turned it over to the children. If he thinks for one second that I'm going to make any comments on Mr. Zanuck to a couple of gossipy people like you, he should see a doctor. We miss you and send you our love.

Patsy Brice was a graduate student at UCLA.

February 12, 1954

Dear Miss Brice:

I don't suppose anybody can isolate the particular quality or event that influenced his life to the end it reached. A biographer examining the evidence objectively might be able to do that, but not the man himself. But I will make a speculative guess in my own case, and I make it quite seriously. I think that being fired from jobs so many times led me to where I am now. If I hadn't been fired I might have been sitting today in any of a half-dozen less attractive positions. I never liked being fired, it staggered and depressed me each time it happened, but the result was that I kept moving around looking for work and this led me, step by step, to the movies. I never aimed for them. It was just that looking for a way to make a living and support a family brought me around to them.

You asked for something that might be profitable for you in the planning of your future. I doubt that this fills the bill in that respect, but it might suggest to you that there are jobs from which it is better to be fired than anything else.

Very truly yours.

February 27, 1954

Dear Betty:

I'll tell you exactly how things are. We went to the Screen Writers' Guild dinner the other night, as Irving Lazar's guests, and I didn't win one single award. But the truth is, I have something else up my sleeve. *How to Marry a Millionaire* is up in the Academy contest for Costume—color, and I've been spending all of my time getting people behind that. I've already got Ira Gershwin, for one, to support it.

Ira's an honest man. He hasn't seen a picture since *Mrs. Miniver* and can support anything a friend suggests with a perfectly clear conscience. It was a pretty good evening, if you don't mind being with so many writers. Most of the sketches were very funny and Groucho, the MC, was tremendous. In his introduction to one sketch, which was about the effect of movie making on the natives in Africa, he said that there were more pictures made in Africa last year than at RKO. "As a matter of fact," he added, "there were more pictures made in my back yard last year than there were at RKO."

The cast was all blacked up like Amos and Andy and the leading man, a Swahili nance, had changed his native name to Montgomery Congo. They got all their messages by tom-toms. "Catch it," the nance would say, and this secretary would pick up the drum. After one long exchange of beats, he turned and asked in a very puzzled voice, "Who's Paul Small?" [the agent]. If Bogey had been there, he'd have been the only one in the house who didn't bust out laughing. At the end of the sketch, Montgomery invited some of the other cannibals to dinner. "We're having Sam Zimbalist," he promised. "Dressing?" asked one. "No," Montgomery replied, "just an apple in his mouth." So you can see for yourself how things went.

Lazar really spread himself and his other guests were the Vidors, Charles Vidor, the director, and his wife, Doris Warner Vidor just back from yodeling in the Alps, the Bill Goetzes, the Billy Wilders, the Ira Gershwins, and Alfred Vanderbilt. Alfred and I had a nice long talk together. He talked about Native Dancer and I told him about Christie's horse. We fascinated each other.

Your son Stevie was a pleasant visitor in our home yesterday afternoon and a good time was had by all except Scotty's parents. Stevie looks just fine and seemed to be in the best of health. This is the sort of thing I deplore. I find that I am able to love a child better when he or she is a little sickly and doesn't feel like throwing a toy truck at me. You can have your healthy kids. What I like is one that the doctors are worried about.

Winchell is around here and can now empty a room in thirty-two seconds flat. I heard him the other day telling about how many dynamite secrets he has. "I know so many things that I can't reveal that sometimes when I go to bed at night it scares me." But inadvertently he let one of them slip. Did you know that professional wrestling is not on the level? Now, for Christ's sake, don't repeat this! We don't want to get Walter in a jam, do we?

When are you coming back?

Around here they are describing Marilyn Monroe as a ball player's ball player.

My love to you.

P.S. I forgot to tell you that Montgomery Congo claimed to have been offered the title role in *The African Queen* but his agent slipped up on the deal.

TO JEAN NEGULESCO

March 5, 1954

Dear Jean:

What on earth are you doing there all this time? Remaking *How to [Marry a Millionare]*? Already you've missed not only Eisenhower but also Darryl's earnest explanation of why Eisenhower wasn't visiting the Zanucks. It was sheer eloquence and very closely reasoned and when he finished it in the dinning room, I don't think there was a dry eye in the house.

And if you're not back here by Sunday you will miss the Photoplay Award banquet at which *How to* will be one of the pictures to be honored. *The Robe* isn't. The editor of *Photoplay*, a fellow named Sammis, and the publisher, whose name I didn't get, came to lunch today and Darryl asked them point blank how come about *The Robe*. You never saw two fellows go to such complicated lengths to keep from saying that insufficient people voted for *The Robe*. It was finally agreed that it must have been because their contest ended before *The Robe* got adequately launched. Everybody was so happy with this solution, in which no one's honor was stained, that I forwent reminding them of the fact that *How to* came out more than a month later than *The Robe*, so how the hell did it manage to get picked? . . .

But cut out all that nonsense and come on home. New York can't be all that attractive. We both send love to you both.

TO RICHARD BURTON

April 3, 1954

Dear Richard:

If you really feel so strongly about iambic pentameters, the answer is unquestionably Johnson's dialogue. In all literature there is no greater range than [that] between Shakespeare's stuff and Johnson's. I work on *The Wandering Jew* between other assignments, the way W. C. Fields used to juggle while trying to remember his next joke. Nobody will be more surprised when, or if, a script comes out of it than Zanuck, except possibly myself. But I still hope. I still think it smells like money.

The Masons have an itinerant critic from London visiting them for a few days, Kenneth Tynan, who admittedly came to whack Hollywood over the head for *Punch* and is now, he tells me, dismayed by the fact that he likes it around here. But after an evening with George Cukor, who wouldn't! He tells me that at his last meeting with you, you felled him with a right hook to the breastbone; apparently your secret weapon. He went on to say that for the rest of your little chat together, he held a chair out in front of him, like Clyde Beatty entering a cage full of lions and tigers. You do have the God damndest social gatherings in London. The provocation for this attack, he said, was something he wrote about Claire Bloom. Little did I ever think I'd live to see the day that you were defending, not after, a lady's honor, professional or otherwise. It's certainly not the thing Gielgud would have been caught at.

I met Tynan and his wife at a party that the Masons gave for them last Sunday night. Either they haven't been giving these parties recently, or Dorris and I haven't been invited. But it was rather like old times. Various representatives of Pam's tribe, blood and technical, mingled among the other guests. Freddie de Cordova [a television and movie director] fetched a drink from time to time. . . .

I have no idea what I'll do next. I wrote a script about people wearing neckties and so they put it on the shelf. No neckties in CinemaScope yet. Then I wrote another, *The Man Who Never Was*, from Ewen Montagu's book, and I doubt if it'll be done either. No tommy-guns in CinemaScope. On the other hand, I'm still being paid.

There's a lot of juicy gossip around here but I'm a son-of-a-bitch if I'm going to put it down on paper and jeopardize my soft berth here. That'll have to wait until you and Sybil get back here, which I hope will be before long. Meanwhile, Groucho is about as ever. He took Christie out for dinner the other night and as usual she stopped him cold. After dinner they were going to see his television show, and after his first quip as they sat down in the Brown Derby she studied him for a moment and said, "I hope the show's going to be funnier than that." After that, he said, he proceeded a little warily with her. Roxie still blushes at the mention of your name, and when she heard it in the list of nominations on the Academy television broadcast, she dropped her eyes like a shy maiden trying to control her pride in a triumph of her lover. Dorris is more forthright, she begs you and Sybil to come back.

Our best to you both.

May 17, 1954

Dear Frank:

I am coming to New York at the end of this week and will be there for two weeks, at the Plaza Hotel. I'm wondering if by any chance you will be coming down to the metropolis to pick up your royalties during that time. It would be good to meet you in person.

But how should I describe myself, so you'll know me? It is quite embarrassing for rather a shy person to describe himself, or herself, as the case may be, to a stranger. After all our correspondence, you can imagine how often I've wondered what you look like, just as I have no doubt you've wondered about me. As I think I told you once, my eyes are blue, with just a glint of hazel in certain lights. They are not large, not nearly as large as most people say, but they're not small either. Myself, I should say they are just a little larger than average.

Cute is the word that most of my friends apply to me, but of course that would be of little help to you in recognizing me across, say, a crowded room. Cute sounds as if I were tiny. The truth is that I am not at all tiny. On the other hand, you could hardly describe me as large. My own feeling about it, to be frank with you, is that I am kind of large cute.

Ordinarily I could help you to identify me by describing the way I do my hair, but just now I am in a spell where I change the arrangement almost every day, to suit the mood I find on myself when I awake in the morning. Today, for instance, since I felt very stern when I awoke this morning, it is brushed straight back, very severely, with utter disregard of the bald spot forward. But what tomorrow? Quien sabe!

But this is futile. I simply cannot bring myself to observe myself objectively. Besides which, who knows which of the myriad me's will be present the day we meet? To save trouble, it might as well be that I wear something distinctive by which you could spot me across this crowded room. (But for God's sake, don't sing!) I think I'll wear my green, and to make doubly certain, a red, red rose in my lapel. And to make still more certain, I will carry a sunflower in my left hand and a Remington Rand adding machine in my right. I don't see how you can possibly miss me.

Yours till then.*

* At the time of this letter, Johnson and Sullivan had been friends and drinking companions for more than twenty-five years.

Stephen Watts was an editor at the Bodley Head, the English publishing house, and husband of costume designer Margaret Furse.

TO STEPHEN WATTS

July 19, 1954

Dear Stephen:

I had rather have your lovely words about *Night People* than even lovelier ones from Miss [C. A.] Lejeune [an English film critic]. And if Maggie has anything comparable to say, let her waste no time in getting to it, for I have no intention of moving until I hear from her. The opinion of one you respect is the only opinion worth a nickel (three ha'penny).

I can't say that the London reviews weren't good. It seemed to me that the picture, on the whole, got a very satisfactory reception in the papers. Two or three had their reservations, but then so did I. Miss Lejeune, like you, didn't go for the prologue, but your objections to it were on much more sensible grounds than hers. She apparently just didn't like such an alteration in the traditional way of beginning a picture.

As for your reason, that it drew you into the dramatic illusion and then jolted you out of it for no acceptable reason, this view of the trick had never occurred to me. But now that it does, I can very well see the harm that it can do. I haven't used it arbitrarily, though. In fact, I don't like it myself, as a general rule. In that respect I'm like Miss Lejeune. I like to get the credits, etc., out of the way and get right into the telling of the story without further interruption.

I used it in Rommel [*The Desert Fox*] simply because I had two excellent openings, neither of which I wanted to give up, but which could not be used together in the ordinary pattern of a picture. There was a conflict between them in chronology. So in order to retain the values of both openings, I hit on the device of using one of them as a prologue leading up to the title.

In *Night People*, I hated to launch into the story in Berlin, then jump back to Toledo, Ohio, and then back again to Berlin for the rest of it. For some reason, this offended my sense of neatness, so again I tried to get out of this disorder by making the kidnapping itself the prologue and devoting the body of the picture to what happened after the snatch.

But I assure you that I have no intention of following such an irregular pattern in whatever pictures I do in the future. Unless I run up against such a problem again, they will open in standard style with the title and credits and then unfold as long as the people will stand for it. I am no revolutionary.

I had a session or two with Tynan here some months ago and greatly enjoyed the time I spent with him. He's abominably young, of course, and that gets harder and harder to take, but he makes up in part for this by not looking much healthier than I do. Nothing wins me like the spectacle of an Englishman not in the best of robust health.

Now tell Maggie to drop whatever she's doing and sit right down and write that letter. If necessary, speak sharply to her. That woman can't intimidate us.

TO THORNTON DELEHANTY

August 18, 1954

Dear Thorny:

Your picture from Plymouth, Vermont, really took me back. It was below zero during the ten days I spent there waiting for old Colonel Coolidge [father of President Calvin Coolidge] to die, and there was no indoor plumbing. We members of the original death watch slept on army cots in that Odd Fellows hall on the second floor of the general store. And for ten days, until the death rattle actually began, the *Herald Tribune* printed about a paragraph a day from me. It hardly seemed worth all I was going through.

I don't know whether you remember this or not, but when the old man died and the Presidential train arrived (the President, knowing how God damned cold it was there, didn't leave Washington until he was guaranteed in writing that the old man was going, with the result that rigor mortis had already set in by the time he got there) and Boyden Sparks took over the lead story, I asked him what he wanted me to do. He suggested that I do a background story and let it run. So I really did one. During those ten days I had discovered what an incredible bastard the old man was and how many lunatics there were in the family, including old Caesar Coolidge, a demented uncle who took a phonograph in a wheelbarrow around the countryside and tried to convert people to Jehovah's Witnesses or something like that, and I did a column and a half of real filth, denying it all, of course. I just wrote the truth, branded it as gossip, and nailed it as a lie, in clear defense of a fine old pioneer figure. I was never happier writing a story and put it on the wires feeling that God had been good to me.

Needless to say, it appeared as three paragraphs, all that was left after the blue pencilling had done its indignant duty on it. But apparently it had been set up in type in its original form and many proofs were struck from it, for many reporters and editors told me about it from time to time during the following years. I forget the name of the managing editor, the one that Stanley [Walker] used to refer to as the good grey bastard, but once in Bleeck's* he told me that he lectured a good deal on journalism and that one of his most successful lectures was on this story I had written, citing it as an example of every known fault in reporting. He said in all of his years, which seemed to extend back to Greeley, he had never found so many violations of the journalistic code embodied in one piece of writing. I could not help but glow with pride as he told me this. And I imagine that's why the old *Tribune* never sent me to cover a Republican funeral again.

TO FRED ALLEN

September 4, 1954

Dear Fred:

Out of a clear sky, after twenty-five years of sleep, the short story "Twenty Horses" came up twice in one week, once by this Armstrong Circle Theater, and once by some kind of General Electric program. How that happened I don't know, though it may have been in some kind of anthology that got picked up by two different people last month. I don't know yet how much General Electric was willing to invest in this little work of art, but the Armstrong Circle people took the rubber band off their roll and went all out. They were ready to pay a cool $250 for it. I sent my answer to this handsome proposition orally.

It wasn't that I place any particular value on the story, but the idiotic insolence of such an offer outrages me. Nothing could be nicer than to nestle down in a program between E. B. White and Saki, very elegant company indeed, but not for $250. Those people treat writers like bootblacks. Worse. They had an hour program on, I think, Lux Theater a couple of months ago using a script of mine

---

* The New York watering hole for newspapermen.

verbatim. It starred Charles Laughton and I forget the name of the woman. My script was an adaptation of an Arnold Bennett play. Not one word of my script was changed on this program, but do you know who was the only person credited with it? Was it Johnson? Was it even Arnold Bennett? It was described finally as by some fellow whose name again I can't remember. It's an odd world.

I have a number of short stories that might very well be of use to television, but I refuse to go along with this contemptuous pattern that they have set for writers. Let them continue to get their stuff from the geniuses who turn out Red Skelton's stuff every week.

On the other hand, if ever you run across any of mine that you want, it is yours. Or if you find yourself up for a half-hour comedy plot, let me know and I'll look over the stuff to see if there is anything that might please you.

My best to you.

TO GENE FOWLER

March 17, 1955

Dear Gene:

In case you are doing something on Lucius Beebe, I may be able to add a note or two. Stanley Walker gave him his first newspaper job, on the *Herald Tribune*. I remember Stanley coming to me (Stanley had some kind of fierce loathing for the Ivy League of colleges) and whispering: "I've just hired a man, by God, who was kicked out of Harvard AND Yale!" . . . Lucius is reputed to have been the first student ever to wear plus-fours at Yale. An enormous fellow even then, Lucius's plus-fours were unbelievably long and voluminous, and the story goes that on beholding him one day, a near-sighted professor demanded, "What are those two girls doing on the campus?" . . . Don Skene [a reporter for the *Tribune*] (there's a fellow for legends!) ran Lucius crazy by hailing him always either as "Loosh" or "Beeb," rhyming with Hebe. . . . There is also a curious by-product of the legend that Lucius has a sister named Phoebe B. Beebe. Not certain about that. . . . During his New York period, Lucius was an enthusiastic fancier of firearms. When his name was up for membership in The Players, he was taken down to the club by his proposers on the customary visit of personal appearance, so that the other members could see what a fine and attractive candidate he was. In the course of the visit, Lucius took out a pistol and fired it, and since there are few members of The Players under 70, you can see for yourself why Lucius isn't a member today. He used his mastery of firearms to better purpose on another occasion. Billy Guard, then press-agent for the Metropolitan Opera House, came into Bleeck's one afternoon and was moody about the presence of hundreds of balloons spotting the ceiling of the opera house. They had got loose during a performance of *Aida* the night before and since nobody knew how to get them down, they presented a ridiculous appearance up there. Lucius picked up the challenge at once. Out came some of his air rifles, and with a few other old squirrel hunters like Stanley Walker, he and his colleagues spent the afternoon shooting down balloons in the Met.

If you are writing about Bleeck's, don't forget the Ghoul Pool, or Grim Reaper's Sweepstakes, which went on for years. It was a hat pool, with a hundred names in it. The names were of celebrities who were either aged or likely to die through violence. You paid two dollars for a name, for a pot of $200, and the pay-off was two or three times a week. There was also quite a bit of trading in these names. If you drew William Murray Butler* who looked like he was going to live forever, you would be doing well to get rid of it for 75¢ or a dollar, whereas Elihu Root, around 90 at the time, was worth up to $7 or $8 regularly. But many a man damn near went broke on Root, who refused to pay off for a long, long time. Also you might remember the time Jack Bleeck installed his own afternoon shower. The place, as you know, is a real subterranean grotto, the only opening at that time being a window on an airshaft about 12 floors deep. Bleeck noticed finally that when rain fell around 6 in the evening the patrons were inclined to remain for one more and so business was quite flourishing. But in long dry spells, the customers hurried on home quite promptly. So Jack fixed up a kind of shower bath effect over this one window and would turn it on around 5 or 5:30, whereupon the customers would glance toward the window, see the downpour, and decide to have another until the shower passed over. It was very successful for many months. Before the dark day when the bars were lowered and women were allowed in the place, the waiters had one standing answer to all women's voices who called up: "He just left." Maybe you should get from Stanley an account of the Battle of No Wits in Bleeck's. Stanley and another fellow got to arguing at the bar about which of two high officials on the paper was

---

* *Sic.* Nicholas Murray Butler (1862–1947) was president of Columbia University for more than forty years.

the stupider man. It developed into rather a heated affair until finally Stanley offered to prove that his man was far and away the duller fellow. The two nominees, in fact, were to be brought down to the bar and encouraged to air their foolish views publicly, with an impartial referee to evaluate their dreariness. So Stanley went upstairs and invited his man down for a social cocktail while the other fellow went up and got his, and so presently the two champions sat face to face across a table in a titanic battle of idiocy. Certain rules had been hastily thrown together, among them being that a sponsor could lead his man into a field where he was most potent in dreariness but could not actually put words into his mouth. A quiet nod from the referee marked a point, and 10 points made the winner. So when Stanley's man would say, "Paris is a woman's town, London is a man's," Stanley claimed, and got, a point. For your own information, Stanley's man was Arthur Draper. I can't remember his opponent. But Stanley has quite a saga about it and it's worth asking him about. Stanley's address is Lampasas, Texas; that's all of the address needed. As a matter of fact, I think he and Mrs. Walker are the only inhabitants.

Alva Johnston told me once that while there had been hundreds of fights in Bleeck's, no human standing directly in front of a gladiator had ever been harmed; the dead and dying had always been felled by elbows. There was a time, during Prohibition, when Bleeck's was incorporated as a club, the Artists and Writers Club. Only one member was ever posted throughout this period, Mrs. Dick Maney [wife of the theatrical press agent], who, according to Alva, was barred for biting other members. I don't know the lady but she must have been what they call quite a character. Stanley told me he went into the backroom one night on the way to the can and found her methodically piling all the furniture up in the middle of the floor. When he came out of the can she had crumpled up a newspaper and lighted it with the apparent purpose of burning down the whole building. When Stanley stomped out the fire, she looked at him in some disgust and said, "Well, you would seem to have very little to do." The match game flourished in Bleeck's for a while, and Lucius once staged a world championship in Bleeck's for the title. Engaged a small ballroom at the Madison, everybody in evening dress, champagne and caviar, and Lillian Hellman and Stanley fought it out before a distinguished audience. Maney came to my table one night and said he had just withdrawn from a large match game for an odd reason. There were 9 in the game, including Wolcott Gibbs, so tight that he couldn't even recognize the other players. Gibbs was the first to name a number when the fists were put on the table. He guessed "None." Nine players! And before God, he won! Not even Ripley would have believed that. Maney said he wouldn't play in a game subject to miracles.

If I think of any more of these things that I think may be of some use to you I'll jot them down and send them along. I scarcely need say that I expect you to elaborate on any of these incidents in your own Homeric style and fashion; I offer you only the bones, you add the blood and meat. I do hope you are getting along better—and I'll see if I can get [Joel] Sayre to chip in with something.

Johnson's longest movie, and one of his most successful, was *The Man in the Gray Flannel Suit*, released in 1956. It starred Jennifer Jones, Gregory Peck, and Fredric March and was based on the best-selling novel by Sloan Wilson. Johnson also directed. When he realized that Peck was afraid to play comedy, he modified the screenplay accordingly. Jennifer Jones was difficult to direct, a difficulty compounded by the great interest David O. Selznick took in his wife's career. Johnson was inundated with memos from Selznick, some a great many pages long. Finally, Johnson sent David a note: "In case your wife is too modest to tell you this, I think the scene she did today was absolutely superb, and she couldn't have been better. Please do not answer this."

The Johnsons were friends of Fredric March and his wife, the actress Florence Eldridge.

TO FREDRIC MARCH

November 25, 1955

Dear Freddie:

A group of us tried to get you and Florence on the phone last evening, Thanksgiving. Venturing out-of-doors for the first time, Harlan [Thompson] was at my house, with Marian.* They were jubilant over this important moment, and I was additionally happy about the word from you and Florence about *Gray Flannel Suit*. As two old reporters, Marian and I tried to track you down, but were stopped dead when two local references pinpointed your dinner en-

* Harlan Thompson was co-author of a play, *Sleep It Off*, on which Johnson based his screenplay for *How to Be Very, Very Popular* in 1955. Thompson also wrote the screenplay for *Ruggles of Red Gap*, and produced many films in the late 1930s and early 1940s, including *College Holiday*, *Big Broadcast of 1938*, and *Road to Singapore*. His wife, Marian Spitzer, wrote the screenplays for *The Dolly Sisters* and *Look for the Silver Lining*, and adapted *Shake Hands with the Devil* for the screen.

gagement in Rutledge, New Jersey, a town which the American Telephone & Telegraph Company insisted did not exist. Obviously we are
not the newspaper people we used to be.

I wanted also to tell Florence that the idea of her playing Mrs.
Hopkins had come almost simultaneously with the proposal that you
play Hopkins, and I refrained from mentioning this to her only because it might sound a little indelicate until you had made your decision. But whether you decided to do the part or not, I couldn't
think of anyone who fitted this small but important part better than
Florence, with every quality of social and human distinction in her
looks and the emotional warmth and strength to go with it. Tell this
to her for me.*

We have deferred the starting of the picture until December 5,
and we expect to do the scenes in the Westport home with Peck
and Jennifer Jones first. I will tell the production department to
figure out at once when you will be needed and so to notify you.

Dorris joins me in the very best to both of you.

Sam Berke, Johnson's business manager and a family friend, asked Johnson to
read and comment on a play by his nephew, a television scriptwriter.

TO SAM BERKE
November 28, 1955

Dear Sam:

One great improvement in *The Top Rung* over Reuben's previous script is that he deals in material that is likely to enlist more
general interest. Also Reuben has found and used a good dramatic
situation, to wit, the one in which Paul's friend gets the job that he
was after. And still again, there is a great improvement here in the
dramatic structure of the story.

But I think there are still two aspects of writing that he needs to
sit and think about. One is economy. Dramatic writing is to book
writing as a telegram is to a letter. The ideal dialogue is that in which
each line advances the story at least a fraction of an inch. No line
should let it stand still. It takes some artfulness to do this and at the
same time keep naturalness in the speeches, and I don't pretend that
I do it successfully myself, but that is what I am aiming at. Certainly
it ought to be kept in mind at all times.

* The role of Mrs. Hopkins was played by Ann Harding in the film.

The second thing is the naturalness of dialogue. Reuben is inclined to write entirely proper English. If he will read any of John O'Hara's books, he will see what I mean. Whatever O'Hara is otherwise, he has the greatest ear for natural dialogue that I have ever heard. Such naturalness gives a feeling of life to a character.

There is still another thing he should keep in mind. He should examine every development to see if it can't be shown rather than told about. I am thinking of the scene between Paul and Pat in which Pat at first refuses to reveal the name of the man to be promoted and then later in the same scene, a rather awkward treatment, decides to tell him. I think he should have broken this up into two scenes. Pat should hold his ground throughout this scene, and then show the board meeting, or whatever it might be, when the president of the company makes the announcement. A dramatic writer should never tell anything that he can show.

I should have looked for some other threat for Paul to make against Pat. It may be quite true that the fact that he had an illegitimate child would be a severe blow to his professional position, but Reuben never convinced me of that. It might be true with a preacher, but not with an advertising man. The idea of a threat is all right, it's just the kind of threat that seems to me inadequate.

But all in all, this script is a great step forward on his part, and while I know how anxious a fellow is to have his development proved by a sale, I don't think he should be discouraged if this one is still not quite up to what I would think of as the professional standard. It must be five times as hard to become a proficient writer as to become a proficient doctor, mainly because there is no true and tried educational process for a writer, so every fellow who wants to write for profit, including my daughter Nora, must be prepared for a long, slow, and often very discouraging preparation. But if he's got it in him to be a writer, this won't stop him. If he stops, it's a fair sign that he was never intended to be a writer in the first place.

TO MARY HEALY
AND PETER LIND HAYES

December 7, 1955

Dear Mary and Peter:

Hardly a man is now alive, or a woman either, who remembers my birthday but you. The celebration of the event in my home was, I must say, unprofitable. Scotty gave me a collar pin containing the figures of a cowboy, a saddle, and a sombrero, set with emeralds and rubies and costing 25¢. I suppose I will have to wear it one day anyway. Roxie operated more or less after a fashion set by Nora at one time. She borrowed a dollar from me and gave it back to me wrapped in a small pill box. Getting the dollar back made it a very happy idea.

We saw your show last week and were surprised that you gave in on using your stuff. Why don't you make them give you some scenes in return?

I have started shooting the picture and all is confusion. The actors now want to know what the lines mean. At that rate we'll never finish.

We all send love to you.

Lynn Loesser was the wife of songwriter Frank Loesser.

TO LYNN LOESSER

May 8, 1956

Dear Lynn:

I take my pen in hand to congratulate you and Frank on two successes. Frank's success with *The Most Happy Fella* may be the most formidable one-man success in the history of the American Theatre. Dorris and I read the reviews with awe and happiness.

But this is also to tell you of a success of yours that we witnessed, to wit, Johnny's [the Loessers' son] performance as the dashing prince on horseback at the Westlake May Day Fete. Johnny, as you may not know, has always been our favorite performer since the days of Vilma's dancing class in Beverly Hills. Nobody has ever done a back-bend like Johnny in a buttoned-up jacket. There, I said, and you may quote me, is a performer! In the May Day Fete, though, he outdid himself. His arrival on his horse, circling the Tiny Tot Woods that surrounded the Sleeping Princess twice, and his awakening of the Princess with a smack were histrionics that for happy bravura have not been equalled in my time.

And then he topped even that. Called on to dance with the enamored Princess, he insisted on including his horse. The Princess made some effort to discourage this crowded gavotte, with the understandable feeling that a horse is out of place in such a romantic moment, but Johnny, like the hero of a Western before they all became adult and offbeat, was resolute in his attachment to his faithful steed. So round and round they went, him and the Princess and the horse, in one of the finest exhibitions of terpsichore that Westlake had ever know. He was easily the star of the entire afternoon and it is a sad thing indeed that you and Frank could not be present at his triumph.

Must close now. Dorris will be home from the foundry soon and I haven't even got the dinner on the stove. Hoping you are the same, I remain, yours in Christ.

When writing his biography of Charles MacArthur, Ben Hecht asked Johnson for reminiscences. Johnson and MacArthur had collaborated on the play *Stag at Bay*, based on an escapade of John Barrymore's.

TO BEN HECHT

September 5, 1956

Dear Ben:

Not being a jackanapes myself, I never shared in Charlie's antics of the kind that made up his legend. And I seem to have only a few stories that might be of use to you. But first I hope you agree with me when I say that I never, repeat never, caught Charlie at work on his legend. I know a number of "living legends" and all of them with the exception of Charlie seem to me to be putting in a few hours a week on their own personal masterpieces.

I saw Charlie from time to time back in the Twenties but it was not until around 1939 or '40 that he and I began to hang around together. We left a party to go to a saloon, where you don't have to wait for the host to give you another drink, and in the course of a couple of days we decided to work on a play of his suggestion. It was about Jack Barrymore and Diana. We based it on Charlie's story about the time Barrymore, after about fifteen years of never remembering he had a daughter, decided to look into her welfare. After calling Diana's mother in Europe and bawling her out for not being a better mother, he went down to the boarding school near Baltimore where Diana was a student. According to Charlie, the female members of the faculty of the school were not aware of Jack's more recent activities. They recollected him only as that beautiful and brilliant young comedian and then as a great Shakespearean actor. So they welcomed him with such warmth that he remained on the premises for a week or so, having his wicked will of more than one of the lady teachers.

This anecdote resulted in the longest and most fruitless collaboration in the history of American letters. We wrote and rewrote and consulted, mainly in saloons, for a year or so, or until my money gave out and I had to return to Hollywood. We never actually finished the script, and I remember asking you at one time how you ever managed to get a piece of work out of Charlie's hands and into those of a producer. I guess we must have submitted a half-dozen versions of this play, none complete, to as many producers—and I still have it in my files. But it was a merry experience and we became very good friends to the end. It was worth all the waste of time, and health, to have come to know him as well as I did.

Out of this collaboration I am reminded of two incidents. Once we gave the script to Producer X. (The real name of Producer X is Gilbert Miller.*) Presently we went together to hear his word on it. What Gilbert had to say was, to me, so windy and useless that when we got outside I told Charlie that I was appalled by this exhibition by the great theatrical producer. I told him I was used to producers who showed some knowledge and authority in what they had to say about a script and that I had expected to find Miller, a man of great distinction, the very epitome of dramatic editorship. But so far as I could see, I told Charlie, this was a big bag of wind that we had been talking to. And that was all I said to him.

A few months later I met Miller, said how do you do, and the hand that he gave me was like a wet fish, and he turned away from me so quickly that it was clear that I was far from his favorite character. Since I didn't think that a bad script should have had this sort of effect on a man, I remarked on this icy greeting to Charlie, whereupon Charlie replied that he was surprised that Miller hadn't struck me with his glove. "But for what?" I asked, as innocent as Christ. "For what I told him you said about him," Charlie explained. And when he told me what he had told Miller I had said about him, I was also surprised. For Charlie, who detested Miller and bore with him only because of Helen,† had taken a very clever advantage of this situation to get a few things off his chest to and about Miller. Attributing everything to me, he had told Miller what he thought of him, in round and ringing terms, all the way from criticism of his

* Among the plays Miller produced were *The Cocktail Party*, *Gigi*, and *Witness for the Prosecution*.

† Helen Hayes starred in many plays produced by Miller.

physique to stern comments on his intelligence. "I'm surprised," Charlie told me, "that he didn't knock you down."

During the same collaboration, Charlie exhibited a genius for improvisation not possible in many other people. Here in Hollywood, I suggested that we send the script to Jed Harris in New York. Too polite, as always, to express his derogatory opinion of Jed, he very carefully explained to me how unwise this would be. In effect it was this. If we sent the script to Jed, Jed would read it, catch on fire, hop the next plane, and be with us the next dawning. Ideas, he said, would fly from him like sparks from an emery wheel. And so we would catch fire again too. We would work, work, work. We would be tireless. From eight o'clock in the morning we would work on until four, five, six, seven, then eight, then nine, then ten, and so on.

I would be later and later for dinner, Charlie said. At first Dorris would understand. Then presently she would begin to wonder. The next step would be to put a private eye on my tail. This fellow would follow me day and night, and eventually, of course, would catch me.

Then the divorce. Dorris, with a airtight case, would take all of my dough. I would be broken in spirit and nerve by such a blow, and my value as a screenwriter would soon disappear. The next thing people knew, I would be down on Main Street, cadging drinks and picking up butts out of the gutter. From this it would be only a step to prison.

"That's why I don't think we should call Jed," he told me. "I wouldn't want to see you wind up like that."

When I saw David Selznick at Charlie's funeral I couldn't help but think of David's toothmarks in Charlie's arm that he still bore there in that casket. You remember the fight he had with David and Myron [Selznick, the agent and David's brother]. I was reminded also of the futility of a tycoon like David in trying to compete with Charlie in a contest of playfulness, and of the Case of the Cloth-covered Buttons, which I will remind you of briefly, though you probably know its details even better than I. To me it was a fine example of the brilliant deadliness of Charlie's ingenuity when the occasion called for it.

As Charlie told me about it, it started at one of those highly social dances that took place weekly at a restaurant called the Montmartre some twenty years ago. Selznick wore that night a fine set of white tie and tails fresh from the seamstress and very proud he was too of its last cry in styling. In fact, you couldn't have found a happier little producer in the entire room until MacArthur, dancing past him, commented on this fine new suit of clothes and then gave a start at the sight of the buttons. "Cloth-covered buttons?" he commented and danced on. Not two minutes later, at MacArthur's suggestion, [Charles] Lederer repeated MacArthur's praise of the suit but started also at the buttons. "Not cloth buttons!" Lederer said and danced on.

I can only assume that Selznick hadn't the security of his wardrobe, for as friend after friend lifted an eyebrow at the buttons he became infuriated with MacArthur and Lederer, whom he very properly suspected of spreading this little sartorial trouble, and in a scene of some indignation (the two Charlies were working for him at MGM at that time) he banished them from his employment. It must have been a very dramatic moment.

But the next morning, apparently feeling that his position left him open to some criticism, David was misguided enough to try to turn the whole affair into a joke in which he was having as much fun as they were. He wrote one of his wordy letters to them, explaining that you would have to go far to find a man with a keener sense of humor than himself, and that he was quite surprised that they should have taken his firing seriously. The truth of the matter, he said, was that he had fallen quickly and cleverly into the spirit of all of this larkishness and would no more think of firing them for such a joke than he would think of not dictating a letter when there was a secretary available. This turned out to be a sad mistake on his part.

MacArthur and Lederer took the letter to a psychiatrist, who accommodatingly wrote out a diagnosis of the writer's mental condition, which seemed to be calamitous. The man who wrote this letter, the psychiatrist reported in effect, needed immediate attention, preferably in an institution. The two Charlies then had David's letter and the psychiatrist's report mimeographed and mailed to everyone connected with MGM. I don't know what you can do about a story like this, but it pleases me very much.

There is another story about the two Charlies (if I ramble on through incidents that you already know, forgive me) that has always amused me. This one concerned the time that they went into Twenty-one and asked for a particular brand of Scotch and soda and were urged by the waiter to take Ballantyne's Scotch, which Twenty-one was then pushing. Irked by this exhibition of hard selling, Mac-Arthur called for a phone and got Sherman Billingsley on the wire at the Stork Club. When Billingsley informed them that he gave his customers whatever they called for, without pleading, Charlie ordered two Scotch and sodas to be delivered to him at Table 7, 21 West 52nd Street. Billingsley said he would be happy to serve them.

When presently a Stork Club waiter in a red jacket brought the drinks to the table in Twenty-one, MacArthur and Lederer were so pleased with this service that they not only ordered two more but asked for the Stork Club menu. When the Stork Club man returned with the second drinks he was accompanied by a captain of waiters with the menu. Our two gourmets then ordered a fine hearty meal from Billingsley's place and it was brought through 53rd Street, down Fifth Avenue and into Twenty-one by quite a staff of serving men. Since there was very little he could do about this, Jack Kriendler (being much too smart to write a David O. Selznick letter to them) accepted the situation philosophically. Such a man will live long. Or would have if he hadn't died shortly thereafter.

Incidental intelligence:

Item. When Alexander Woollcott was appearing in his first play in New York there was no question in his mind, as you can well imagine, that people thought and talked of little else. That was why Charlie would every now and then give Woollcott a ring and invite him to dinner, "If you have nothing better to do tonight." It never failed to set Woollcott on fire.

Item. I rarely received a letter from Charlie that didn't contain some wonderful arrangement of words. He described Helen once as being apparently determined to be "the water wings of the world."

Item. During the war I read in the paper that he was in the hospital in Washington. It turned out to be an explosion of his ulcer. He wrote to me that he had blacked out while talking to General Porter, with whom he served as aide during the war. "But I don't think he slapped me," he wrote. "The Generals around here are being very careful about that sort of thing since the Patton incident. At any rate, they siphoned a lot of blood into me and I suspect that some of it was coon blood, because I caught myself cake-walking to the can this morning."

Two items about Charlie's wife:

It's a question whether you'll want to use either of these anecdotes but they may amuse you. The first is from a letter Charlie wrote me in 1947.

"I was faced with a parental dilemma last week and wonder how you would have solved it. Helen and I flew to Dennis, Mass. to catch a dress rehearsal of a hunk of marzipan by N. Coward, in which Mary [their daughter] is appearing with Lillian Gish. In the play a goony youth with pimples rushes at her, demanding kisses. 'Once, twice, thrice!' he cries, and each time Mary pulled away from him so hard you could hear her neck crack. Whereupon Mamma summoned her outside with the lad and insisted on a kissing rehearsal that lasted an hour, until Helen was satisfied with the sincerity and warmth of the embrace. She was yelling, 'Kiss him on the mouth. He hasn't got halitosis,' etc. On the airplane coming home I said to Helen, a little sadly, 'Mary's going to meet four young men in the same role this summer. What responsibility do you take for her virtue?' My Iron Bride coldly replied: 'The only responsibility I accept is for her Art.' "

The second is to show Mrs. MacArthur's consistency. When Helen opened in *The Wisteria Trees* in Boston a few years ago Charlie disappeared and was heard of no more until at the end of the performance Leland Hayward and Josh Logan grabbed me as I came up the aisle and told me that Charlie had fallen in the lobby of the theatre and hit his head on a marble stair. Although it knocked him out for a few minutes, I was told that the injury was not serious and that he was back at the hotel in bed having a drink with the doctor. They wanted me to go backstage and inform Helen of this without frightening her out of her wits, so she would not delay getting back to the hotel.

When I got to Helen's dressing room it was filled with those worthy looking old ladies who are often to be found in her dressing room, and after what I hoped were suitable compliments on her performance (I could not bring myself to say anything about the play itself) I stood around for a moment or two wondering how to go about this business. Then I thought, oh, the hell with politeness, and grabbing her by the wrist I pulled her out into the corridor and told her what had happened. She gave a little squeak at the first news but I convinced her pretty quickly that there was no need for great alarm. Just don't sit around all night with these old bags.

A few minutes later when we were in her car on the way back to the hotel she began to giggle. "This makes me so ashamed of myself that I oughtn't to tell you about it, but now that I know the situation isn't serious, it was a very funny thing," she explained. "When you came into the dressing room I could tell that you hadn't liked the play and that you were lying like a dog when you said you had. Then when you grabbed me wildly and pulled me out of the room I thought to myself, oh, my God, he's going to tell me that this is a dreadful thing and I must get out of it immediately. Then when you told me about Charlie, and this is what I'm so ashamed about, I couldn't help it, I had a little flash of relief. Isn't that the most dreadful thing you ever heard?"

Item. Only a year or two before Charlie died he planned a lovely birthday gift for Helen. He was going to join AA. Naturally he didn't want to, but nevertheless he went very resolutely up to their offices to sign up.

In the waiting room when he got there was another candidate with a hangover, a melancholy colored gentleman. Then when the young lady entered to call in the next one to be interviewed she beckoned to Charlie, giving the white man priority. As Charlie described it to me, it was like a message straight from heaven. Knowing that Helen would never be happy with him a member of what was practically a branch of the Ku Klux Klan, he denounced the young woman for race prejudice, probably the only time in his whole life he ever gave any thought to that particular matter, and told her he wouldn't be caught dead in such an organization. Five minutes later he was at a bar. Narrowest escape you ever heard of.

I doubt that these items are much of a contribution to your book but I send them along nevertheless because they may suggest other matters to you. I know you will do him well. And I hope that you agree with me when I say that I don't believe Charlie ever passed a moral judgment on any other human being. When I asked him what he found to like or admire in Errol Flynn, he said he liked him because Flynn never assumed a false pose. This wouldn't have been enough to satisfy me, but then I wasn't Charlie. He was really the most tolerant and understanding man I ever knew.

I had one theory about Charlie, the validity of which you would be in the best position to judge. It suddenly occurred to me once that Charlie never thought, never went through the processes of thinking, apparently never had to. The more I went back over my experiences with him the more I was convinced that this might very well be the truth about him. Instead of thought, he seemed to be gifted with instinct and intuition, like an animal or a genius. Myself, I plod through ideas and you can literally hear the grinding of wheels when I tackle something. But everything from Charlie seemed to fly right out of the top of his head. I am still pretty well convinced of this.

One of the results of this indifference to thinking was that he never had more than about one-fourth of a hangover. Three-fourths of a hangover is ordinarily a horrible combination of remorse and guilt and so on, which is what Charlie's seemed to have been spared by nature. . . .

If I think of anything else that might interest you I'll send it along. My best to you and my best to the book. It's a great thing to look forward to.

Joe Bryan, a friend from Johnson's journalist days in New York and a former editor of *Holiday*, was one of several to join the Arthur Sheekman for President group. Sheekman, a screenwriter who had written many of the Marx Brothers' movies, ran a valiant though poorly timed campaign.

TO JOSEPH BRYAN III

November 5, 1956

Dear Joe:

I got your message from Ted Emory but I'm afraid I can't give you much time at the moment. A group of four or five of us, possibly six, are trying to get Arthur Sheekman elected President and as this is November 5 you will readily see that we will have to hurry.* So I'm sure you will understand, etc.

It is a purely spontaneous idea and it may very well be too late, what with the start that Ike and Adlai have on us, but we're going to have a go at it anyway. The way it happened, we were all sitting around together one night last week when Arthur said he wished he could be President of the United States. No reason in particular, just thought he'd like to be. Well, why not? As you very well know, Arthur is as nice a fellow as you would be likely to meet in the entire county of Los Angeles, and speaking for myself, I couldn't think of anybody that I had rather see in the White House.

Well, we all knew that it wouldn't be easy but if you like somebody, a little extra effort shouldn't stand in the way of doing him a favor if possible. So right then and there we signed up Mrs. Sheekman and Mrs. Johnson and a fellow whose name I didn't catch. The next day I told David Niven about it and although he didn't know Arthur personally, he said he had never heard anything but good about him and he thought it a perfectly corking idea. So there, already we had five grass-roots Sheekman men. Then last night Ginger Rogers said that she couldn't see why not either. So you see, we are snowballing already.

* Election day was November 6.

There's no question about it, it will take a lot of our time and effort between now and tomorrow morning to get this thing off the ground, but there is not a man among us who is not convinced that it can be done. But obviously, in a situation like this, I cannot sit around here on my ass writing letters like this to you. I've got to get out and ring doorbells. At the same time, if this reaches you in time, you might want to get aboard the band wagon.

My best to you.

P.S. Just in case, Arthur promises all of his friends weekends at the White House. He says he expects to treat everybody fair and square and not to start any wars. And if some of his pals would like to make a buck or two on the side, he sees no reason why they shouldn't help themselves and their families a bit. Now after all, Joe, you've really got to go along with a fellow like that, don't you think?

TO JOSEPH BRYAN III

November 11, 1956

Dear J.

I don't think we'd better mention any names until we get this thing pretty well organized. Those other people, you know who I'm talking about, they already suspect there's something in the wind and there are no lengths to which they will not go to find out what it is. So for the time being, I'll just refer to AS (Sh—km—n) as The Chief. I'll refer to myself as I or me, and to you as you. We've simply got to play it cozy until we have all the ends tied up.

Anyway, following recpt of your idea, I caucused with The Chief the other night and laid the whole plan before him. You may be interested to know that he never looked better, the same old fox, or Old Pol, whatever the fuck *Time* means by that. The truth is, he's forgotten more about politics than you and I will ever know, you especially. And you don't have to worry about his health, either. I took a psychiatrist in with me, introducing him as a wealthy oil man from Rhode Island, though I don't believe this fooled the Old Man for a second, with instructions to tell me the Truth about him. No point getting stuck with another Ike. "I give this man another fifteen years, not counting hospitalization," was the way he put it afterward. "I took a long hard look at the hard core of him," he continues, for he reads *Time* too, "and he's as good as he ever was, whatever that means."

Well, to make a long story short, The Chief was immensely pleased by what you suggested and said give him time to think it over. Meanwhile, he sends a Well Done to you, and his personal regards. What I suspect is this: The Chief likes the idea but wants to talk it over first with a friend of his, named Harry Levy. He wants to get Hal's opinion. But in any case, he hinted, it's much too early for a move that significant. The way he put it, "It's much too early for a move that significant." His strategy, the way I get it, is to lay back until the others make their move. He feels that too early is about as bad as too late. "Too early is about as bad as too late," he said. Let them commit themselves first and then we'll see.

Meanwhile, keep your eyes open and your mouth shut. Don't communicate directly with him. Send any information to me here at the studio, where I am known as Herbert Bayard Swope, Jr. And now in closing, I heard a wonderful joke the other day but have forgotten the tag line. I got a great laugh out of it. Remember me to GK, TM, RGT, RLS, GBS, TR, and FDR. We'll write the peace terms in the White House yet!

Yrs.

TO JOSEPH BRYAN III

November 21, 1956

Dear Joe:

I suppose you saw by the papers what happened. Arthur couldn't have been more magnificent about it. He conceded shortly after the polls opened (9:13 Eastern Standard Time) with a simple statement that he would have no part in a situation that threatened to divide the country.

He had the idea for a little quip to lighten the situation, something about losing an election but gaining a grandchild, but unfortunately he had no grandchild. That's the sort of rotten luck that dogged us throughout the campaign.

Immediately after conceding, he returned to his farm at 423½ South McCarty Drive for a much needed rest. Within a month or so he intends to announce his future plans. But for the time being he hopes to be able to relax in (on?) the bosom of his family (Gloria).

And now for 1960! A battle was lost but not the war. But the first thing we've got to do is raise some kind of a big slush fund for the next campaign. My own idea is that we should make a careful selection of one thousand outstanding citizens who have faith in

Sheekman and ask each of them to prove this faith by a donation of $100,000. That should be the limit. In spite of the work I have to do in my private practice, I am prepared to handle this sum personally. But only on certain conditions. I must not be pestered and harassed by questions as to what I do with it. The people must have faith in me too.

Meanwhile, if you would like to get in on the ground floor, let me have your check at once. We must get under way immediately. So much to do, so little time. They must never catch us napping again. Or any part of $100,000.

I must add that before retiring to his hogsty, Arthur expressed the deepest appreciation for what you did in the great crusade. Somewhere, as he put it, so simply and yet so eloquently as always, somebody dragged his foot, but not J. Bryan III. And if I may drop you a word in the strictest confidence, you will not be forgotten when we reach the White House. I can't go any further than that—but have your bag packed for 1960. Say nothing of this to the papers.

Courage!

1957–1966

For those outside the industry, it was hard to grasp the extent of Hollywood's troubles in the late 1950s. But those inside were assuming mantles of self-protection: successful people in every area of movie-making were demanding higher salaries; the studios were turning out fewer pictures, in hopes of drawing bigger crowds to their expensive productions; and theater owners raised admission prices.

Resentment against the studio heads was building. Stockholders were appalled by their high salaries, and employees found their methods outdated, even tyrannical.

L. B. Mayer was forced to resign from MGM in 1951; Harry Cohn remained at Columbia fighting for his position until his death in 1958. Darryl Zanuck left 20th Century–Fox to pursue independent production.

To many, including Nunnally Johnson, the loss of Darryl Zanuck meant the loss of the best source of creative energy at 20th Century–Fox. Although Johnson and Zanuck's relationship was not a close personal one, they shared a great deal of mutual respect. In his authorized biography* Zanuck was quoted as saying: "I knew I was surrounded by yes-men. Sometimes I encouraged them, purely for the sake of amusement: if I said green and knew damn well it's red, just to see what they would say. They were not really yes-men, they were want-to-please men. . . . Nunnally was brutally frank, a Rock of Gilbraltar. If he thought something stank, it stank." Johnson on Zanuck is equally clear: "He was a great editor of a script. . . . He was far and away the most valuable man I've ever been associated with in the business. One of the very few who really made contributions and was a collaborator. . . . He knew what action was, and

* Mel Gussow, *Don't Say Yes Until I Finish Talking* (Garden City, N.Y., Doubleday, 1971).

as I say, he had some sort of Geiger counter in his head when he was reading one of these scripts, any script." Buddy Adler, who replaced Zanuck as head of production, was quite different, in Johnson's opinion: "I'm afraid that was like working with nobody. Adler looked like a very fine, intelligent man. He was a real façade, or maybe he'd have stopped me from making some of those pictures."

Spyros Skouras, president of 20th Century–Fox, had served in that position since 1942. He had survived a fight for control of the company in the early fifties, vastly helped by the success of CinemaScope. When Zanuck left Fox, Skouras's influence on film production became more direct. Unlike Zanuck, however, Skouras concentrated on the financial rather than creative aspects of movie-making.

TO SPYROS SKOURAS

January 9, 1957

Dear Spyros:

Now that you ask . . .

I have talked to most of the other producers and we are agreed that the new policy of information about the box-office results of our pictures was the most important product of your meeting with us the other evening.

But there were a couple of other aspects of the meeting that seemed to me to leave room for improvement or correction in the future. For one thing, so much emphasis was laid on the foreign fate of our pictures that some of us left the meeting with an impression that was both erroneous and discouraging. The domestic results were either dismissed lightly or in some cases not even mentioned. It is all very well to make the point that musical pictures fare badly as a rule in foreign language countries, but the argument was pressed so far the other evening that I, for example, came away with the bewildered impression that *The King and I* was a failure. All I heard was that Burma, Pakistan, and Rangoon didn't care for it. This impression was so real and so strong that I called on Buddy the first thing the next morning to see if it were actually true that *The King and I* was a flop.

In other words, the report from New York headquarters could have been more balanced. In your concern for a selection of stories that should have been acceptable to foreign markets as well as Ameri-

New York, c. 1946. Left to right: Celia Ager, critic for *PM* (back to camera); Johnson; William Morris, Jr., then one of the partners (with Johnny Hyde and Abe Lastfogel) of the William Morris Agency; Dorothy Parker; unidentified.

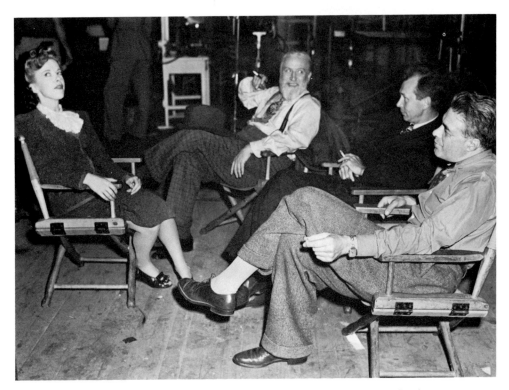

On the set of *Life Begins at Eight-thirty*, 1942. Left to right: Ida Lupino, Monty Woolley, scriptwriter Johnson, and director Irving Pitchel.

The Johnsons' home from 1945 until 1960, Mountain Drive, Beverly Hills.

Nunnally and Dorris at home. This photograph was taken to illustrate a story by Pete Martin in the *Saturday Evening Post*.

From an extensive story in *Life* magazine showing how the big Hollywood studios celebrated the completion of a film (the magazine had requested that the studio give a party that it could cover): The studio was Universal-International Pictures, the movie *Mr. Peabody and the Mermaid* (1948), written by Nunnally Johnson, and starring William Powell and Ann Blythe. The party was given by Johnson and his wife, but the studio paid for it. The small mermaids were placed at each table setting; two life-size ice mermaids each held eight pounds of caviar. Above: Ann Frederic (in mermaid tail), Louis B. Mayer, Doris Kenyon. Below, left: Dorris and Nunnally Johnson with Peter Lind Hayes. Below, right: Lady Elsie Mendl, William Marshall, Michele Morgan.

Above: Johnson (left) directing Reginald Gardiner and Ginger Rogers on the set of *Black Widow*, 1953, which he also wrote and produced. Below: On the same set, with Scott and Roxie.

A party celebrating the Johnsons' eleventh anniversary and Humphrey Bogart's departure for Nairobi to make *The African Queen*, 1953. Left to right: Lauren Bacall, Bogart, Johnson (in the background), and Dorris.

A birthday party for Johnson, 1956, with props borrowed from *The King and I*. Inset: Among the guests (right to left): Mrs. Dan Duryea, David Niven, Joan Fontaine.

Above: With Joanne Woodward and Lee J. Cobb (right), preparing for
The Three Faces of Eve, 1957. Johnson wrote, produced, and directed it.
(See his letter to Pete Martin on page 156.)
Below: At the 1957 Academy Awards ceremony, with Joanne Woodward,
who won the Best Actress award for her performance in *The Three Faces
Of Eve*.

Above, left: During the shooting of *How to Marry a Millionaire*, 1953. Johnson wrote and produced the picture, which starred Betty Grable, Lauren Bacall, and Marilyn Monroe. Jean Negulesco (right) directed. Johnson had a precise idea of how the comedy lines should be read, and Negulesco allowed him to direct the three stars.

Above, right: On the evening of the premiere of *How to Marry a Millionaire*, at the Johnsons' home (left to right): Dorris Johnson, Monroe, and Bacall. (See Johnson's letter to Edwin P. Hoyt on page 201.)

On the set of *The Angel Wore Red*, which Johnson wrote and directed, Sicily, 1959. It was his first and only independent production (MGM distributed the film). At left, Johnson with Ava Gardner and his son, Scott; at right, Johnson's teen-aged daughters, Roxie and Christie.

Nunnally Johnson, 1959.

can, a valid and valuable concern and reminder, the discussion got off on a long account of calamities abroad that left me, for one, discouraged and depressed, which I know of course was furthest from your thoughts and intention. It became difficult to remember that these pictures had also played in America, and many of them to handsome grosses. It reached a point where, to me anyway, there seemed to be an implication that we should never have made *The King and I*, because Burma didn't like it.

For another thing, I thought that a more balanced view would have taken into consideration the part that the New York headquarters plays in a picture's fate. To put the situation into arbitrary, if not official figures, I believe that from 90% to 95% of a picture's ultimate fate lies in the picture itself, its quality or lack of it, which is largely the studio's responsibility. But that would leave from 5% to 10% of responsibility which the New York headquarters must assume in the exploitation and sale of these pictures. But if any mention was made of this the other evening, I failed to hear it. Is there never a failure in the very complex and difficult operation of making the most out of a picture? The attitude the other evening was that there was no fault or failure or misjudgment or stupidity that did not lie at the studio's door. All other departments functioned flawlessly, brilliantly. Is this a correct assumption? Or should some examination and criticism be made of that end of our company?

I think there were mistakes in the meeting, but I know also that they were unintentional and can and will be corrected. As for further meetings, I not only think they should by all means be continued as you suggest, but I will go further and suggest that monthly confidential reports to the producers would be of great benefit and value; reports on the approximate final results of pictures that have just about run their course as well as on how current pictures are doing; and not only our own pictures but also, generally, how those of other studios are being received by the public. I believe also that in such reports it would be immensely useful for you to add a comment on each picture mentioned, such as why in the light of your observation and information it had done well or badly. This is the kind of information we would profit by.

I apologize for the length of this letter, but I have taken your request for comment seriously and I regard the whole matter as important. I think it calls for honesty and frankness. When you admonish your producers to keep in mind the necessity of material that will be acceptable abroad, I am sure your words will be taken to heart. When you urge caution about the cost of a particular subject, one that is worth a picture but not an expensive one, this is advice to remember. And when you announce a policy of light and information about the results of our effort, we appreciate it and accept it as wise and beneficial. But we should all be sure that the broad and complete version is understood, not a discouraging fragment of it.

You asked for it!

Now to change the subject for a second, Dorris and I send you and Mrs. Skouras our very best wishes for a happy New Year.

Oh, Men! Oh, Women! (1957), the first film Johnson wrote and produced for 20th Century–Fox after Buddy Adler had replaced Darryl Zanuck, was a comedy about psychiatry, and not a great success. One critic felt that the "overblown production distorted the simple comedy," and Johnson reflected that "the material didn't sound interesting to a great mass of people, and [David] Niven was not a great draw, and neither was Ginger [Rogers] by that time."

TO ROBERT GOLDSTEIN

January 11, 1957

Dear Robin:

The Negulescos are back and being feted all over town. Absolutely united. But there must have been something in that story about him and Sophia, for he is telling everybody that Lollobrigida has practically no bosom at all, hardly more than Scotty, and that the whole thing is an engineering product and publicity. Do you think that possible?

The way I heard it . . .

NURSE   (to patient) I'm sorry to have to tell you, Mr. Jones, but you have cancer.

DOCTOR   (stamping his foot) Oh, darn it, *I* wanted to tell him!

Oh, Men! Oh, Women! is now in the can, as we say in the biz, and I am flying to Savannah tomorrow morning to look for locations for *The Three Faces of Eve.* Not being able to get a star, we think the only way to do this picture is with a new face. Joanne Woodward's. Not only new but pretty. And a good actress. On the other hand, we have an old face for the psychiatrist. Lee Cobb's. Old but very good, of course. And a pixie face for the young woman's husband. David Wayne's.

Your in haste.

T O   R O B E R T   G O L D S T E I N
January 24, 1957

My dear Robert:

We (our little group) are very happy that Princess Kelly had a little girl. We believe it will give Rubirosa something to look forward to. Some of us were beginning to worry about him.

We had Frankie [Spitz, wife of Leo] and Jessie [Landau, executive secretary at 20th Century–Fox in New York and at International] and Cy [Jessie's husband, a lawyer] over for dinner the other night and then came over to the studio to see *The King and I*. It made Frankie very homesick. I don't know if you know it or not but Frankie is right in the middle of that Siamese bunch. In Siam. She said that *The King and I* was just a slice of life as she knew it in Siam. It was a very pleasant evening.

I was in Savannah when Dorris called me about Bogey's death. I had to finish some work there and in Augusta but got back here in time for the funeral. Niven, Romanoff, Leland Hayward, Irving Lazar, looking like the upper third of Yul Brynner, and I were ushers. We did nothing but stand back and let them come in. We were supposed to seat the gentry in certain choice locations and the peasants otherwise, but I couldn't tell the gentry from the peasants, and neither could any of the other ushers.

The occasion brought out more oddities than any I've attended since Barrymore's funeral. We had nothing really as horrifying as John Carradine afflicted with grief or W. C. Fields at eleven o'clock in the morning, an unbelievable sight, but there were a few singularities. One was an Indian wearing a flat hat and his hair in two long braids with three white squaws in their early twenties. I passed them along to Romanoff, whom I put in charge of Indians for the day, Mike steered this Vanishing American up to the balcony, which he described as a temporary Indian reservation. We figured him to be Geronimo Bogart, an uncle on Bogey's father's side. . . .

I think there was genuine grief for Bogey's passing. There are a lot of people who still detest him, people he had deliberately affronted, and God knows he could do that viciously, but there were many more who were drawn to him because he was a lively fellow. I myself feel the loss deeply. It must have been some twenty years ago that I first ran into him, in a saloon, and his first words to me were to get the hell out here, back east. As you know, he was never slow to offer advice, even to strangers. But between us we knocked off a lot of bottles together over the years and I'll miss him. It's not a good way to start the New Year.

Harry Brand tells me that Jayne Mansfield now wants to live, as she described it, like a real Hollywood movie queen. She consulted Harry on the purchase of a house with about ten bedrooms and ten baths, which she said she could get for a hundred and fifty thousand. A house that size, if she only knew it, she could get for ten thousand, because who the hell else wants it? She said she planned to put a nude statue of herself on one side of the driveway and one of Mickey [Hargitay], that muscle fellow, on the other side. Sounds right pretty. She told Harry she intends to marry Mickey as soon as the law will permit her to, with the biggest wedding ever heard of, with the swimming pool filled with champagne. Harry says he's beginning to think she's not a very sound girl. And as for Mickey, who is Hungarian, Harry feels that he is liable, single-handed, to ruin this entire sympathy for Hungarians.

Jerry Wald is going fine. No pictures, just going fine. Last week he instructed our story editor to line up Dickens, Walt Whitman, and Voltaire for scripts. Ought to get some good stuff out of those fellows.

We all send our best to you.

TO ROBERT GOLDSTEIN

February 14, 1957

My dear Robin:

This young lady, Gaby [Lalonde, a French-Canadian writer living in Rome], writes much too well and sounds much too intelligent to be messing around with the likes of Henaghan. If he's the fellow I mean, he wrote the gossip column in the *Hollywood Reporter* once, and on his first day out he wrote a line I didn't think a man could be cruel enough to write: "George S. Kaufman is sicker than he knows."

As for that story about Bogart, it made me sorer than a bastard. This little English correspondent whom I've seen around for years came to me with an urgent appeal for help. The *Daily Mail* wanted about four thousand words about Bogey at once. So on condition that I not be quoted I gave him as much stuff as I could think of and he didn't quote me! He just signs my name to the whole God-damned story!

They're incredible people, these movie correspondents, and what's more, it wasn't for the *Daily Mail* at all, but for a paper that's even trashier, if that's possible. I don't suppose he had any idea I'd ever see it.

They're previewing *Oh, Men! Oh, Women!* Friday night and it opens around the country the following week. I wrote a story about it, demonstrating that it was in the great tradition of American classics, like *The Five Commandments*, just *War*, and *Halfway Around the World in Forty Days*, which Einfeld* has persuaded the *New York Times* to run Sunday. I informed him at once that the *Times* could have it on condition that Crowther not rewrite it. If it's to be rewritten, I would prefer it to be rewritten by a writer.

Now let's cut out all this horsing around and get down to the real situation. What's with Philip and Liz [Prince Philip and Queen Elizabeth of England], and I don't mean Liz Taylor. Has that hot-rod kid been cutting up again with Vivian Blaine? And what the hell does Liz expect him to do, ramble up and down the corridors of that big palace every night? I sure would like to hear what they had to say to each other about the matter. So you just drop whatever you're doing, excuse yourself from Sir Carol Reed, and give us the facts. We're depending on you.

Meanwhile I'm shooting *The Three Faces of Eve* with a young lady named Joanne Woodward and enjoying it very much. I think she's going to be a star. And if she becomes a star, that won't make me look bad, eh?

Little remains to be told. Rod Steiger and his wife are making up, Richard Ney is still available, and it's hot as hell here. We send our best.

Although Johnson had written many screenplays based on the lives of real people, *The Three Faces of Eve* provided a unique challenge. It required detailed, exacting research. Johnson read the papers of the psychiatrists who had worked with the real Eve, and was in constant consultation with them during the writing of the script and the filming of the movie. The main difficulty in the writing, according to Johnson, was "trying to get some form

* Charles Einfeld was head of publicity in 20th Century–Fox's New York office.

that would convince somebody that this wasn't simply fiction." Part of his solution was to have Alistair Cooke introduce the movie, a touch that gave the film its needed documentary form.

Casting the film also proved difficult: Johnson received rejections from eight or nine leading actresses, including Doris Day, June Allyson, and Jennifer Jones. Judy Garland saw films of the real Eve at Johnson's suggestion, but though Garland was immediately enthusiastic, negotiations were never begun. Joanne Woodward, finally selected for the part, gave an Oscar-winning performance.

Johnson approached the directing as he had the writing, stressing the documentary nature of the film: "I didn't want any trickery about [the transformations from one character to another]. I wanted to do it exactly like I'd seen in the films that the doctors made." Woodward was particularly easy to work with: ". . . she could have almost directed herself. She's very, very knowledgeable."

TO ROBERT EMMETT DOLAN

March 26, 1957

Dear Bobby:

I am delighted that you will do the score for *The Three Faces of Eve* and so is Al [Alistair Cooke]. A few weeks ago at a party Buddy Adler asked why we didn't get you out here to score a picture or two for us. I didn't pick up the ball at that moment because you were negotiating in other fields at the time.

But as *Three Faces* began to shape up, the matter of music became more and more important. I doubt if the picture will ever rival *White Christmas* for popularity, or even *Oh, Men! Oh, Women!* for that matter, but it's a curious affair and seems to me to present all kinds of challenges to a composer. It ranges from almost slapstick to scenes and situations that aim at deep emotion, and the transitions themselves will call for what should be unusual treatment.

I finished the picture yesterday except for a few pick-up shots one day next week. Alistair Cooke will interview the real young woman by way of preface or prologue but I won't be able to shoot that until April 24, which is the earliest that Cooke can make it out here.

As for the rest of the Johnson world, Christie is here for her spring vacation and becomes more and more of a delight to be with. Dorris spent nearly two weeks at Sun Valley learning to ski and now grabs for the sport section to see how Toni Sailer came out in the slalom the way I grab it for news on Ted Williams and Mickey Mantle. (Toni Sailer is a skier. A slalom is either some kind of antic on skis or you are drunk and your tongue gets stuck on the roof of your mouth.) It now occurs to me that another wife of mine, Marion, took up skiing some ten years ago and promptly broke her left leg. . . .

The other day Louella Parsons called me and after hemming and hawing and shuffling her feet a bit told me that she had just been informed that Dorris and I were breaking up. Breaking up [were] her words. I told her I had no idea about Dorris but that I had no intention of breaking up. She said she was very happy about this and by way of calling my attention to the impregnability of her journalistic standards, she told me she would even print a denial. And that's why you haven't seen anything about that in the paper.

We all send you our love and so forth.

The Wandering Jew, one of Johnson's few unproduced screenplays, had occupied his time and interest for several years. "I thought this script had a kind of dramatic, or melodramatic, understanding of that legendary story of the wandering Jew from the time he spat in Christ's face, popping up all over history."

TO ROBERT GOLDSTEIN

June 24, 1957

Dear Robert:

I can't say that things are much different around here. Darryl is back, cutting that picture about the man (in the Gray Flannel Suit).

Island in the Sun has had an odd beginning. At the big preview, with invited guests, the whole thing was out of sync. But what dropped everyone into the depths of despair was the fact that every time the story came to a big dramatic climax, the house roared with laughter. They thought at first that this was just that particular audience. But it continues to be the case wherever the picture is shown. Every time the fine old mother turns to her daughter and says, "There is no coon blood in you, because the coon who claims to be your father is not. Your real father is a white man, whose name I forget for the moment."

Nevertheless, the picture is mopping up. Everybody thinks they're going to see Joan Fontaine and Harry Belafonte hop into the hay together, just like the yokel who kept going to see that old picture where a car raced a railroad train across the crossing. Some day, he figured, there was going to be a wreck. According to an unprejudiced observer (DFZ), the picture is doing the biggest business since *The Robe*. Which was all white people. Or almost, anyway.

Meanwhile, I'm in a very nasty situation. Buddy wants *The Wandering Jew* to cost five million dollars. Like a DeMille picture. Except by C. B. DeJohnson. Now how the hell can I get rid of five million dollars on a picture? I couldn't even count to five million. As you and Hedda Hopper know, there are twenty million light years between me and DeMille. (Incidentally, in an interview with Hedda the other day, the Great Man was quoted as referring to "those other great men, Winston Churchill and Bernard Baruch.") For one thing, my interest is in people, while DeMille's is in splitting Red Seas. If I was interested in splitting seas, I could spend five million dollars too. But as it stands, I will be doing good to get rid of three million on it.

Scotty (now 8) is planning to write you a letter today. Planning, anyway. Among other interesting features of the watch, it doesn't have to be wound by hand. It winds itself through the natural motions of the hand during the day. This worried Scotty at first. "I'm so active," he said anxiously, "maybe I'll overwind it." I assured him that this was impossible, but couldn't explain why not. Now when he is in public places he puts on quite a puzzling show. He keeps shaking his wrist. This doesn't make any sense but it attracts quite a bit of attention.

May I take advantage of this opportunity to express my appreciation and Mrs. Johnson's for your many courtesies while we were in foreign parts? If ever you are in our country, will you please let us know. We should like to reciprocate.

We send our best to you.

TO ROBERT GOLDSTEIN

July 10, 1957

Dear Bobby:

Christie returned from her trip to Ecuador engaged to a young Honduran who, she says, speaks quite a few words of English. He looks a good deal like Tab Hunter. Just a little darker. He's apparently an up and coming lad, for he is already quartermaster on the banana boat that Christie travelled on. In addition to everything else, he is very sincere.

There is also a fellow in Brooklyn that she was going to marry last month. Or rather, last month he was the fellow she was going to marry. He is 100% American and his name is Mitzlan. The Honduran's name is either Bruce Wong or Bruce Davis. So that's the way it stands today, either the American Mitzlan or the Honduran Davis.

That's the kind of confusion that Christie can create on a brief vacation.

There seems to be some doubt that I'll ever get the script finished, to say nothing about looking further for locations for *The Wandering Jew*. I have all the time in the world and nobody speaks to me on the lot and still I don't seem to be able to get along with it very fast. We may get into the sequel before we get the first one made. Not that it matters, I suppose. Everybody else on the lot is making pictures hand-over-fist and they are all mopping up. All but a few. Jerry Wald says that *An Affair to Remember*, which is a carbon copy of *Love Affair*, may very well be the best picture he has ever produced. And you know how cautious Jerry is.

As for the rest of the people around here, Sam Engel has desegregated himself from the studio and set up his own company. After a nationwide search for a name for this company, he finally decided to call it Sam Engel Productions. And since he is still in the same office, with the same secretary, and eats in the same chair in the dining room, I can't see how this is much of a change. Just made him feel happier, I suppose. . . .

And now in conclusion, Harry Ruby has kindly contributed an advertising slogan for my next picture:

> *The movie fans are flocking to*
> *The Wandering Jew*
> *By Eugene Sue.*

This particular Wandering Jew doesn't happen to be by Eugene Sue but Harry doesn't think that should matter. He says this is the day of the New Look. He says they will no longer go for the same ideas, treatment, etc., that they used to go for. He says that what Groucho still calls "knockers" are now referred to as milady's "mammary glands" or "love bubbles." He says Groucho is a decade behind the times.

Repent!

TO ROBERT GOLDSTEIN

July 22, 1957

Dear Robert:

I get more publicity in Hedda Hopper's column when she's with you in London than I do when she's here. Incidentally, the day after she wrote that we had walked out of *The Summer of the Seventeenth Doll* after the first act (it was after the second act, wasn't it?) Hecht-Hill-Lancaster* bought it for $300,000. That's the least Harold Hecht pays for anything—$300,000. Even a copy of the *Ladies' Home Journal*.

That's a very mysterious organization. They paid $350,000 for *Lucy Crown* and now I hear it's on the shelf. On the shelf with *The Devil's Disciple* and the original screenplay that Axelrod wrote for them. Meanwhile, Harold has bought a big lot with a big house on it on the south side of Sunset Boulevard near Alpine and is tearing down the house to make way for an entirely new one. He told Charlie LeMaire [executive director of wardrobe at 20th Century-Fox] that he figured the whole deal would cost around a half million. He's going to have a stream running right through the living room, so he can go fishing any time he feels like it. He's also bought a yacht, a big one, around a hundred feet long, and is having it done over at eight times the cost of the boat. This is probably so he can go fishing outside of his house. Dorris and I went there to dinner the other night and he showed us an El Greco that he said he paid $125,000 for. Also a Modigliani for around $75,000. Now where on earth do you think all this money is coming from?

I also saw Groucho's new house. Only a quarter of a million. Eden has a round marble sunken bath. She can't possibly use it for anything but a shower, for it would take thirty-two hundred gallons of water to fill it. A person could drown in it. She also has a new round bed. Groucho said that this was his idea, to keep from bumping the corners when he was chasing her around it. It certainly takes all sorts, etc.

We had dinner with the Gar Kanins the other evening and they asked about you most affectionately. They are headed for Europe shortly, with Thornton Wilder. You may use this information in whatever way you think best.

The Wandering Jew gets tougher and tougher, but the way it is beginning to shape up it may be the first picture in the history of the industry to affront all three great religions—Christianity, Judaism, and Islam. I am now working on something that will make the Aga Khan's crowd sore. That's a hell of a dynasty—all of the males are

---

* Harold Hecht, a former dance director and literary agent, joined with Burt Lancaster and producer James Hill to form an independent production company. Their films include *Run Silent, Run Deep*, *Sweet Smell of Success*, and *Separate Tables*.

royal and all of the females used to work for Dior. We all felt very bad about Aly Kahn.* How is he taking it?

That's all for now. We both send our best to you.

P.S. Thanks for the clippings. I read quite a few of them.

MEMO TO HARRY BRAND

August 16, 1957

Dear Harry:

Before we go any farther, I think it only fair that Charlie Einfeld should be notified that Johnson makes no speeches.† Johnson doesn't even give an informal little talk. In fact, Johnson says nothing standing up. He is available for interviews, private or en masse, and for photography, either alone or in groups, or if the occasion calls for it, in the conventional nude. But no speeches. So Charlie should be advised that none should be scheduled either by his minions or the local authorities in either Augusta or Atlanta. If he feels that this condition is unacceptable, we'll just have to call the whole thing off.

I send this information to you because the communications lines are evidently down between the New York office and myself. Yours is the last remaining outpost for messages from headquarters. Tell them we intend to hold out to the last man.

TO ALISTAIR COOKE

September 24, 1957

Dear Alistair:

I didn't think the *Time* review was so snide. The fact that we have no camera capable of dollying through a woman's soul is not my fault. I've been begging for such a camera for years. But you know the front office. The chief trouble with the *Time* man is that he's heartless. He keeps laughing at people because they haven't his talent.

You missed something by not remaining another night in Atlanta.

---

* Refers to the fact that Aly's father had by-passed Aly and named another son to succeed him as the Aga Khan.
† In charge of 20th Century–Fox's New York publicity office, Einfeld had suggested that Johnson participate in publicizing *The Three Faces of Eve.*

You missed meeting Miss Fried Chicken. When I came back up to the room for my bag after breakfast the morning after you left you never saw two such females as were waiting for me in the corridor. One looked the Spirit of the Old South at a Webster Hall ball—sweet, sweet face, golden ringlets, and a crinoline garment so voluminous that it covered us all in the back seat of the car on the way to the airport. She explained that she was a reporter from some paper I never heard of and had a big notebook and six pencils, different colors, to prove it. She wanted an interview. She also wanted a contract and was prepared to go to unheard-of lengths to get it. With her was a duenna who looked like a Mexican Madam. She carried a Kodak with a flashlight that never worked. Snap, snap, snap—oh, shucks! Don Yarborough [member of 20th Century–Fox publicity department] was with me, naturally, and so I never came to grips with either of these two hobgoblins, though both made it more than clear that they were prepared for any eccentric arrangement my pretty little fancy might dictate.

So we settled for the interview in the car on the way to the airport. It was then that she showed me her credentials. Among them was a layout in *Life* two or three weeks ago showing her in some kind of trick photograph wearing a hundred different bathing suits. Just a hobby, she said. Also some other cheesecake guaranteed to galvanize any full-blooded man, of which I am one. It was then also that she confided (as Leonard Lyons would say) that she had just returned from New York, where she had been named Miss Fried Chicken. (Champagne all around for Miss Fried Chicken!) And a good part of the trip was taken up with a good-humored debate between the two ladies over whether Miss Fried Chicken looked more like Elizabeth Taylor or Dana Wynter, except blond. However, I have no wish to burn you up with envy, so I will tell you no more than that in the course of discussion of writing, the duenna asked me if I wrote genetically. That's right, genetically. I said no, I kept strict business hours. But your guess is as good as mine. So you see? . . .

T O   P E T E   M A R T I N

April 14, 1958

Dear Pete:

If Joanne [Woodward] had a discoverer, it was probably Dick Powell. He is one of the owners of a television affair called, I believe, the Four Star Playhouse, and she appeared with him in a little play in which she was an unhappy boarding school girl who had no parents to go home to on holidays, or something like that. She was superb. Very touching.

The kinescope of this TV show was submitted to the studio and that's when I first saw her. Buddy Adler was also very much impressed by her and told Zanuck that he wanted to sign her. Buddy was already scheduled to succeed Zanuck and was going through a kind of training period. Buddy says Zanuck was puzzled. He had seen the kinescope and could see nothing in the girl. But Buddy was so urgent that Darryl finally said, "All right, go on and sign her. Like everybody else in this job, you're going to make mistakes. So go ahead and make your first one." That's why Buddy cabled Zanuck the other night, "You remember my first mistake? She won the Oscar last night."

But having signed her, Buddy couldn't find the right spot for her. So the studio loaned her out for a couple of pictures with other studios. I never forgot her and when I finished the script of *The Three Faces of Eve* I still had her in the back of my mind. But I confess that my first choice was Judy Garland. After seeing the doctors' film of their patient, Judy got very excited and anxious to play it. But as often happens with poor Judy, there were all kinds of complications and, to tell the truth, I never heard any more from her. Now the New York office, after reading the script, was insistent on a star. But both Buddy and I were anxious to give the part to this new girl. And finally we had our way. She flew out from New York and came in to see me.

After talking about the part for a while, she asked me if I wanted her to use a Southern accent. I told her, over my dead body. I had heard some of the phoney Southern accents in *Baby Doll* and I didn't want any part of that kind of acting. "But mine wouldn't be phoney," she said. "I just have to slip back into it." Then she made a few remarks to me in pot-likker talk and I recognized it for the real thing. Actually it hadn't occurred to me that she could be from the South. She had had no accent of any kind in the television show. Now it turned out that she was from Thomasville, Georgia, and had lived around in a number of Georgia towns and small cities where her father was superintendent of schools. . . .

I was delighted by the fact that she was a Southerner. To be able to use this dialect properly was a great asset both to the character and to the picture. As fellow Crackers, I think we hit it off very well from the first.

When I suggested that you keep my part in this story to a minimum, I had in mind the fact that no actor or actress is too pleased by even the slightest implication that their success in a part was due to any talent but their own. I don't blame them for this. A director's contribution to a performance is rarely much. His usefulness is to the scenes and the picture as a whole, not often to an individual performance. He can govern it a bit, keeping it from going overboard usually, but for the most part the actor is operating out of his own ability. As proof of this, Joanne has been excellent in varying degrees in everything else she had done, always with different directors.

In 99 cases out of 100, it is the part that leads a good actor or an actress to an Oscar. Orson Welles read my script and called the turn immediately. He said he'd never read a part more likely to lead the girl to an Academy award.

In this case the part found exactly the right actress. Joanne, in my opinion, has even more than Bette Davis had to start with. One of these extra assets is a feeling for comedy. It is idle to speculate whether another actress could have done as much with the part, or more. The fact remains that, as you know as well as anybody else, it was an extraordinarily demanding role, and this new young girl was up to it. It was lucky for her that she got it, lucky for us that we got her for it.

I found that directing her was easy and satisfying. She knew what she was going to do and she did it. She had studied the doctors' book and film and thought about the character with great care and intelligence. When she came to the set she was prepared. It happens occasionally that an actor or actress makes all these preparations and comes to the set equally prepared, but prepared for what seems to me the wrong conception. Joanne's seemed to me right. She rarely asked even for advice. She simply rehearsed it and looked at me to see if I thought it looked okay. It nearly always did. This is the kind of acting that makes a director look very good indeed. To make an arbitrary ruling on it, I would say she was 95% responsible for her performance. Certainly no less.

I hope this gives you what you want or need. Yours in Christ.

TO JAMES THURBER
September 3, 1957

Dear Jim:

I look forward to your stories about Ross more than anything I've heard of in years. You're exactly the man to do Ross and Ross is exactly the man for you to write about. Nothing so right has turned up around here since Boswell met Johnson. The fat one.

I once made a half-hearted effort to get on *The New Yorker*. I say half-hearted because I had begun to sell stories pretty regularly to the *Saturday Evening Post* and I was a happy fellow not to have to hold a salaried job anymore. This must have been around 1929 or 1930. But still at bottom a little nervous about no pay envelope every Saturday night, I asked Ross about reviewing movies for *The New Yorker*. This probably struck me as a job calling for the minimum in time and talent, and I simply couldn't get it through my head that [John] Mosher was doing it through either his choice or anybody else's. He seemed to be doing it resentfully, as if Ross had got him into it through a sharp trick, and he was getting back at him by doing it as badly as he could. The whole set-up seemed so temporary and unsatisfactory that I had no qualms about asking for another man's job. (As it turned out, Mosher was reviewing pictures exactly as Ross wanted them reviewed and as he apparently always insisted that they be reviewed. The *Daily Worker* has no party line stronger than *The New Yorker*'s about movies.) Anyway, Ross turned me down flatly. ("Reviewing movies," he said, "is for women and fairies. Why don't you write me some pieces?")

Once I heard Frank Capra ask Ross why he didn't fire [John] McCarten.* "Wouldn't think of it," Ross said. "McCarten's my ace in the hole. If ever I need to, I can always get $30,000 cash from the movies by firing McCarten. As long as I've got him, I'll never go broke." In spite of all this, Ross saw an awful lot of movies. When we went fishing with Chasen once,† he astonished me with his knowledge of current pictures.

I saw Ross only from time to time, mostly out here. Either he or Chasen called me when he got in town and we spent our evenings together drinking and talking in Chasen's back room.

One night (this may not be a delicate thing to publish) Ross had a very pretty Confederate girl with him. . . . Around one o'clock

---

* McCarten reviewed movies for *The New Yorker*.
† Ross was a large investor in Dave Chasen's restaurant.

Chasen shut up shop and we went to my house for a swim. I must have been really soaring, for ordinarily I wouldn't go in a pool in broad daylight, much less at midnight. (I was unmarried at this time.) We were no more in the house than [she] proposed an evening of utter abandon, nude bathing, and such were her high spirits and my hysteria that in less than a twinkling she and I were splashing around together in the deep end. It was not until then that I realized that neither Ross nor Chasen had been swept along into this lark. While I was trying to catch [her] to spank her playfully (I can hardly stay afloat, much less swim as fast as [she]) Ross and Chasen were pacing up and down discussing the parsley situation. Ross, I believe now, was shocked by what was happening, and Chasen, so beholden to Harold, was trying manfully to string along with the boss. But both [she] and I were immediately cooled off by the sight of this business consultation and its disapproving implications and so we climbed out of the pool (gallantly I let her go first) and presently all four of us, fully clad, were delving into the matter of parsley. And that little girl, I gasped and turned crimson with shame when I read about it, was presently Mrs. Ross. I had no idea!

One summer Chasen and Ross and I went fishing in Nevada, around Reno. It must have been the summer before his death, for the following summer, when Chasen and I were to meet him in Denver for some fishing around there, Chasen got a call that Ross had been taken to that clinic in Boston, and he died a few weeks or months later. But if you think Ross was sartorially a man of undistinction in the fashionable world of smart New York, you should have seen what he looked like on a fishing trip. I can't even imagine where he got such garments, unless they'd been discarded by Joe Jackson, the tramp bicyclist. He looked so villainous that he attracted worried attention in a truck drivers' diner where we stopped for breakfast on the way to Nevada. To twist one of Stanley Walker's remarks, I never saw anybody who reminded me less of Lucius Beebe. To prove this, in fact, we called on Lucius in Virginia City on the way and I was right.

Ross had to see Joe Liebling* in Reno the night we got there. Liebling was there to get a divorce, and to finance this project he had persuaded Ross to assign him to do a piece to be called "The Reno Story." After being there for several weeks, Ross said, Liebling wired

* A. J. Liebling was foreign correspondent for *The New Yorker*.

that it was his considered opinion that the story should be expanded into "The Nevada Story" in order to include Las Vegas, and for this he wanted *The New Yorker* to buy him a car. Ross said he refused, but authorized an 18-cents-a-mile allowance, the same being that of a United States Senator. Also, as it turned out, Liebling couldn't drive a car. So he arrived at the Riverside Hotel with a lady candidate for a divorce as his chauffeur. Ross gave him some money and Liebling and his chauffeur went out to dinner. Around nine o'clock, as we were passing one of the joints on the main street, the lady chauffeur lunged out and barely made a lamp post. Ross checked them into the nearest hotel for the night. Why should he let one of his valued writers be driven back to their divorce-ranch boardinghouse by a crooked chauffeur?

Ross played poker all night in one of those open games on the main street. He won $36. After all night. But he liked the people, he said. All poker games in Reno, he said, include one Chinaman with more dirty money in his left shoe and a one-armed brakeman.

He was a wonderful companion on such trips, never too much interested in fish, and very talkative. Once, in a boat with a fishing guide, a gray-haired old fellow, Ross got into a long encyclopedic explanation of why certain trouts were to be found both on the East Coast and the West. It had to do with streams that were split by the Great Divide. Just as he gained cruising altitude in this discourse, the guide looked at him with contempt and said, "Bullshit." I never saw a man so taken aback. "But God damn it," Ross kept saying later, "I'm recognized by everybody as one of the finest conversationalists since Oscar Wilde. So how the hell does this son-of-a-bitch get off saying 'bullshit' to me!" I have no explanation for this. . . .

These occasional meetings with Ross gave me a genuine affection for him. So much so that till this day I can hardly bear to look at Winchell, whose vitriol about Ross during his final illness is still hard to believe. Winchell was apparently convinced that Ross was pretending to be ill just to irritate him, Winchell, but why Ross should even think about Winchell is not easy to understand. Anyway, either the day of Ross's death or the day before, Winchell printed something to the effect that people were saying Mrs. Ariane Ross was going to be the most popular widow in town. (Don't ask me. I don't know.) Then after the funeral he printed a line unprecedented in journalism: he knocked the funeral. "The *New York Times* reported there were 1,200 people at Harold Ross's funeral; it was nearer 600."

I do hope that you'll find this strange sidelight on Ross's death interesting enough to have it looked into; I know of no more horrible misuse of a horrible profession's horrible liberties.

I'll see Chasen in a few days and I'll ask him if he has anything for you about Harold, if you haven't already asked him. Oh, yes, Sam [S. N.] Behrman told me not long ago that Ross fired a Mr. Broadwater, husband of Mary McCarthy, because he couldn't hear him coming down the hall.

I wish this were better and more helpful. My best to you and Helen.

TO JAMES THURBER

September 9, 1957

Dear Jim:

Two more nothings about Ross. He once claimed that he wouldn't take anything for his ulcer, because it always got him an immediate table in a crowded restaurant and the promptest of service. All he had to do, he said, was to walk up to the headwaiter and say, "Captain, I've got an ulcer." All headwaiters, he insisted, either had ulcers, had had them, or were getting them, and not even the Masons had a closer brotherhood than ulcer victims.

His sister (who looks exactly like him) told me that Harold's city ways were occasionally a little baffling to his fellow Coloradans. Once she and her husband and Harold had to stop and get out of their car to put on tire chains before going farther over an icy mountain road. Since Harold looked like the toughest man in the Last Chance Saloon, his brother-in-law was a little startled at the way Harold went about this more or less ordinary motoring chore. After piddling around with the tire chains for a moment or two, he got out a bottle of Elizabeth Arden's hand lotion and kept washing his hands in it every two or three moments. Nobody in Colorado ever saw anything like that in their lives.

My best.

TO ROBERT GOLDSTEIN

October 22, 1957

Dear Robert:

The fish arrived and it is now out on the lawn, wired as a lamp. I have never seen such a handsome beast. It must have taken you three or four minutes to bring it to boat. Many many thanks.

Did you want to know about Tallulah Bankhead? I sat at a dinner table with her the other night. She's really a caution. Inflamed with wine, she was attacking Josh Logan, far down the table, for being solvent, which seemed to be an unpardonable crime to her. You never heard such screams and yells and walloping around, while poor Josh, to whom the charges never became quite clear, tried to crawl up the wall behind him. Mrs. Jennifer Selznick, our hostess, kept signalling frantically to me to talk, talk, talk! Anything to create a diversion. But as all men know, and most women, there is a limit to my courage, and Tallulah is well out in front of this limit. I had just as soon walk in front of a Sherman tank. Later, in case you haven't already turned the page, she called across the dance floor to Cecil Beaton, "Don't try to show off in front of me, Mr. Beaton! Don't forget that it was I who taught you how to make up your eyes!" That's the way to make a party go!

Beaton told Dorris (assuming you are still with us) that he sat between Hedda and Tallulah at a dinner a few nights before. He said Hedda recounted her first view of Tallulah, a vivid drama in which Hedda claimed to have been in the audience the night that Tallulah made her debut in London. "The curtain rose on the most beautiful girl in the world: you, Tallulah!" To which Tallulah replied with a short ugly word, described Hedda as a Republican bitch, and declared that the occasion was of such social elegance that Hedda would not have been allowed in the same neighborhood, much less the theatre. Hedda retorted in kind, and since her voice isn't many decibels below Tallulah's, poor Beaton must have been threatened with concussion. The shouting got more and more acrimonious, and when finally Tallulah offered to bet a thousand dollars that Hedda was not present on that occasion, Hedda made the very good point that Tallulah didn't have a thousand dollars, whereupon Tallulah looked around the room and replied, "No, but I will make a thousand dollars before I leave this house tonight." . . .

And now in conclusion, all I care to say about this winsome Alabama belle is that I'll bet there are no black children who would like to go to school with her. . . .

Johnson adapted Romain Gary's *The Colors of the Day*, retitling it *The Man Who Understood Women* (1959). He tried, in his screenplay, "to see if great tragedy couldn't properly mix or be used with broad comedy." The result was less than satisfactory, and Johnson admitted, "It can be done, but I couldn't do it." Some of the fault lay in the screenplay, but Johnson also thought the casting was wrong. The lead role, written for Orson Welles (whom the studio refused to employ), was played by Henry Fonda. Johnson, as director, did a lot of cutting as he filmed; his daughter Marjorie Fowler was the final cutter, as she was on many of his films.

TO ROBERT EMMETT DOLAN

December 17, 1957

Dear Bobby:

You know about as much as I do about what's going on out here. Last night we had a staff meeting here at the studio, mainly because Skouras likes to make long, dull, unintelligible speeches to a captive audience, and he defied the world on behalf of 20th Century–Fox. This studio will up its annual releases from 60 in 1957 to 70 in 1958. This of course includes a pack of little pictures made by [Robert] Lippert for around $125,000 apiece.

Lippert himself, who is also owner of a few theatres in small cities, said that in two of his locations the sentiment against pay television was violent and overwhelming, between three and four to one, because everybody said they didn't want to add one more nickel to what they had to spend. They are afraid that pay TV would be but the first step toward the complete elimination of free TV.

In the only other contribution to free speech, Jerry Wald wanted to know why *Kiss Them for Me* with Jayne Mansfield hadn't done better abroad. Or even in this country, for that matter. He was informed, in effect, that there was an international resistance to the picture. It seemed to be one area of happy coexistence between Communism and the free world. Here they stood shoulder to shoulder against it.

Other than that, all you hear here is the blues. Every other studio seems to be making pictures reluctantly. Warner Bros., I am told, exists only by grace of *Giant*, though *Pajama Game* must have been successful to some degree too. RKO is of course dead, and Paramount is being cultivated by sharecroppers. You never hear anything about picture making at MGM, just about voting for or against Vogel. It's a very gloomy Christmas season for pictures, and I wonder sometimes whether I'll be writing episodes for "Maverick" or "Have Gun—Will Travel" a year from now.

Nearly a year of my time went down the drain last week when Skouras decided to shelve *The Wandering Jew*, on the grounds that it was anti-Semitic and anti-Christian, leaving us only the Moslems to support it. This was in spite of the fact that I had a small pack of rabbis, from orthodox to reform, who found nothing to object to in the script or the picture. And also a Catholic scholar, head of the department of English at Loyola, who gave his Christian approval to it. The script was generally admired, so far as I can tell, but you know what they say, you can't fight city hall. Sooooo, back to the old drawing board.

I'm fiddling around now with *The Colors of the Day*, but not with much heart. We are told constantly that the ruination of this business is the in-between picture, the picture that is not either about a girl from outer space or a blockbuster, and if there is anything I have done all my life, it is in-between pictures. And *The Colors of the Day* would seem to be right down the middle of the in-betweens. It may, in fact, be the death knell of the whole industry. However, I shall press on. What the hell else can I do? . . .

In short, the Russians can't drop that thing any too soon to suit me. As a matter of fact, it's beginning to look like our only hope. Merry Christmas.

TO ROBERT EMMETT DOLAN

April 16, 1958

Dear Bobby:

One of the privileges denied to people who live in New York is to be a guest at the SPG's [Screen Producers Guild] annual Milestone Dinner. But of course you'll want to know all about it. As it happened the other night, when the speeches finally ended at something after twelve o'clock Mary Livingstone stood up and fell in a swoon on the floor. I think that will give you the idea.

The last time I went to one of these things Dorris and I sat at a large table with people we didn't know. Naturally I spoke to nobody. As we finished the shrimp cocktail the young woman on my left said to me, "Shall we have a little small talk?" It didn't seem to me necessary to answer her. Turning to Dorris, I said, "Will you excuse me, darling? I've got to go to the can." So I went to the can, at home. And never came back.

This time we stayed a little longer. During the confusion when the coffee was served we both went to the can at home. All I had to do was look at that line of people on the dais and I knew that this was not the place for me. Skouras, Henry Cabot Lodge, Clare Luce, Jennifer Jones, General Van Fleet, and a man named Pappas, a banker from Boston, among others.

As I heard about it afterwards, Mr. Pappas, Skouras's oldest friend, was assigned to the emotional delivery. He choked up so much at this, I'm told, that his entire tribute to Skouras was one long gargle. The only interesting thing about it was that Skouras fell asleep as Mr. Pappas began his emotional charge and woke up only when it ended. Then when he got on his feet to speak, everybody else in the house went to sleep.

At a dinner the night before, I sat beside Mrs. Luce. [Sam] Engel sat on her other side. Somebody once told Clare that she looked like a pale goddess and clearly she has never got over this. Everything about this woman fits. She is the phoniest snob I have ever come up against.

It didn't help, of course, when Sam, inflamed with wine, launched our small talk by asking me, across her, "How the hell are we going to clear up this mess that Clare left in Italy?" This is not the sort of humor that Mrs. Luce takes well. As nearly as I could get it, she was doing her best to be gracious among colored folks. The dinner was in the Escoffier room at the Beverly Hilton and when a tulip glass was placed in front of her for the champagne, she asked incredulously, "Is this really the way champagne is served in Hollywood?" The wine waiter, who probably knows about two hundred and fifty times as much about wine and its service as she does, said it was. Whereupon she shrugged as if to say that if this is the way it's done here, who am I to question them? I suppose I should have brought up the point at the time, but I didn't think I should be as rude as she was. But the tulip glass is the one favored by Andre Simon for the service of champagne. Sometimes I wonder why I'm so polite.

Later she told me that the explanation for the killing of Johnny Stompanato by Lana Turner's daughter was obvious. Subconsciously, she said, the child was following a script. She was following the dramatics of Hollywood. That settled that.

As a matter of fact, I hated a great many other people there too. You know yourself that I don't confine my antipathy to one person. But I must admit that Clare was way out in front. Talking with her reminded me of the story that George Kaufman once told me. When *Margin for Error* [an anti-Nazi play by Clare Boothe Luce] was in Philadelphia and needed help, Clare accosted George on the street in New York and invited him to come down to Philadelphia and do what he could to help them out. For reasons that I don't remember, George said he wouldn't be able to do it. Clare then said reproachfully, "I think you should remember, George, that after all, this is for your people." It was of course as generous an offer as George had ever heard. But still, "Clare," he said, "all the Jews need now is to have you take us up."

We've had many more adventures here, but I think I could sell the accounts. For one instance, they're thinking of throwing Christie out of George School. For another, they're thinking of throwing Roxie out of Westlake. For still a third, Scotty can't make up his mind between his Brooklyn Dodgers cap and his Los Angeles Dodgers cap to wear at the opening game here on Friday. Otherwise I have no problems.

Thank you for the report on Nan. Mrs. D. A. Doran told us the other night that Nan was in line for a television show. What about that? Also, what about that first act?

We are all just dreadful.

TO ROBERT EMMETT DOLAN

May 6, 1958

Dear Bobby:

In the first place, the announcement that Marilyn Monroe would play in *Can-Can*, like the one you saw about some girl being cast in *The Colors of the Day*, was the idle work of the publicity department on a dull day.

I talked to Henry Ephron* the other day about *Can-Can*, wondering what was going to be done with it, and while he spoke of it as a possibility at some future date there didn't seem to be any genuine expectation in what he said. As you know, musicals are regarded as dangerous projects these days, especially at this studio. Our various European representatives turn pale at the very suggestion of a musical and say that not even *The King and I* was able to do anything outside of England. So, for the time being, I doubt very much that anybody has any plans at all for *Can-Can*.

As for Jeanmaire and Petit, I hardly know what to say. When I wrote to them and when I talked to them in France there was no question in my mind but that the picture would be made. Zanuck had

---

* Henry and Phoebe Ephron wrote the play *Take Her, She's Mine*, which Johnson made into a film.

assigned it to me and I had his okay to approach several people about playing in it, including Jeanmaire and Petit. In other words, I had authority for as far as I went and my negotiations with all of the players were of course in good faith.

Nevertheless, they were negotiations only. I gave them the date that I hoped to be able to start the picture but always with the proviso that a leading man could be engaged. We were talking about it with Cary Grant, as who doesn't. Eventually, as so often happens, Cary withdrew himself, after giving me every reason to think that he liked the part and the script. He was even exercising his singing voice with Ken Darby. Then Zanuck removed the picture from my hands. I wrote this to Roland immediately. I expressed my regrets about this and told him how grateful I was for the patience Jeanmaire and he had shown. I added that I would do all that I could do under the circumstances, which was to make recommendations to Ephron, who had succeeded me. The only project of his own that Roland mentioned to me was a revue scheduled for September 1956. I wrote him about my giving up the production of *Can-Can* on January 6, 1956.

But it seems to me a matter that had better be handled by the legal department, not me. I regret it deeply if all our discussions of the script and the projected production caused them any loss in any respect. I can't feel that they would be justified in regarding these talks as a commitment. They involved too many conditions and other ifs. It seemed to be more as if we were exploring the situation with an earnest hope on both sides that a deal could be worked out. I have done this, as I know you have, without such exploratory conversations being taken to be an actual commitment in any sense except that of a hopeful one. As I explained to them when I saw them in France, I had no authority myself to make a deal. As the producer, it was my job to line up the various elements. Then and then only would the boys with the contracts step in.

If they really feel that they have a case, which I must say I doubt, the only way to test it would be by legal procedure. I would hate this, naturally, because I like and respect them both and would regret the implication that I had dealt in any way unfairly with them. Or that the studio had, for that matter. But as I say, it is up to them to take the next step. Incidentally, Roland never answered my letter telling him about my withdrawal from the production. If he had any such feelings of disappointment or resentment, that would have been the normal time to express it. Nor have I ever heard from him since then.

This just about covers the topic of *Can-Can*. There is one bright side to the situation. If they take it to court, I could very well be called to the witness stand. This is what I have been wishing for for years. Already I can see myself making a monkey out of their lawyer. And compelling even the judge to fake a cough to hide a smile at the brilliance of my ripostes. So as much as I would deplore litigation, I can't help looking forward to that day. Would you ask them if they would be good enough to retain a rather stupid, slow-witted lawyer? My guess is that that's the kind that would show me off to best advantage.

I won't say anything about *The Saturday Night Kid*. Behind Nan's back they put an ad about it in last Sunday's *New York Times*. Ordinarily this would make it an open secret, but I will continue to respect her wishes and make no mention of it.

Production of Johnson's screenplay for the Western mentioned in this letter to Robert Goldstein was postponed because the costs of making a Western were considered too high. The movie was finally released in 1960 as *Flaming Star*, with Elvis Presley as the lead. Although the script was Johnson's, he reluctantly agreed to share screen credit with Clair Huffaker, the author of the original book. When Johnson saw the movie some years later, he found Don Siegel's direction commendable and was pleasantly surprised by Presley's performance.

TO ROBERT GOLDSTEIN

May 12, 1958

Dear Robin:

The beautiful ties arrived in the nick of time. I was having to tie my old ones almost at the end, to hide the dirt in the middle. As you very well know, I never buy ties or anything else. Except now and then a tube of brushless shaving cream. So any time you see anything, that's exactly what I need.

I understand that you will soon have a pleasant visitor in the shape of Mr. Jerry Wald. It is his first trip abroad and so far as he is concerned, to hell with Westminster Abbey and all that jazz, where are the newspapermen? Harry Brand has come to turn white when Jerry's name is mentioned. The other day Dick Powell dropped the remark that he had brought Jerry out here. Harry stepped back, took off his coat, and said, "Get out of that car and say that!" At the last Screen Producers Guild meeting, at which Sam Engel wound up his term as president, Sam was delivering an eloquent farewell to his troops. Full of Schnapps and weeping like a baby, Sam had his audience enthralled. There were only two dry eyes in the house. At the climax of his address, Frank McCarthy felt a nudge and Jerry slipped him a note. The note said, "Have you any ideas how I should handle my publicity while I'm in Europe?" Making movies is only a hobby with Jerry, his main business is getting his name in the papers. I trust you will do all that is expected of you as a loyal member of the 20th Century–Fox team. . . .

Just to bring you up to date on the situation, all of Jerry's pictures so far have grossed $38,000,000 each. He has 126 stories in the works now. His telephone bills alone cost more than *The Ten Commandments*. This man operates on a very high level, and would send out just as many memos as David Selznick if he could spell. . . .

I have just about finished my Western, on which we had put the title *The Brothers of Flaming Arrow*. When we consulted with New York, it turned out that Mr. Skouras didn't care for *Flaming Arrow* or *The Brothers*. He had nothing against *of*. After a great deal of cerebration (look it up, God damn it) our brain trust in New York came up with *Flaming Lance*. All of these fellows who cooperated to think up this title are said to get more than $10 a week each. We've sent the script to Brando and nothing can be done until he sends a reply. But according to his agents, he must be approached very carefully, on tiptoe. It sometimes takes them weeks to get his attention. For he must speak first, you know. I wish I'd never been born.

Scotty has turned into the wildest baseball fan ever heard of. But he's still loyal to Cleveland. He told me straight to my face that if the Dodgers and the Cleveland Indians should meet in the World Series next Fall, a possibility that no human older than Scotty could ever have dreamed of, he would be for the Indians. Tell Spud [Robert's brother, road manager of the Cleveland Indians] that. The thing is, he's going to have a nervous breakdown if the Dodgers don't go East soon. This business of listening to the game on radio in the dark when he is supposed to be sleeping is affecting his health. The morning after a 14-inning game the other night he was too weak to go to school. Meanwhile, their games are nothing much to listen to.

We all send you our best.

TO ROBERT EMMETT DOLAN

May 15, 1958

Dear Bobby:

You're a very crafty fellow. You had beaten down your play so much that I was prepared for almost anything. Thus it was that I read this first act with surprise and pleasure. And when I came to the end I was sorry that I didn't have the rest of it to enjoy.

I know you will accept it that I am on the level in what I say about it. First, the subject matter. The situation, as you know, is a pretty familiar one, but still worth stating and restating if it can be done with a fresh point of view. Whether yours is a fresh point of view or not I must confess I don't know. I can only say that the situation as you dramatized it interested me, and I still want to know how you solve it and what statements you have to make that are pertinent to the theme. These are yet to come. I don't mean preachments, of course, I mean dramatized statements.

The act is written literately, clearly, and with good humor. Your own criticism of the act shouldn't be taken too seriously. A blue pencil could clear most of it up without difficulty. The fact is, you have overwritten your dialogue. You say too much. You apparently have no faith whatever in the ability of actors to convey the message without spelling it out in words.

For another thing, your dialogue is often dialogue to be read, not spoken. It is literary at times rather than dramatic. But this again seems to me an easily corrected fault. I think it is possible to be colloquial without being illiterate. Colloquial dialogue always eases up the situation a bit. Strict dialogue is inclined to become didactic and consequently you give an audience the wrong impression, often a rather stuffy impression.

I doubt if I can be specific about more than a few points. Take Bedford for one. If I may go back to something of my own, when Freddie March went through his first rehearsal of his first scene in *Gray Flannel Suit* he was the standard equipment tycoon, with too much heartiness, too quick a laugh, all that kind of stale stuff. That was the way he had rehearsed it, he said, with Florence. But I suggested that I would like for everybody, in the audience as well as on the screen, to like and respect him. I didn't want him to make fun of himself. I wanted him to play it with a measure of natural modesty, or perhaps I should say naturally. Freddie, as you might guess, unlike the ordinary ham, was delighted with this conception of the part. The result, for better or worse, was as you saw it on the screen.

I think this kind of reasoning should apply to Bedford. For one thing, I would never let him be called by his initials. That's not only out of date, but it kind of dates you. It's a worn-out device. Beginning with that, I would try to humanize him a little more. Don't let him be a stock-figure Philistine, but a man who, try as he will, simply can't understand anyone who doesn't put money and what money can buy first. One of the things that I usually try to do, but rarely succeed, is to make a character sympathetic, whether I agree with him or not. In such a play as yours, people don't set out to be heavies, the circumstances sometimes make them so. But I think it's always better if the writer tries to assume an honesty in all of his characters, and especially should this be true in such a play as yours.

As for Bill, he seems to be very close to a good character, not another variation of Marchbanks. Why don't you keep Jack Lemmon in mind for the part? Then he could be ingratiating, bright, with a measure of wit, but still solid in his view of music as a way of life. He's only a fragment so far, and I really need the whole of the play to form any kind of valid opinion of him.

As I said on the phone, the Woodward vs. Bedford situation is very nice indeed. And now I will make an effort with one of their scenes to show you what I meant about dialogue in such a case. I will enclose it.

Also as I said on the phone, the more natural comedy you can get, the better for the play. Character comedy, I mean. The Woodward-Bedford situation is a perfect example of this. There are no jokes in it. It all comes out of the occasional encounters of two people who will never understand each other if they live to be a million. This is the best of all comedy situations. That was also wonderful when Bedford tried to find out from Sidney what the hell kind of business Bill was in. That was as natural as water, and beautifully and deftly handled.

Little remains to be told. Christie is pretty well convinced that she is going to be flang out of George School. In another somewhat awkward situation, Dorris was elected assistant room mother by a landslide for next year at Westlake. The question now arises, will she still have to serve if Roxie, as seems possible, is flang out of Westlake? Scotty is getting along fine with but one real weakness—he's still hitting at bad balls.

I will now lie down.

John Crosby was the television critic of the New York *Herald Tribune*.

TO JOHN CROSBY

June 26, 1958

Dear John:

The trouble with you 21-inch people is that you don't realize the hold that actors have on us Robber Barons these days. They want half the studio just to show up! If they are also expected to speak distinctly, holy jumping Jesus Christ!

Just to give you an example, you know what box-office dynamite Jack Palance is. ("Leave the dishes in the sink tonight, Mother! There's a Jack Palance picture in town!") For a good standard incomprehensible appearance in a picture, Mr. Palance's agents ask $125,000. (Among those Mr. Palance draws into a theatre is Mrs. Palance, whom he immediately reconciled with when the court worked out what he would have to pay her after the divorce, and Mrs. Palance's lawyer, to say nothing of a distant cousin on his mother's side in St. Paul, Minn.) But if Mr. Palance must part his lips from time to time and unknot his tongue and pronounce words like Bergen for Chrissake Evans, the tag is $150,000. Never thought of that, did you!

As for Orson [Welles] he's got a secret. It's what he's saying. As long ago as *Jane Eyre*, which he played in English, he wouldn't tell the audience even then. To hell with 'em. They want to know what it's all about, let 'em go somewhere and read the book! Jerry [Wald] tried to get him to dub the lines in *Long Hot Summer*, but not only did he refuse the suggestion but he wouldn't even let Jerry get the Kingfish to dub them for him.

To sum it all up, I quote from a recent letter from Stanley Walker, the shrewdest Corinthian in Lampasas, Texas: "No matter which way you look these days, pardner, it's tough tits in the sunset!" And if that ain't the God's truth!

TO ROBERT GOLDSTEIN

August 20, 1958

Dear Robert:

Mr. Skouras has gone back to New York leaving us just about as he found us. No hits, no runs, no errors. But while he and his Mafia were here, having lunch in the executive dining room was a little like

Russian roulette. You couldn't tell who you were going to be trapped with. My God, what a fuss the man makes!

Hecht-Hill-Lancaster rejected *The Visit*. From what I hear, they are all about to reject each other too. Friction. Jim Hill talked to me about doing *The Visit* with Rita [Hayworth], but I haven't heard from him since, and it won't matter very much anyway, because Fox has indicated that it will meet any outside offer, as it has the right, to keep it here on the lot.

One of the fellows that Abe Lastfogel [president of the William Morris Agency] and I talked to about this outside project was Spyros Skouras, Jr. He said his company was in position to finance a picture. But I don't think he can be altogether wrapped up in this business. When he came into my office he explained to us that he couldn't give us but five minutes. He said he had to get to a meeting of his board of directors to help in the selection of a new president for his ice cream company. There's no business like show business. He did return an hour or so later, but I had a feeling that his heart was still in the freezer.

This has been a big week for Author Nora Johnson. Her book is out and has received excellent reviews in the big New York papers. One mentioned her in the same breath with Salinger. Gene Fowler said she wrote like a literate Françoise Sagan. This is all pretty heady stuff and I look for her to go into orbit any minute. On top of everything else, she sold an article to *Sports Illustrated* on, of all things, football. This I don't understand at all. As for my part in this fracas, if you can get back here by the 31st you will be able to see me from 1½ to 2 minutes on a television program called "The Cavalcade of Books." This is my second time to post (the first was in a salute to Joanne Woodward) and if I don't click this time, to hell with it. I sent that column about the father who wanted to borrow a sports car for a weekend to Nora. Maybe she can get a story out of it. If she can do a story on a game that she has never seen so far as I have ever heard of, she ought to be able to get a story out of anything. Whatever can *Sports Illustrated* be thinking of!

Scotty spent six hours in the Coliseum last night, from 6 p.m. until midnight, to see the Dodgers clobber the Braves twice. He said he enjoyed every second of it. These younger fellows have stronger bottoms than their elders. I don't think I'd sit in the Coliseum for six hours to see Mickey Hargitay clobber Mrs. H. On second thought, I think I would. . . .

We send you our best.

TO ROBERT GOLDSTEIN

September 2, 1958

Dear Robert:

Martindale's is mailing you a copy of Nora's book today. I didn't know you couldn't wait. The book has had excellent reviews, particularly in New York. I suppose it has sold well enough for a first novel but it could hardly be called a best seller. I do what I can for it, handing out copies here and there, and Sunday I had a full minute on a TV program called "Cavalcade of Books" to make a pitch for it. I don't know what good it did for the book, but I can tell you right now that it did me no good. I always thought that TV personalities were simply deluged with fan mail. I haven't even got a postcard. . . .

I'm leaving today with my entire family for a week of carefree discomfort in a hotel at Laguna Beach. This business of getting a rest is pretty well established now. You leave a nice big comfortable home, where everybody can get away from each other, and shack up in two rooms where two people have to sit on the same chair. The food will be bad, the pillows on my bed will be too thin, and some fellow will run into my car on the way down there. This you can get for as little as seventy-five dollars a day. Goodbye, everybody!

I am having an awful mish-mash around here with the studio. To tell the truth, I'm pretty well fed up with the way it's being run now. Some people think that Skouras, having conquered the rest of the world, would now like to produce the pictures here. This is the man who didn't want to make *The Diary of Anne Frank* because Bernie Gimbel [owner of the department stores, and a friend of Skouras] told him it was anti-Semitic. Bernie Gimbel also told him that *The Wandering Jew* was anti-Semitic. I wonder what he thought *The Young Lions* was. In *The Young Lions*, the American heroes were a drunken bum who had to be kidnapped into the Army to fight for his country and a Jewish goon who was surrounded by loyal Americans who beat the be-Jesus out of him every day. On the other hand, the representative of Nazi Germany was one of the nicest fellows you ever met in your life. He hated Hitler, had no idea that they were throwing German Jews into the cooker, and clearly wished he could get in with a friendly American crowd. So what do they do? They shoot him. Where was Mr. Skouras when all this was going on?

At any rate, I think Buddy Adler is being crushed to death. Last week he turned up with an ulcer. His first. I feel very sorry for him. He apparently has to get approval from New York before he can even sharpen a pencil. He got a little tight at a party the other night and really sang the blues to me. I may get out of here if I can. Buddy has all my sympathies but I can't afford to go crazy in his behalf, since that wouldn't do him any good anyway. He's got enough crazy people around him already.

That was a very interesting story on Groucho. I know that he hates every minute he's away from his own home. I was sorry to hear that his TV project didn't go through. But I doubt if he cares. All he seems to want is to be let alone.

We send you our best.

TO ROBERT GOLDSTEIN

November 28, 1958

Dear Robert:

Jack Warner is back in town, but when I reached that point in the story where it said he was making jokes and wisecracks I turned to something else. It makes a man shudder just to think of the wit that is trickling out of him at this very minute.

The widow Bogart is very excited about her return to Blighty. She says she's had it here. I think it's the best thing that could happen to her. Because everybody knew her and Bogey together, she has a feeling that she is being watched 24 hours a day by curious people, which I think is quite true. It's an uncomfortable situation for her and I think it very wise of her to pull out of here and live for a while anyway in an area where she isn't subjected to this scrutiny.

Nothing but funerals this week. Ty Power, Parkyakarkus, and Bert Allenberg's today.* Bert suffered the same fatal hemorrhage as Leonard. But he had about 24 or 48 hours of warning, headaches, but like many others, he suspected nothing serious.

This is the sort of thing that will never be said of me. I suspect everything. Now and then you see in the papers some such line as, "Mr. So-and-So had a slight pain in the elbow on Thursday night but thought nothing of it." In my obituary this line will read, "Mr. Johnson had felt a slight pain in his elbow off and on for 20 years and always thought something of it. In fact, every time he felt it he nearly went crazy." Nobody's going to catch me overlooking a symptom.

I am having the usual idiotic difficulties with the starting of my picture [*The Man Who Understood Women*]. Miss [Leslie] Caron

---

* Parkyakarkus was a comedian of the 1930s and 1940s. Bert Allenberg had been Johnson's agent at the William Morris Agency in the early 1950s.

is in London and Mr. [Charles] LeMaire is in ladies' wardrobe here and is dressing her by air mail. This is as unsatisfactory as undressing a woman by air mail. I suspect that she regards this as our fault, because after all there was no particular reason to build this studio so far from Montpelier Square, London SW 7. The problem with Mr. [Tony] Franciosa is also international. He wants to bring a make-up man from Italy, a fellow whose handling of the powder puff he admires very much. But we had to disappoint him. The union won't let a Dago make-up man even point at a powder puff on this lot. Mr. Franciosa will just have to be satisfied with one of Shotgun Britton's colleagues.

Edward Leggewie [formerly Paris representative for 20th Century–Fox] is back here and the production department is trying to find something for him to do. I have asked him to keep an eye on the French settings in this picture. The art director has never been any nearer France than West Street and is liable to turn up with a street that looks as much like the Rue de la Paix as Central Avenue. Edward tells me that when the first money reports on *The Roots of Heaven* reached Darryl, Darryl didn't leave his room for two days. *Look* had a lay-out this week of John Huston's simultaneous double blockbuster on Broadway. No mention was made of the amounts of money that these two pictures will lose. If a studio wants to commit suicide I have the perfect arrangement for it. Get Leland Hayward to do the producing and Huston to do the directing.

I am turning *The Goldstein Story* over to [Robert] Lippert. It sounds like dynamite to me. If he doesn't want it, we'll have Jerry Wald announce it anyway. Jerry and the studio have reached an agreement. Jerry doesn't want to make any more pictures here and Skouras doesn't want him to make any more here either. Something ought to come of this.

You may be interested in the fact that all of your letters and cartoons are being filed in a time capsule which will not be opened for 100 years from this date. Let them work it out for themselves.

Happy Thanksgiving to you and yours from us and ours.

TO ROBERT GOLDSTEIN

January 17, 1959

Dear Robert:

The enclosed is a good sample of the reviews that *The Sheriff of [Fractured Jaw]* has got here—all very good. Now that I'm shooting,

I don't read the trade papers, so I don't know what the business is. But I'm sure you take it for granted that the picture will lose money. All Fox pictures do. Look at the figures.

Skouras has a quarter-annually day of horror. That's the day when he has to give out the quarter-annual report on the company's business. In Skouras's case, this is enough to make a man want to cut his throat, because he's got to cook up a report that makes the stock-holders glow with pride in the management and at the same time convince the employees that only ice every other day in the cooler will prevent bankruptcy and the arrival of the sheriff—of Los Angeles County. This isn't easy. They are all out here now—sweating away in Adler's office this very minute—working on a financial report with slide rules, invisible ink, qualified forgers, and unfrocked certified public accountants. Any honest man discovered within one hundred yards of that office will be shot on sight. Nine men arrived on planes, first class, and are bivouacked in suites in the Beverly Hills and Beverly Hilton hotels. All eat high on the hog, on an expense account. They will spend three days repeating to each other what they have already said to each other on the phone. Leonard [Goldstein] could have produced an entire TV series on what this trip will cost the studio.

Judging from the interviews printed here, the Widow Bogart has sought political refuge in England. Did you hear what my darling told 'em? She said something like, "I want to be where someone will listen to what I say." My darling must have dropped a few of her marbles on the way over. To the best of my recollection, if somebody didn't listen to what my darling was saying, either here or anywhere else, my darling was liable to belt somebody. Get that Clyde out of here! Give her my love—and tell her I'm listening.

Richard Griffith was Curator of the Museum of Modern Art Film Library.

TO RICHARD GRIFFITH

February 2, 1959

Dear Mr. Griffith:

My recollection is that CinemaScope and other wide-screen de-vices received a very cold welcome indeed from the movie reviewers. They probably resented, and quite understandably, the classic Ameri-can industrial practice of insisting that every gimmick to goose up sales be accepted as still another glorious contribution by selfless institutions to the eternal happiness of every living human being from one end of the earth to the other and pax vobiscum. But instead of accepting this familiar dido for what it was and passing on to less idiotic matters, the reviewers, who are often as much the victims of their own dreamy nonsense as the producers, chose to assail it, and on, of all things, aesthetic grounds.

Much of this gallant stand seemed to be based on the premise that three actors can perform more artistically in a telephone booth than in an open room. There were also many who recoiled like stricken interior decorators at all that space that would now be empty on each side of the screen while the players, unable to break themselves of old habits, serpentined about each other exactly in the middle. Many lamented the passing of "the historic proportions" of pictorial presentation, i.e., the 35-millimetre frame, historic dimensions that went all the way back to a technical limitation met with and accepted by Mr. Eastman. This all sounds pretty ridiculous now, and I doubt that many of these reviewers still hold such opinions, but they were widely and strongly advanced at the time.

In any case, I doubt if many will still argue that the shape of the screen, assuming it not to be downright perverse, can have any more effect on the quality of a picture than the color of the director's eyes. The quality of a picture will always come from the quality of the picture-maker's competence, whatever the geometrical pattern of the picture's presentation. It will always be the picture, not the frame.

As a matter of mechanics, it is another story. Actors, directors, and cameramen shared the worry and uncertainty of those reviewers who were knowledgeable in this area. They confronted this innovation with many misgivings. Now it happens that as a director I am a child of the wide screen. God was good enough to keep me on the bench until the mechanical circumstances of supervising performances had undergone this rearrangement, and for that I am deeply grateful to Him. For as it turned out, the wide screen improved and made easier everything that goes into the effort to achieve something approximating reality in a picture. The actors unhuddled and moved about more naturally. The director found himself with two or three times as much space within which to operate. And as for the cameraman, the toughest convert, it was not long before his eyes began to glisten too at the new possibilities presented to him.

I can now think of few things more horrible than the idea of directing a picture within the confines of the old 35-millimetre limitations. And my hat is off and my bow is low to those directors who did work in such constriction and still produced excellent pictures. Ask them the difference.

Very truly yours,

Johnson's contract with 20th Century–Fox allowed him to make a film off the lot, and in 1959 he and his family went to Rome for the filming of *The Angel Wore Red*, to be released by MGM. Johnson set up his own production company, Spectator, and worked with the Italian company Titanus. *The Angel Wore Red* was the only film produced by Spectator.

Johnson had a great deal of difficulty working in Italy. He confronted unusual labor problems, as he was forced to balance communist and non-communist interest in every aspect of actual production. *The Angel Wore Red* was the last film he directed: "And just then I said to myself, 'What . . . am I doing here? Two o'clock in the morning. In Sicily. At the age of sixty. On a slippery rock. On a cold night. Saying "Put the camera here." Look, this is the end of it. From now on, let somebody else say "Put the camera here." I'm going to be at home in bed.' "

Although Johnson's contract gave him the right to make the first cut, he discovered that the Italian producer, Goffredo Lombardo, was recutting the film simultaneously. Johnson realized there was no way to control his rights short of a lawsuit, a step he was unwilling to take. His final work on the film was in London, where he worked with stars Ava Gardner and Dirk Bogarde on dubbing dialogue. He never saw the completed film.

TO LAUREN BACALL

May 26, 1959

Honey Chile:

I know why you hung around London until you saw Mike Romanoff, but not me. He's older than I am. You've got to break yourself, God damn it, of this necrophilia!

The way it is in Rome, I rented a house there for eight months beginning around the end of June. Jet to NY, June 11. (Whole family.) June 13, see Christie graduate at George School if still unthrown out. June 17, sail on *Liberté*. (Steamboat.) June twenty-something, to Rome. July something, Scott and Roxie to camp in Switzerland. In September, Scotty and Roxie enter Overseas School in Rome. Meanwhile, back at the typewriter, Johnson writes screen-play about horny priest and virgin-type prostie. October, if we have a cast, will shoot same. Where it will all end knows God.

We've rented the house here to Judy Holliday. You should have seen the negotiations with [. . .] whatever the hell his name is, Las

Vegas fellow, who was willing to pay rent asked but not over the table. Firm rule against over the table negotiations. Brings own table to conferences. Wants everybody to get under it with him. I flatly refused. This outraged him. He thought he'd just flushed an honest man. But it wasn't honesty. I just wasn't sure I'd be able to get up again. He did everything but draw a pistol on Scotty to compel us to accept his plain unmarked bills. What it was, he has presented a picture of himself to the Guvmunt as a small business man, barely making both ends meet, and if he shelled out a check for $2,000 every month it would spoil the picture and the Man from the Guvmunt might come nosing around and asking how he can afford so much. But for a while there it was like we were mixed up in a Bogart picture. Or else! He finally withdrew with the explanation that the sofa in the living room was faded. This is true not only of the sofa but of everything else in the house, including me.

I saw Geo. Kaufman in NY. He and her are back together. Geo. told me he probably sees [Irving] Lazar oftener than anybody else. Local friends just see him now and then, when they feel like it. Lazar, busy with a contract, calls on him every time he comes to NY, and he comes there about 45 times a year. "And we have so little in common," Geo. said, "that we would have to have just a bit more to have nothing in common."

I don't know what we're going to do after Rome, which will be certainly through Feb., and perhaps until next June. Maybe I'll get another picture to do over there. The future is uncertain. I can only hope that there is a Betty in it. You, I mean. I've got to go now. I'm parked double. I love you.

Following the filming of *The Angel Wore Red*, Dorris and Nunnally moved to London. And in Hollywood, 20th Century–Fox underwent another management change: Robert Goldstein became production head of the studio. Goldstein persuaded Johnson to help finish the trouble-ridden *Cleopatra*. Johnson did work on the screenplay, but found the director, Rouben Mamoulian, impossible to satisfy. He sensed that Mamoulian was never going to get the movie into shape. When Joseph L. Mankiewicz was brought in to replace Mamoulian, he took over the writing as well as the directing, and Johnson returned to his own projects.

TO GROUCHO MARX

February 7, 1960

Dear Grouch:

You would have heard from me before now if I hadn't been making monkeys out of Shakespeare and Shaw by writing dialogue for Twentieth Century–Fox's *Cleopatra*, which Rouben Mamoulian had been signed to direct. But now that I'm benched I can write and thank you for the Carl Reiner record, which is wonderful, and *The Age of Roosevelt*, which will take me a little longer.

Did you ever have anything to do with Mr. Mamoulian? Well, sir, he is quite a character. After a couple of meetings with him I managed the first successful prediction I have made in my whole life. I bet Walter Wanger [producer of *Cleopatra*] that he would never go to bat. All he wants to do is "prepare." A hell of a preparer. Tests, wardrobe, hair, toenails. You give Rouben something to prepare and he's dynamite. I bet Wanger two pounds (32 ounces) that he would never step into the batter's box. If you make him start this picture, I said, he will never forgive you to his dying day. This chap is a natural born martyr. If you don't martyrize him he is going to be sore as hell. The rest is history.

But by then I was in the showers. It turned out that he wouldn't even read what I was writing, which created something of a bottleneck. The writer he wanted, next to himself, was Paddy Chayefsky. (It's all right, I don't expect you to believe one word of this, though it's God's truth.) It seems that Elizabeth Taylor told him that Chayefsky was just the man to pick up where Shakespeare, Shaw and I had left off and old Rouben didn't want any better recommendation than that.

Myself, I don't see it. I don't think there's that much difference between Chayefsky and me, especially when it comes to writing dialogue for an Egyptian goddess and a Roman god. We're both right for it, nobody denies that, we just approach it a little differently.

Chayefsky writes about "little people" while my folks are about medium height and a little round-shouldered. Chayefsky's little people keep saying the same thing over and over again (he gets paid by the word) while my medium folks sometimes can't remember to say it even once. Otherwise there is not much to choose between us. It just depends on how little or medium you want Julius (Groucho) Caesar to be. Hell, I'll make him any size they want. Just tell me what size and I'll take a hack at it. (That's why they call me a "hack's hack.")

Well, little remains to be told. Lady Diana's confession cleared Derek and he rejoined Jillian, who had enlisted in Lumumba's Foreign Legion (battalion of vegetarians), and when last heard of they were being served with yams and Bearnaise sauce at a state banquet in Leopoldville. Bye bye Derek and Jillian! Bon appetit, Mobubu!

I've got to go now. They're waiting for me.

GODOT

Betty Baldwin was Johnson's secretary at 20th Century–Fox.

TO BETTY BALDWIN

February 13, 1960

Dear Betty:

The decision to remain over here was not made without a monstrous soul struggle. Two things determined it. After being over here for 9 months, it seemed foolish not to try for the keep-money that another 9 months would give us. (It's idiocy to think that I am ever going to get any profits out of Fox.) The other was my depression over returning to both Fox and the living rut we were in. Fox was the worse. And I was genuinely astonished when objections were raised to my asking for my release.

This has been a struggle and I'm not sure yet what my status will be. Lastfogel & Co. are still working on it. My aim was to buy *The Visit* and make it over here through Spectator with Ava, who wants very much to do it, but in the flurry of shouts when I said I wanted to get out, Fox rushed in and bought it (at more than twice the price it could have had it a year or so ago) and threw it at me to make— over here! There were two other stories I wanted to do—*Twist of Sand* and *Stranger in Gallah*—and since I had talked them over with Skouras and feared he would buy them away from me too, I have bought them myself, with my own money! So Spectator now owns properties—and Fox or anybody else will have to buy them from me. I am assured that Fox will go along with my remaining over here but I am not yet sure of the terms. But that, I am given to understand, will be through Spectator too, which of course is and has been my aim. One of my numerous tax advisors laid out the plan for me—make Spectator, not yourself, affluent. Get the tax benefits if I can, but don't break my neck about that. (I refused to commit myself to some of the demands of the tax benefit residence here; it was like a kind of reverse captivity.) So that's what I intend to do—work for Spectator. This means I'll have to live, or have a residence, in Switzerland and pay taxes there. But that doesn't bother me. In fact, I like the idea of being with Roxie. But the immediate future is not clear. I still have two or three weeks more work on *The Fair Bride* [original title of *The Angel Wore Red*], dubbing and cutting, and Fox is puzzled what to do with me and *The Visit* now, since I go on strike the minute I finish here, so what! Or rather, so what? Anyway, we are really living from day to day, or week to week at the outside, and can make no plans. . . .

We hate to give up so much in Hollywood. I'll miss seeing Marjie and Gene and the kids, but I hope to get them in on Spectator in some way, though don't mention this to them. We have friends that we will miss, and the house and all the things in it that we have accumulated through the years. But it won't be forever. Just two or three years. I won't miss the company-town atmosphere, the gossip, the trade papers, the rumors, the eternal luncheons with the same people, the politics in the studio, all that stuff. Somebody else can have it. I'm tired of it.

I hate very much giving you up, and actually, I can never bring myself to admitting that I will have to. So I will continue to try to hang on to you for a little longer anyway. Maybe something can be worked out.

In any case, this is not the last you'll hear from me. Meanwhile, I send you love from all of us.

Cecil Johnson was Nunnally's older brother.

TO CECIL JOHNSON

June 24, 1960

Dear Cecil:

I heard about Presley in *Flaming Lance* only the other day. It doesn't bother me. It was the result of a bit of trickery on the part of the studio but there was nothing I could do about it, particularly if I wanted to stay over here for a while. The fellow who is rearranging the script writes me that in the end Presley sings at the Indians. This is the kind of secret weapon that we might try on the Russians. . . .

I am now at work on the script of *The Visit*. I'd like to get either Ingrid Bergman or Ava Gardner or Deborah Kerr to play in it, but nothing can be done about that until the script is finished and they can see it. And also I am monkeying around with an English television series, and while it looks good so far, you mustn't count on anything in show business until it's actually in existence. My hope is that I will be able to make some use of my old short stories in this series.

In Italy the picture I made in Rome was called *The Fair Bride*. It won't be released in the U.S. until sometime in the fall, and the title there—you'd better sit down for this—will be *The Angel Wore Red*. Let's not think about it.

I got my periodic pathetic scrawl from Aunt Minnie the other day accompanied by a note from Evelyn. She wrote that she and Curtis were off on a long trailer trip, as nearly as I could get it, so Curtis could fish in the Rocky Mountains. I wish to God I knew how they do it. I have not heard of him working in twenty years, and it never seemed to me that he made any extraordinary money when he did work, but such holidays as safaris in Africa and month-long tours of the West, fishing, can't be paid for in chopped chicken liver. I certainly couldn't afford it. He must have something on somebody. Evelyn wound up her letter with a denunciation of sin in the movies. She's against it. At her age she can afford to be.

We are all well enough so far as I can find out. We still have not got settled but I expect that will come in time. It was good to hear from you, to get the news about everybody, and we all send love to you all.

Mr. Hobbs Takes a Vacation (1962), a family comedy based on a novel by Edward Streeter, was a particular pleasure for Johnson. Streeter had written for the *Saturday Evening Post* for many years, and Johnson thought him a genuine humorist. The screenplay marked the beginning of what Johnson referred to as his "children's series."

Jerry Wald was the producer of *Mr. Hobbs Takes a Vacation, Johnny Belinda, The Glass Menagerie, Peyton Place,* and many other films.

TO JERRY WALD

October 23, 1960

Dear Jerry:

At this hour of the day (late afternoon) it seems simpler to write to you as Dorris Johnson than go looking all over this torn-up flat for some other kind of stationery.

B. Goldstein showed me your wire to him. This is the way the matter stands: I have done about 25 pages of *Mr. Hobbs' Vacation* (which I prefer to think of as *One Big Happy Family,* its original title) just to see if it felt all right. This puts nobody under any obligations whatever. If I hadn't been doing that, I might have been playing with myself or some other mischief like that. Result? It feels quite good (the 25 pages, not the idle diversion). Whether it reads good to somebody else or not, I don't of course know. But it tickles me.

But I've done this without first arming myself with your ideas or notion of approach or anything like that, and these I would appreciate from you if you want me to press on. My only inspirations so far have been the visualization of Jimmie Stewart as Mr. H. and the enthusiasm you are reported to have for the project. But since I have never known you not to be enthusiastic about a project, this second inspiration may be a little naive.

Now shall I go on? Do you want me to send you the pages I've done, to see if they seem to be heading in the direction you think they should go? And how is Connie, bless her heart? In case you don't know it, you can always speak frankly with Johnson. He has heard it all before anyway.

It suddenly occurs to me that if this whole thing folds up, the Brooklyn *Daily Eagle* is gone but I'm sure I can still get work on the rim of the copy desk at the *Post* or the *Herald Tribune.* But what about you? Because where is the *Graphic*?

Our best (my love to Connie) to you both.

P.S. This is all assuming, of course, that the William Morris Agency is able to make a deal that makes everybody happy.

Julian Symons, author of many mystery novels, was chairman of the Crime-writers Association.

T O   J U L I A N   S Y M O N S

January 16, 1961

Dear Mr. Symons:

I am sure that all friends and admirers of Dashiell Hammett will appreciate your fair estimation of him in the Sunday *Times*. But your conjecture that he was destroyed either by Hollywood or himself calls for examination, and as a friend of his from as far back as his *Black Mask* days I can provide some testimony on the point.

Hammett told me that he stopped writing (at the top of his career and success) because he saw no more reason to write when he not only had all the money he needed but was assured of all that he would ever need the remainder of his life. This turned out to be a mistake, but it was a sound enough belief at the time, for the curious reason that I think I can explain. Money was pouring in from his books, movies made from his stories, and radio series and comic strips based on his works and characters, and most of these projects extended into the future indefinitely.

Apparently there was nothing in writing that interested him but the money. He had none of the usual incentives that keep writers at their typewriters for as long as they have the strength to hit the keys. He had no impulse to tell any more stories, no ambition to accomplish more as a writer, no interest in keeping his name alive, as it is often described, or any other vanity about himself or his work. This is not to say that he was not gratified by the respect with which his stories were received, nor should it be taken to mean that he did not apply to his work all the conscientiousness of a self-respecting craftsman. But once he had made his pile, that was all there was to it. Out went the typewriter and he never wrote another book or story. If there is a precedent for a decision like this in a writer I have never heard of it, and as a writer myself, with all the urges and secret vanities of a writer, it took me a long time to be convinced of the truth of it. But time provided the proof. And I can't tell you how awed I was and always have been by such astonishing resolution.

To say that the decision turned out to be a mistake calls for a second explanation, and my testimony on this point I must confess is speculation, but speculation based on a good deal of knowledge. From the day I met Hammett, in the late twenties, his behavior could be accounted for only by an assumption that he had no expectation of being alive much beyond Thursday. He had had a severe case of tuberculosis and he told me that he now had but one lung. Once this assumption was accepted, Hammett's way of life made a form of sense. Even allowing for exuberance of youthfulness and the headiness of the certain approach of success, not to mention the daffiness of the twenties, no one could have spent himself and his money with such recklessness who expected to be alive much longer. For once in my life I knew a man who was clearly convinced that there would never be a tomorrow.

The money rolled in fast and out just as fast. And it would continue to do so for many years to come, long after he expected to be here to collect it. But life persisted in him. Lusty friends sickened and died, and Hammett, for whom we all drew a deep sigh every other day, survived and carried on. As frail as he was, as appallingly as he mistreated himself for many years, he came to be accepted by the Army and served during World War II in the harsh outpost of Alaska. I would give much to have shared his amused reflections then, with his financial springs running dry and him still here (though now very well behaved) when so many of those who had sighed for him were long since with their fathers.

I suppose that by the time he came to realize that he would in all likelihood be here not only next Thursday but for many Thursdays to come it was too late to sit down at the typewriter again with much confidence. When the end approached, it was thirty years later than he had expected it, and Death owed him a genuine apology when eventually it made its tardy appearance.

But could this be called destruction, either by himself or some other agency? He stopped writing of his own volition, for reasons satisfactory to himself if not to everyone else. And if he did indeed die poor, it was due to the sort of miscalculation that frightens the wits out of insurance companies.

Respectfully yours,

November 12, 1961

Chris dear:

This is a footnote: *The Grapes of Wrath* was a picture for its time, which was about 1938 or 39, I believe. Even then, in those pre-McCarthy days, it took courage to make a statement that there were mistreated people in this country. Americans have always liked to believe that everybody was doing all right, Jack!—except possibly the Negroes. White folks not doing all right, it was their own fault. But in the 30's the winds blew the Okies' land away and since they were ignorant and in the main helpless people they didn't know what to do about it. All they could think of was another place, California, where everybody drank orange juice all day and had good teeth. California, understandably enough, began to get worried about all these poor folks streaming in like locusts and showed their resentment by misusing them and taking advantage of their need and hunger in every way they could think of. Human nature all down the line. John Steinbeck lived with the Okies for several weeks and what he wrote in his book was a kind of glorious journalism. This was exactly what was taking place.

Nevertheless there were plenty of people who resented the picture (the book as well) and cried Commie at it. Though Commie wasn't as pat a charge as it became later. (If the picture had come a few years later somebody would undoubtedly have been called up before McCarthy and questioned as to how much gold from Moscow went toward the hiring of Dorris Bowdon and Hank Fonda, et al.). The Russians, as a matter of fact, were as much misled in this respect as certain Americans. They stole prints and showed the picture in Russia as a sample of the truth about a capitalistic tyranny. But it was quickly withdrawn from circulation when to their horror the mujiks keened with envy. Even people like the Joads owned an automobile! And not only that, but everybody had shoesies too! It was thought best to recall the picture. Nevertheless, the Russkies who called on us that time in Beverly Hills had all seen it and kiss-your-little-hand-Madame to their hostess who had played Rosasharn in it. They love Mommy in Ooomsk!

The last time I looked at it was when I ran it for Helen [Hayes], who had never seen it. Helen was moony about it but it seemed to me interminable—and how dreary! It belonged back in the lavender and old lace, a souvenir of another day, good enough to remember in retrospect but not to be exhumed for present day examination. Sic semper!

Love, Dad

P.S. Helen doesn't want to hear news of us. We write. It was simply her diffident way of wanting to hear from you about yourself. She is fond of you and is hurt by your not letting her hear from you from time to time.

Footnote to footnote: *The Grapes of Wrath* came out in 1940.* After writing this letter, out of a box came a bronze plaque celebrating its selection as the best picture of that year by the NY Film Critics Circle. End of footnote to footnote.

Johnson, as screenwriter and producer of his own screenplays, rarely ran into trouble with either management or actors. *The Visit*, his adaptation of Friedrich Dürrenmatt's play, was a rare exception. Johnson had transferred the scene of the play to an American Western setting and wanted Ava Gardner and William Holden in the leading roles. He agreed to have Ingrid Bergman as the lead only at Skouras's insistence. Although she initially agreed to play a fairly unattractive woman, Bergman objected strenuously when she read the screenplay. Johnson felt that her demands for changes were an encroachment on his authority as writer and producer, and told Skouras, "Now, either I'm producer of this picture or Ingrid is, and if Ingrid's going to produce it, she can get her own writer and do whatever she wants, but I can't take orders from her." Eventually he abandoned the project.

Gene Lerner was a William Morris agent in Rome.

T O   G E N E   L E R N E R

November 14, 1961

Dear Gene:

Your cable of cheer and encouragement was well-timed. I needed it. (Still do, in fact.) Thank you for your thoughtfulness.

Now these are the conditions that prevail. The other day Mr. Skouras summoned me to tell me that he had been talking to Miss Ingrid Bergman, who was irked that I had been quoted as saying that I preferred Miss Ava Gardner to her for *The Visit*. He reported that she said she had no wish to impose herself, etc., etc., all of which

---

* This was the year of its general release. The movie had its premiere in New York at the Roxy Theater during Christmas week 1939.

was a little staggering to me, since I had never heard anything from anybody that gave me any reason to assume that she was really interested in the project. Needless to say, anybody who dismissed Miss Bergman's interest in anything would be out of his mind. But what happened with Mr. Skouras was that I was given no choice in the matter. He simply said flatly that Fox would not make the picture without Miss Bergman. That's all.

Result: After a chat with Miss Bergman on the phone that afternoon, during which she acknowledged a serious interest in the picture, I made arrangements to fly to Paris tomorrow, Tuesday, and expect to meet with her tomorrow evening. (Meanwhile, Dick Brooks* is with her today discussing a picture he wants her for.) Now you know as much as I do.

I let you know about this because of your mention of Ava in one of your letters. As you know, I have had her in mind from the beginning, and blabbing around about it is what brought Miss Bergman's interest to a head. I want you to know the way the situation is now shaped, in case you have to tell Ava about it. I regret this ultimatum for many reasons, not the least of which is the removal of Ava's name from my hopes. I regret also that if Miss Bergman doesn't care for the way I've told the story (I've made many, many changes since the first draft) all of my time and efforts will be down the drain. Did you say that's show business? Well, I guess that's as good a philosophy as any.

Alas! alas!

TO ROBERT GOLDSTEIN

Thanksgiving Day [1961]

Chief:

Mr. Skouras has had his problems and I've had mine, on different levels. But we met long enough for him to rebuke me for permitting Miss Bergman to say that she could [not] make *The Visit* until next September. "You should have told her that that was up to Mr. Skouras and Mr. Goldstein," he said. It was a courageous statement and I wished I had been equal to it. But since she still hasn't seen the script I doubt if it would have worked. Nice try though!

He went on to say, in effect, she's GOT to do it! I said: Has she really? He said: Absolutely. I bought it for her. I said: I thought you

---

* Richard Brooks, screenwriter and director, won an Academy Award for the screenplay of *Elmer Gantry*.

bought it for me. He said: No, I bought it for her, because she kept asking for it. (He'd never told me any of this before.) He said: I sent Buddy [Adler] to her and he said, Ingrid, if you really want *The Visit* we'll get it for you. And we did. So now she's got to make it. When I left him he was trying to get her on the phone in Paris to tell her this, I suppose. I hope he's right, but I have yet to see a star as big as Miss Bergman who has got to do anything I ever heard of. He said: I'll call you this evening and tell you what she says. That's the last I heard from him.

I've been working day and night on the rewriting and this afternoon I finished all I can think of to do and will mail it to her tonight. I'm mailing her a carbon of my working copy. No use of further delay for mimeographing. Now we'll see! . . .

Dorris stayed on in Paris for a few days and got Roxie and her roommate to join her there. Dorris said they went to the Ritz for lunch and Roxie, who was playing the part of a woman of the world for the benefit of her roommate, said to the waiter without even looking at the menu: "I'll have caviar, chateaubriand, and crepes Suzettes." Dorris said she looked up at the waiter and said, "No, no, and no." So they got their hamburgers as usual. . . .

Papers here like the *Daily Telegraph* have kept a close and serious watch on the *Cleopatra* affair. Not that they have been able to clarify things. Skouras keeps announcing that Fox will never desert Elizabeth Taylor, by God! Lot of nobility around here these days. I wouldn't desert Elizabeth Taylor either if I had her for a picture; I'd be just as loyal as anybody. What I'm trying to do now is get myself in a position where I can tell the world I'll never desert Ingrid Bergman. In fact, I'll be loyal to anybody with a first-rate box-office rating. I can never understand Wanger. Whenever I talk to him about *Cleopatra* he talks as if it were somebody else's production. Once I said to him: Is she due to work yet? He replied: I hear she's overdue. What the hell does that mean?

We send our best to you and your two charming sisters.

T O F R A N K S U L L I V A N

Friday night—1961

Dear Frank:

So far as I've heard, Thurber is still alive at this minute but he may not be by the time you get this. It sounds pretty final. I am happy to say we saw a great deal of him and Helen earlier this year.

He was here for five or six months trying to find out whether his *Thurber Carnival* was going to be put on here or not. It was not. He really got screwed on that deal. But every son of a bitch in town and his brother interviewed him and that made him happy. Nobody ever had to draw Jim out! He gave freely. It would have been terrible if he didn't talk so well. But he did, very well indeed. He was triumphant about the man who came to interview him from the *Guardian*. "All I let him say was Hello and Goodbye," he told me. "He was here a half-hour and I never let him get one word in. I knew that if I paused, the son of a bitch would ask me, first, when did I start to hate women, and second, had I ever owned a dog. I really stopped that son of a bitch." He was still a steady man with a bottle. To give you an idea, one night around two o'clock he announced that he was the greatest actor alive and that there was no role he couldn't play. I said, how about Ophelia? He said he thought with a little warming up he could do her.

The first time he came over to our place, after some fumbling around he said to me, "This is always a little awkward for me. I can't truthfully say it's been a long time since I saw Dorris but then on the other hand I don't think it would sound right for me to say it's been a long time since I felt your wife." The blindness; well, it's hard to say. My father was blind during his last four or five years, after a lifetime of reading, and to see him sitting there in dull and lonely darkness was heartbreaking. So it's no use for me to try to believe that Jim was as indifferent to his blindness as he seemed to be. I daresay other blind men make jokes about their infirmity, but Jim's were really kind of merry. He had some auditions for his play here and once when for some reason one of the young ladies slipped out of her dress on the stage and Helen told him, "There's a beautiful girl just about naked up there," Jim said, "I lifted my face and said, Lord, there are times when this goes just a little beyond a joke." He claimed that he was the only man ever heard of who hadn't had to receive some kind of psychotherapy when he went blind. We were talking about what Ed Duffy has been going through. I guess it must have come on so slowly and steadily that there was never any actual shock. He quickly became used to a room and its chairs and doors, and in his hotel suite Helen rarely bothered to do anything when he got up to go to the can. He knew how to get there and back. Here at our place I had to accompany him each time, and I don't mind telling you that during some evenings we spent a good deal of time in our can together. But never any selfconsciousness or anything like that.

Over here he talked a lot about our generation and how many were gone. "Ten percent," he insisted. I urged him to stay here and buck for internment in the Abbey [Westminster]. In fact, I'd have a go at it too. Package deal. Maybe we could start an Old Newspaperman's Corner.

He was pretty bitter about *The New Yorker*, and I must say it sounded justified. I was astonished, and indignant, at the number of pieces he said they'd turned down, one with a letter which he insisted was a lecture on comedy in the theatre of today from some young fellow. Nor would they answer any of his letters, he said. He seemed to take it for granted that this was all due to the Ross book. He said he'd written five letters to Andy [E. B.] White without an answer. This was hard to believe but he insisted that it was so. He blamed it on Katherine [White's wife]. He said she'd come between him and Andy. You think that's possible? At any rate, that's what he believed, and he was deeply hurt, which I could well understand. He talked of it again and again, and I urged him to hell with *The New Yorker*, send the stuff to any other magazine and they'd be delighted to get it. Helen finally sent one of the rejects to *Esquire*, which took it, and also took advantage of the fact that it had been rejected and paid him only $700 for it, according to Helen. That's why I was glad to see a piece by him in *The New Yorker* about a month ago, a very good piece, full of his excitement about words, "The Manic in the Moon," I believe. (Ken Tynan had one recently that he would have liked. Tynan was trying to describe Frankie Laine, the singer, an obnoxious fellow, and said something like, "he is full of the opposite of bashfulness" (blashlessness, I suppose). Jim said some drunk dame at a party said, "I'd like to have a child by you, Mr. Thurber." Jim said he replied, "You mean by unartificial insemination?"

We talked about you a lot. He has a great devotion to you. So we got along well along those lines. And as long as we are on these sad events I was very sorry to hear about Corey [Ford] and hope he'll be able to scuffle through it.

Next time I'll be cheerfuller.

April 23, 1962

Chris dear:

The word from Roxie is that her new fellow, an American this time, is a writer and "if the world doesn't accept him it will be missing something wonderful." Thus the torch is passed from hand to hand, lighting the way through all eternity. She writes cheerfully and is resolved not only to catch up with her class but to continue on to graduation at Ecolint. She says she wants to enter Sarah Lawrence and is going to work hard to make it.

I hate to exhibit my ignorance but who is Lorca? A new one or an old one? An old one I might be able to understand, a new one is just out of the question. I may go back to Thackeray.

I had my third round with Miss Bergman last week, this one in Paris. No hits, no runs, no errors. As I was leaving her she asked me to write her a letter outlining the changes we had agreed on in the script and repeating what I expected to do about them. So I wrote her a letter to the general polite effect that I had scuffled with this script as long as I intended to without a definite commitment from her that she would do the picture and would she very kindly say either yes or no and let's all get back to the mainstream of life in the mid-Twentieth Century. Since I deliberately wrote it to make her say No, I imagine that's what she'll answer. I'm sick of her and the script too and would just as soon never see either of them again.

The notion of your skipping a year at Pembroke is not one that disturbs me if you feel that way about it. You are certainly of an age to examine the situation independently. But my guess is that "skipping a year" is only a euphemism. Do you really think you'd ever go back? Separations are usually hard to mend, especially as you've never indicated any deep devotion to Pembroke. I think you had better think of this possibility. . . . (Based on many years of observation, of restless young women and athletes eager to get the professional coin held out to them, I am a little skeptical of an education to be picked up later. It rarely seems to work out that way.) The question is, is education attractive to you? Do you really want it? What use will you ever make of it? . . .

Our local medico has charged me with cholesterol in the blood, an extremely chic ailment, though I was troubled to find that it is widely prevalent among Eskimos. That blubber diet, I suppose. On the other hand, Koreans don't have it unless they join the army and eat army chow. (These are South Koreans. God only knows what goes on among the North Koreans.) At any rate, I don't get much butter or any diary products or meat fats. Next week I'm going to get another blood check to see if I've made any progress. Win or lose, I may sneak me a little butter anyway.

Lots of love to you, darling.

TO GROUCHO MARX

December 17, 1962

Dear Grouch:

Hundred Dollar Misunderstanding is simply marvellous. It's a classic comedy. John Steinbeck was here last night and I passed it along to him. (I'm like you, when I like something I want everybody else to read it too.) Also I've ordered a couple of copies to pass along to others. I thank you.

John was on his way back from getting the Nobel Prize in Stockholm. He says he holds one record anyway, he's the only American male* winner to be both sober and perpendicular when he accepted the prize. He said Red Lewis was in such a state [in 1930] that he forgot the acceptance speech he'd worked so hard on and ad libbed an entirely different one. The committee [in 1949], after observing Faulkner at work on the local booze for a couple of days, resorted to deception to assure his being sober. They shook him into listening and then told him that he was due on the platform that afternoon. But Faulkner, whom they don't call the Old Fox for nothing (in fact, they don't call him the Old Fox), just smiled. Even while the Swede double-domes were explaining to him that it was Thursday, the Big Day, Bill could hear the churchbells ringing; it was Sunday, not Thursday, and either he had three more days of wassail or he had skipped the whole affair on the previous Thursday. In either case, all was well and he ordered up schnapps for all. John said the Swedes had great admiration for Faulkner, the way he was propped up and spoke slowly but indistinctly. John said he spoke slowly too, he said he had to, to make the speech last six minutes, which they had suggested as the minimum acceptable. It's the only speech he has ever made. I've only made one. This was at the opening of a picture in Augusta, Georgia. I live in such fear of people being bored by what I've got to say that I devised an opening to hold them in their seats for a minute or two anyway. I began, "And now in conclusion," etc. Even so, there was already quite a bit of restlessness.

What you really need sometimes is a gun of some sort. Steinbeck said some fellow wired him, "At last justice has been done." John replied, "You misunderstand. I wasn't after justice. I wanted the prize." He said John O'Hara wired him: "Dear John, you were my second choice." So much for Nobel Prizers.

Again thanks, and Merry Christmas God damn it, and our best to you.

* Pearl Buck got it but I have no idea how she drinks. If she doesn't she's probably got some secret unspeakable vice.

Johnson chose to operate independently on his next project, *The World of Henry Orient*. The screenplay was based on his daughter Nora's novel, which Johnson thought had great potential as a movie. In addition, he felt that it would be an opportunity for Nora to expand her writing market by learning, from him, the skills of screenwriting.

Johnson first offered the script to 20th Century–Fox. When they did not respond within a two-month period, the script was offered to, and immediately accepted by, United Artists. Richard Zanuck, Darryl's son and a producer at 20th Century–Fox, belatedly made an offer for the script, but negotiations with United Artists had progressed too far for Johnson to change studios.

George Roy Hill was finally selected as director; Johnson had hoped that Rex Harrison would play the lead, but was initially pleased with the selection of Peter Sellers. Two nonprofessionals played the parts of the young girls who pursue Henry Orient. Although the movie was well received in New York City (the setting of the story), it did not do well elsewhere. Johnson felt the title was partly to blame, but found that the casting of Peter Sellers was a more serious mistake: ". . . there was no controlling Sellers. . . . He's always funny, but I don't think he was funny in the right places."

Johnson was sending Garson Kanin a copy of the script.

TO GARSON KANIN

January 18, 1963

Dear Gar:

I send this with a prayer that you will not only like it but will direct it. I am so fond of this thing, this kind of comedy, that I would cheerfully direct it for scale, but I'm not permitted to. As you will see, it's got to be done in the US, much of it in New York, and the Guvmunt is against work in the US for non-residents. . . . My business is script-mongering, because writing must be done sitting down in a warm room, which is what I am doing now. . . .

Unfortunately I haven't one single piece of talent as a producer.

About doing business or getting actors, I mean. I'm like the guy who couldn't make a dame in a whorehouse. My general approach to a star is, "You wouldn't like this, would you?" And of course he wouldn't. But how can a writer praise his own stuff? If I were Sam Spiegel, I'd be sitting on Harrison's doorstep until he said yes. I'd push that little girl Hayley [Mills] in a corner and twist her arm, to say nothing of the arms of her father and mother, until she gave in. But when Mills wrote me that Hayley now wants to play older parts, hug-the-boy parts, I could hardly wait to get him on the phone and tell him that I didn't blame that kid for one instant and that she would be insane even to consider my script. I can't tell you what a handicap this kind of contr-will-power is to putting a production together.

Oh, well!

If the script interests you I will be on the next boat (I'm dying for an excuse like this) to see if there is anything further I can do to fix up anything that you don't like or are not sure of. . . .

As for Lillian's [Hellman] invasion of our territory, this may call for a rumble. I'm going to check around with [S. J.] Perelman and [George] Axelrod and a couple of other members of the Laughing Dragons to see when they'll be free to meet Lillian and her mob somewhere down on Tenth Avenue. Better get out your bicycle chain.

Edward Streeter was a banker who had written *Father of the Bride* and *Father's Little Dividend*, both of which had been made into movies.

TO EDWARD STREETER

November 22, 1963

Dear Mr. Streeter:

I read "The Fourth Bride" with the same pleasure I have read all of your other stories, including "The Chairman of the Board," which I fumbled around with a long time before the studio said No. In other days, past years, when picture making was a studio program I would embrace the story, as closely as it comes to "The Father of the Bride" in many respects. But I no longer choose my stories that way. No longer under contract to a studio, I am in the position of being asked to do this story or that, which either a studio or an independent producer has bought. Sometimes I'm lucky and offered a good one, sometimes I have to send it back, with regrets. Since *Mr. Hobbs* I have done another with [James] Stewart and Henry Koster: *Take Her, She's Mine*, and now I am at work on a third [*Dear Brigitte*] with them. This one is a real son-of-a-bitch and I am doing it only because it is such a satisfaction to write for Stewart. I can only think of how much easier, with what greater pleasure, it would be to work on *The Fourth Bride*.

We are both old-timers, and since we will probably go on until one of Miss Jessica Mitford's ghoulish characters comes for us, there is no reason why eventually you shouldn't write another novel and why I shouldn't have the good luck to knead it into a script.

In any case, I take great satisfaction in the fact that I now have three authors who are still on speaking terms with me after my violation of their works. In view of what I know about other screen writing, this is not at all a bad record.

Spyros Skouras resigned from the presidency of 20th Century–Fox in July 1962. He had been sharply criticized for the financial mismanagement of *Cleopatra* and was unable to reverse the declining earnings of the company. Darryl Zanuck, who had remained the largest stockholder in the company during his years as an independent, replaced Skouras as president.

Zanuck took over supervision of two of Johnson's screenplays, *Take Her, She's Mine* (1963) and *Erasmus with Freckles* (later changed to *Dear Brigitte*) (1965). Both were family comedies written for James Stewart, who had been so successful in *Mr. Hobbs Takes a Vacation*.

Johnson's screenplay for *Take Her, She's Mine*, based on the play by Henry and Phoebe Ephron, had been approved by Peter Levanthes, then head of production at 20th Century–Fox. When Zanuck returned, however, he insisted that the last scene be set in Paris in order to increase its appeal in foreign markets. Johnson finally agreed, and "went back and finished up a very lousy third act, all taken on the back lot, and the French didn't understand that any more than the Americans."

Johnson was so dissatisfied with Koster's direction of *Dear Brigitte* that he had his own name removed from the credits.

Other films directed by Koster include *It Started with Eve*, *The Bishop's Wife*, and *The Robe*.

TO HENRY KOSTER

April 18, 1964

Dear Henry:

Your letter with its enclosures of blue pages etc. arrived this morning. I read the letter with a particular interest. I was curious to learn if you were going to complete this project with a flawless record of not having offered me one word of approval or encouragement from beginning to end. You have. Nor is this note merely schoolgirlish pique on my part. It is a solid practical fact that in as difficult an assignment as this one the writer is entitled to know how well, if at all, he is succeeding; he needs this information to appraise the remainder of the work. You have always been most generous in generalities about my stuff but in this case I have not one reason to believe that you care for one word in this script. And indeed perhaps you don't. In which case I feel that I must remind you that you must share in the blame for this failure. . . . In fact, if it hadn't been for Jimmie Stewart's warm words for the work I did in Mexico and the rest of the story that I outlined to him orally I don't think I would have had the heart to go on with it. Even Dick Zanuck offered me more encouragement than you have. And in case you question this wholesale indictment I suggest that you reread the three letters you have written to me since I left there, in comment to something more than 100 pages of script. . . .

The script now more or less speaks for itself. I considered every suggestion in your April 1st letter and have, I believe, used most of them. A few I couldn't bring myself to agree with. One was the idea of dropping the scene in which Pandora goes to Erasmus' bedroom and asks him to help her with her homework. You can, of course, cut it yourself if you feel strongly about it, but I believe that it is the right, and most amusing, way to introduce that aspect of the plot. Also, I don't believe that anything should come between Leaf's effort to keep his son's mathematical gift a family secret and the newspaper headline about the bank computer. This is such an effective dramatic juxtaposition of events that I don't see how you can even consider changing it. . . .

20th Century–Fox asked Johnson to rewrite *My Favorite Wife* (a movie made in 1940 originally written by Leo McCarey) as a vehicle for Marilyn Monroe. Johnson wrote the first draft of the script in London. He then flew to California to discuss it with the producer. Changes were agreed upon and Johnson went to Mexico to make the final changes in the script (under the income-tax laws, his residency abroad did not permit him to work in this country for a long period of time). When he was there Monroe phoned him several times to discuss scenes in the script that concerned her. When Johnson returned to Hollywood they met to discuss her role in detail. Monroe's understanding of her screen image and her suggestions about the character impressed Johnson.

They worked well together and she showed a growing self-confidence. Johnson returned to London before filming began. He soon heard that George Cukor had called in another writer and that the script that had so pleased Marilyn and the producer was being rewritten. Monroe, who had depended heavily on Johnson's support, was unable to continue working. Her repeated absences, illness, and suspension caused 20th Century–Fox to stop all work on the film (*Something's Got to Give*). In Johnson's opinion, "That was the end of Marilyn. She never recovered . . . The whole thing was quite sad for me. I had come to know this girl and found how vulnerable she was, how helpless and how lonely."

Edwin P. Hoyt was interested in writing a biography of Marilyn Monroe.

TO EDWIN P. HOYT

February 2, 1965

Dear Mr. Hoyt:

I don't know Arthur Miller and I probably shared your feeling about him until I saw *After the Fall*, which I went to prepared to be either bored or resentful or both. As it happened, I not only liked the play very much but I thought I understood something about Miller. I thought, for one thing, that his treatment of Marilyn was compassionate and, to me, touching. In any case, I believed everything the character did, both good and bad, and on the whole I thought it was a very sympathetic treatment of a most pathetic girl.

How much she loved him I have no way of knowing but I do know that when she heard of his re-marriage she had some kind of attack of the vapours. As usual, she locked herself in and wouldn't answer the phone, etc. But this also happened when a story appeared in the papers that Sinatra was going to marry a girl named Juliet Prowse. The same sort of reaction. I had just started working with her at the time of the Sinatra announcement and so I know this to have been true.

There will be no need for you to answer this, because I will look for all the answers in your book.

My best to you.

My associations with Marilyn were at the beginning of her professional life in pictures and at the end of it. At the beginning I actively disliked her. When I began work on what was to be her last effort at a picture, then called *Something's Got to Give*, we were together more than we had ever been before and I came to know her better and to have a deep affection for her. The news of her death, by phone from a newspaper here that Sunday morning, was a greater blow than I would ever have guessed. The memory of her last few months still fills me with sadness. I must have loved her more than I thought.

I remember her first as Johnny Hyde's girl friend. Johnny was my agent and close friend. He was a dear and gentle man and was more stirred by female beauty than almost anyone I've ever known. But he was tiny, barely five feet tall, and I have no doubt suffered painful fears that the beauties he devoted himself to accepted his devotions more out of professional self-interest (he was a partner in the William Morris agency) than for himself as an escort or lover. This would have been understandable, in a community of tall and handsome gallants, but exceedingly unfair to him, for he was capable of understanding and an unselfish sympathy far beyond anything his beauties were likely to find anywhere else.

When I saw her at that time I took it for granted that she fell into that category of eager young hustlers. It was usually at lunch at Romanoff's, and when I sat with them from time to time she took little part in the conversation, though both Johnny and I did what we could to include her in what was generally no more than casual gossip. She listened intently, her eyes never left us, as the eyes of most luncheoners at Romanoff's did to see who was coming in, who was with whom, etc., but I'm afraid I can't remember her ever uttering one word.

Sometimes Johnny suggested her to me for a small part in a picture, but she never seemed right to me. Johnny was earnest in his assurances that she had tremendous promise, but even though he was my friend he was clearly too much in love for me to take these assurances very seriously. Moreover, he was still an agent, and agents are automatically given to discoveries of great talent in their clients. At any rate, it was a long time before I found a part for her.

This was in a picture called *We're Not Married*, a series of episodes in which there were a number of stars. The plot was that a justice of the peace had married six or seven couples after the expiration of his authority, a fact that did not become known until several years later. The picture concerned the reaction of the couples to this unexpected opportunity to become unmarried again. Marilyn played opposite David Wayne. She had just won the title of Mrs. Mississippi in a bathing beauty contest, and she was jubilant over her new status, which gave her the opportunity to enter a more glamorous contest and become Miss Mississippi as well. After which she married Wayne.

She irritated me by either her ignorance of the situations or some vague indifference to what she was doing. I am always irritated by professional carelessness, if that is what it was. For example, the final scene was the remarriage, and the groom carried their baby to the altar. But though the baby was crying the bride never so much as glanced at it during the rehearsals. When I asked her about this before the shot it seemed that it had never occurred to her. I don't understand this yet.

Once when I came on the set during this picture she came running toward me and asked breathlessly, "Where's the men's room?" I pointed and off she raced. I have never understood that either.

Also during this picture I remember talking to an extra, a bathing suit beauty who had been in numerous such contests in and around Los Angeles. Extras are often contemptuous of principals in their own areas and I was curious about this young woman's opinion of Marilyn's figure. How would she fare in a real beauty contest? The answer was short and without qualifications: She'd win 'em all.

I saw more of her during the shooting of *How to Marry a Millionaire*, which I also wrote and produced, though I can't say I was any more won by her. She was under the spell of one of her dramatic coaches at that time and was giving the director, Jean Negulesco, a continual headache. Marilyn was turning to the coach after every take, and if the coach shook her head Marilyn insisted on another, regardless of Negulesco's decision. This was not only an intolerable position for the director to be put in, it was costly, for the coach became more and more demanding and the time spent on additional takes ran into important money. When I told Marilyn finally that the coach would no longer be allowed on the set she said nothing at the time but simply didn't show up the next day. There are times when a producer has no choice but to give in to the actress. We endured the coach and the additional takes for the remainder of the picture.

There was but one conversation with her worth remembering during this picture. Again she was in a bathing suit, a fashion show this time, and I suggested a very short beach coat. After giving me her baby stare for a moment she said, "You mean so they'll think I haven't got anything else on?" I said, "I'd like something so startling you'd get immediate whistles." And added, "You don't mind whistles, do you?" She grinned and said, "Where do you think I'd be if I hadn't got whistles?" It was the first inkling of humor or even humanness that I'd ever got from her.

But if this somewhat eased my impatience with her she soon put an end to that. One late afternoon she said something that still dumbfounds me. I was watching the shooting of a rather long scene she was playing with Lauren Bacall and Betty Grable. It was nearly six o'clock, the end of the day's work, and the cast as well as the crew grow edgy at that hour. But Marilyn was blowing take after take, either fluffing or forgetting a line completely. Both Miss Bacall and Miss Grable have very good set manners, but there was a tension that was steadily tightening at each Cut! I seemed to feel the waves of dislike, even hatred, that were centering on her as six o'clock came and then six-thirty. It reached the point where I became sorry for her, for being so conspicuously inept, so publicly and embarrassingly at fault. For now when Cut was called and she made at once for her mirror and further unnecessary touching up of her make-up there was a taut silence on the set instead of the usual whispered chatter and adjustment of this light or that. For at that moment every man and woman on that set was loathing her.

I couldn't help but feel that a word of sympathy or understanding or encouragement to her would be both welcome and helpful, so I crossed to the mirror and said, "Don't worry, darling. That last one looked very good." She looked at me puzzled and said, "Worry about what?"

I swore then that I would never attribute human feelings to her again.

The day of the premiere of the picture Harry Brand, the Twentieth Century–Fox publicity chief, phoned to ask if I would include Marilyn in my party that evening. I can't remember whether she was married to Joe Di Maggio at the time or engaged to him, but in any case she wouldn't care to be seen at the theatre with any other man. And she was very anxious to attend the opening for two reasons. One, she'd never been to a premiere, and two, she had a feeling that she would be good in this one.

I would like to say here that it is my belief that *How to Marry a Millionaire* marked a turning point in Marilyn's career, in the public reaction to her anyway. For in this picture for the first time she played a young woman without complacency or arrogance. This had been her standard role since reaching stardom and whatever else it may have been it was not a winning one. In *How to Marry a Millionaire* she had bad eyesight and was convinced that Dorothy Parker had uttered no more than the truth when she declared that men never made passes at girls who wore glasses. She hastily removed her glasses when a man answered a phone call, she stumbled down steps and into walls, and eventually played a love scene with a man she could see only fuzzily. (Happily, he too was astigmatic and didn't know what she looked like either, and there was quite a touching moment when finally both summoned the courage to produce the spectacles they had always kept concealed and studied each other in focus.) The public had always been fascinated or stirred or appalled by her, but after this role I think they began to like her.

It was hardly a party that I had for the premiere, being simply Bogart and Betty, old friends of ours, and Mrs. Johnson and myself. Marilyn entered with a request for a drink, a stiff one, bourbon and soda, and I provided her with same. Then even though it was to be a quick and early dinner she asked for another. And got it. At the time I knew nothing of her drinking habits but was beginning to admire her for her start anyway. And naturally neither Bogey nor I would have permitted her to drink alone. At dinner she was actually vivacious, her eyes sparkling, eager and laughing and so radiantly beautiful and attractive that I felt myself beginning to like her. It would have been impossible, in fact, not to have liked her that night. Everybody in the house liked her and the dinner was a turmoil, with children clambering around her and the servants abandoning all pretense of work to crowd rooms with offers of assistance to Marilyn. Betty and Bogey they were used to, Marilyn Monroe was a new and shattering excitement.

And she herself was on edge with excitement, nervous and frightened too, terrified about the evening. I know this now but it would have been difficult for me to believe then. I had no idea how naive and youthful she was, how almost unbearably important the evening was for her. Then as we're about to get in the car, a hired limousine with driver, she asked for her third drink, a really stiff one this time. Gentlemen to the last, Bogey and I drank with her on the way to the theatre. By the time we made our entrance you couldn't have found three more amiable people in the whole State of California.

In short, she was tight. She was tight when she had to go to the ladies' room as the picture began. Mrs. Johnson, not tight, accompanied her, for clearly she needed company. She was tight in the ladies' room, and in a tight dress, for she had been sewn in it. Her long white gloves were tight, too, so tight she was unable either to bend her elbows or get the gloves off. It was a wild and exhausting business (my wife told me afterward) getting Marilyn in condition for the john and then properly dressed again to return to her seat. Women who have been sewn into their clothes should never drink to excess.

The next day she called to thank Dorris and me for such a nice evening. "But I'm afraid I got a little tight," she said, and when I dismissed this she explained, "It's the first time I ever tried alcohol." It was true. At Romanoff's, when she and Johnny and I sat together she had always had Dubonnet. And only sipped that.

That was when I first knew Marilyn and it was a period that left no particular pleasure with me. She was either too fey for me to understand, or too stupid, and certainly too unprofessional for me. Sometimes I wondered if I was wrong about this, or if it were something personal, an antipathy for each other that others didn't share. But then there were other stories about her, from other pictures, that supported my feelings. When Olivier directed her in a picture, I was told, he instructed her to sit, count three, and then speak the line. After several ruined takes he was said to have asked her, "Can't you count either?" And then there were the stories from the *Some Like It Hot* set, from Billy Wilder and Tony Curtis and Jack Lemmon, stories of inexcusable behavior. Not so much rude behavior as an almost unbelievable obliviousness to others, as if they didn't exist, as if her clumsiness didn't affect them, as if they had no feelings that she needed to recognize. Dreadful stories.

So when a few years ago I was asked to do the script for *Something's Got to Give*, I suggested to the producer, Henry Weinstein, that it might be just as well if there should be no occasion for me to discuss it with her. Then I got my first surprise. Henry said she wanted to discuss the story with me. He said that when he had told her I had been asked to write the script she had said, "He won't do it, he doesn't like me." Why? "Because," she said, "I once turned down a script of his." This was a point on which I had to reassure her; if I had disliked every star who had turned down one of my scripts, I told Henry to tell her, I wouldn't have a friend in Hollywood.

Her first words when we met in the Polo Bar at the Beverly Hills Hotel were, "Have you been trapped into this too?" I assured her I hadn't, that this was not the only story that had been offered to me, and that I liked this one very much. I told her I thought it would make a very good picture. She stared at me. I know now that she was wondering if her opinion of the story had been wrong. I soon learned that she had no confidence in her own judgment at all. She would make a statement, but if anyone of reasonable experience, and without any visible axe to grind, disputed it she gave up at once and without argument. Everybody knew better than she did!

At the end of three hours and three bottles of champagne (she had come far since three bourbons and soda) she was becoming excited over the project. As for myself, the session was a revelation to me. Nor was it just the champagne. I have rarely spent a happier time with any woman. She was quick, she was gay, she probed into certain aspects of the story with the sharpest perception, and she confessed that she was terrified of the director. Who, I knew, loathed her and was given to blackguarding her in terms that would have brought a blush to Sophie Tucker's cheeks. When we parted all my antipathies were gone and forgotten, I adored her. I see no reason to make excuses for this complete flip. It happened and I regretted every harsh word and thought I had ever had about her, whether they were justified or not. I never stopped adoring her.

She was now as eager about the story as I was, and we found a number of opportunities to discuss it, and to wander from the story to other subjects and people and opinions. (And in case it is necessary, let me assure you that no romance was involved here. None whatever.) When finally she read the completed script she was jubilant, but for an interesting reason. She had liked it, it had excited her, but as I say, she had no confidence whatever in her own judgment. Her call to me had come only when Dean Martin, who was also to be in the picture, had told her he hadn't even bothered to finish it; fifty pages had satisfied him that he should sign for it. Only with this support did she feel free to exclaim that she liked it too. When I left California she was soaring with happiness. She had slipped during the last two years and she knew it, and she was convinced that this was the one that would bring her back.

She couldn't talk enough to me about it, about the casting, about this point in the story and that. She was so excited she almost forgot how frightened she was of the director. At the risk of sounding completely fatuous, she was as much like an excited little girl as an adult woman can be.

The evening before I left she called to ask if she could see me the next morning about something that I have now forgotten. I explained to her that I would be leaving too early for that. "What about six-thirty?" she asked. "That's a wonderful hour," I told her, "I can just see you up at six-thirty." "No, I'm serious. What time are you leaving?" "At nine-thirty," I told her. "When will you be up?" I replied even to such nonsense. I had a call to be awakened at seven-thirty and breakfast at eight. "I'll be there at seven-forty-five," she said. "Honey," I said, "goodbye and good luck."

At seven-forty-five that morning the phone rang. She was in the lobby but they wouldn't let her come up. "Tell them," I said, "that you're a call girl and I sent for you." She giggled, relayed this to the clerk, and said, "It worked!"

She came into the room with two bottles of Dom Perignon, in tight pants, a blouse, and without make-up, which made her look ten years younger. She really had nothing to discuss. She simply wanted to drive me to the airport. And since I don't drink champagne at that hour of the day I returned the bottles with thanks. We were quite happy without the tipple.

In London I heard of the difficulties the picture was having and I thought I knew why. The minute I left, the script that had so excited her was being rewritten by the director who frightened her. Considering the circumstances this was almost criminal stupidity. Since the script had been happily approved by everyone else in authority it may be assumed that it had some call for respect. But quite aside from that, only a foolish or egomaniacal director would so shake and shock as neurotic a star as he had on his hands. He had gone through the same vain shenanigans on a previous picture with her and the result was what might have been expected, a calamity that hastened her downhill slide. But there was no-one at the studio with the strength or intelligence to call a halt to this idiocy and so the damage was done.

I learned later from both her producer and her doctor what happened. When the blue pages began to arrive at her house she was shattered. And more and more arrived, until in the end there were only four pages left of the original script. When the producer saw the distress this was causing her he tried to fool her by having the revisions mimeographed on white paper. But she was much too smart to be misled by that trick.

I don't believe for one moment that Marilyn paid the slightest attention to the revisions. That is, to decide whether they were better or worse than the script I had given her. That wasn't what sent her to bed and eventually to the pills and the booze. What sent her to bed was still another, and this time a final, blow to her poor frail confidence in herself. This time she *knew* she had formed a right decision, a certain judgment. That was what made her so happy with me. Not with me as a person really, but with me as perhaps the agency of this opportunity to make a decision that had turned out to be right. With me as the nearest sympathetic person with whom to enjoy this rare and exalting thrill. And then to have the whole illusion destroyed by the one person an actress like Marilyn stands in awe of, the director. Who always knows all. Once again, after all, she was a dope.

Week by week the news got more and more distressing. She made a wild effort to get me to return and take over direction of the picture. There were a dozen practical reasons why this was completely out of the question, but even if it had been possible I would not have done it. I knew that while she was quite capable of convincing herself that I was the only person on earth who could save her or the picture, she was just as capable, once I had rallied to the cause, to become just as convinced, and with as little reason, that I was out to destroy her. Even as I came to adore her I had come to know a bit about her too. She would have been too neurotic, too unstable, for me to place much confidence in her.

When the then head of the studio made a public announcement that he was going to fire her I phoned him to suggest that if anyone was to be fired it should be the director, reminding him that it was Marilyn who brought people into the theatres, not this director. But by then I suppose he had little choice. She was too far gone in excesses to work for this director or any other. My wife cabled a suggestion to her that she fly to London and visit us for a week or so, in the hope that this change of scene would be of some benefit to her. We didn't understand her answer at the time. "Thank you both but it was not my fault Nunnally." What it meant, as I learned in the papers that day, was that she'd been fired and the picture closed down. I never saw or heard from her after that.

My belief is that Marilyn had the intelligence to appreciate and respect intelligence but not enough to participate in it, and she knew this and it was a destructive knowledge. She was constantly attaching herself to superior men, and it never lasted. In the end, when the fireworks were over, she simply bored them. She had the stuff to win a man but not to keep him. Especially the kind of men that attracted her. She always aimed too high. But there was no solution to this for her. Superior men eventually tired of her, and she was never able to summon up any interest in inferior blokes. You can see where that left her.

I would like to add another word about Marilyn and Johnny

Hyde. Johnny was in his fifties and during the courtship he suffered a serious heart attack. But it looked as if he might recover. The doctors imposed a condition though. To put it delicately, they forecast many more years provided he undertook no undue exertions. In other words, no more courtship with Marilyn. A year or so later he died gallantly, still courting her.

At the funeral she put on quite a show of hysterical grief, pounding on the casket and all that sort of thing until she was led away. Few observers took this with much seriousness, myself included. I took it to be a rather objectionable act.

I don't believe that now. I think she loved him very deeply, as she might have loved a father. (Since copulation was, I'm sure, Marilyn's uncomplicated way of saying Thank You, I don't think that the suggestion of incest would have bothered her.) I am sure also that Johnny was the first man who had ever treated her with almost deferential respect, and was also the only person in the world who was seriously concerned about her at all. When Johnny was buried she was again alone in the world. Just as after Arthur Miller, and Yves Montand, and Sinatra, she was still again alone. That was at the time I was seeing her. When she died she literally had no-one.

During the studio's troubles with her on *Something's Got to Give*, I tried to persuade Joe Di Maggio to go out to the Coast and see if he couldn't help her. He insisted with genuine regret that it would do no good. I could hardly go into his relations with her but my guess was that Joe still loved her but was under no more illusions about any sort of re-union. In short, he'd had it. He promised to call her on the phone but was adamant against trying anything further. So far as he was concerned, she was a lost lady, and while there might be someone to save her, he wasn't the one.

We once talked about Johnny and she was very protective about him. Even though small, she insisted, he had a man's build, a miniature man. She said he was strongly built for his size. She seemed to take great pride in this fact.

One final word, about Marilyn as an actress, or comedienne. I must say I never had a very high opinion of her talent as an actress. She wasn't even in the same league with comediennes like Lucille Ball, Eve Arden, or a dozen others I could name. In fact, the only performance she ever gave that I thought was superior was in *How to Marry a Millionaire*. The others all seemed to me to be imitations of other performances or simply amateurism. I know that many critics rated her much higher than that, but critics are subject to irrelevant influences as well as anybody else. I think that some were being kind, some simply didn't know any better about acting, and some were clearly being bold. But that, as I say, is what makes horse races.

February 4, 1965

Dear Grouch:

Whether we'll be here or not when you get here we still don't know. This is the way everything is, I understand, when you're dealing with David Merrick. (The immortal Mr. Kaufman once said of him: "He seems to be Jed Harris rolled into one.") When he read my script for the musical comedy version of *Breakfast at Tiffany's* he was dismayed. "I expected a Valentine to New York," he said of a story about a doomed girl, a girl hell-bent on destroying herself. Since then he's been in and out, up and down, with that masterful sense of decision we've all come to identify with a smart New York producer. Now he seems to have taken a vow of silence. So I don't know.

All I know is that I've got myself into a streak of no-dough jobs. First, I've spent six months on a couple of stage scripts, *Tiffany* and *Henry Orient*,* not a nickel, and now I'm doing a script for that United Nations TV series, under the producership of U Spiegel. . . .

I don't think you could have a more comfortable place to live here than B. Goldstein's flat, assuming that they get you a house-keeper-cook. And if I were you I'd make sure that they provide you with a car and driver, and for evenings as well as day. As a matter of fact, the flat is the only one in London in the same building with something called the Georgian Pussy Club, featuring Georgian pussies. Goldstein claims it gives room service. I only mention this in passing.

Twenty-five years ago today Miss Dorris Bowdon of Memphis, Tennessee and I were married at the MacArthur county seat, Pretty Penny, and she's still with me. Or was a few minutes ago anyway. You can never tell about these things, can you!

Our love to you all.

* Johnson and his daughter Nora wrote the book for the 1967 musical, *Henry, Sweet Henry*, based on Nora's novel *The World of Henry Orient*.

January 17, 1966

Dear Bobby:

Although I am definitely through with the theatre and let's have no argument about that, every time I re-read the script of *Roxie Hart*, which I have done three times now, I get excited again about its potential as a musical. A period musical. Chicago! Chicago!

I have been told by my agent in New York, Marvin Josephson, that this property keeps popping up from time to time, but is my recollection right that you were dubious about it?

(As you might guess, this is the kind of speculation that comes on me when I'm not at work on a picture script. There are two or three proposals in the offing but the matter of financing continues to be elusive. My guess is that one of them will come through sooner or later, but meanwhile I fiddle around nervously with other ideas.)

I regret that you're not here, or I'm not there, so we could both take a close look at *Roxie*. But the merits of the piece are, one, that the story already has the nutty air of a musical comedy, and two, the part of Roxie is really something for a star. A musical comedy may very well be successful for other reasons but its chances are always two or three times as great when there is a dazzling role for the leading lady. In this story Roxie has everything.

It seems to me that with an opening number establishing the wildness of the 20's in Chicago, the place and period could be slammed home immediately and with great effectiveness. In case you don't remember the story, when Roxie is arrested for the shooting of a mysterious stranger, a newspaperman sets off one of those big murder stories of the period by tagging her as "The Most Beautiful Woman Ever Indicted for Murder in Cook County." Even before she is hauled off to the cooler a booking agent has signed her up for stage, screen and radio. Whereupon she becomes the happiest little murderess you ever saw.

The complications are so many that the chief problem would be the embarrassment of riches. Roxie's husband raises $5,000 to get a great mouthpiece to defend her, a part that was played with beautiful style by Adolphe Menjou. His job is first to create sympathy for her and second to rehearse her for the trial. So, when another female killer threatens to take some of the limelight, he announces that Roxie is pregnant and points out that the State has indicted only one person for murder whereas it will now be trying two. Needless to say, Roxie enters into the spirit of this situation with great gusto.

The trial is a wild burlesque of one of those daffy trials of the 20's. It is broadcast directly from the courtroom under the sponsorship of a company selling Peruna or some such alcoholic tonic. Phil Silvers, in what I think was his first picture part, played a demented news photographer. In the end, you may remember, Roxie is found not guilty but just as she faces all the beautiful rewards of her celebrity, a redhead mows down three guys and that was curtains for Roxie.

I wonder if you could get a copy of the play from Samuel French. It was called *Chicago* and it was written by Maurine Watkins, I believe. While I was in New York, Leland Hayward tried to get me to do a musical comedy script for him, but this was impossible at the time. I have thought of writing to him now, about *Roxie Hart*, to see what his reaction would be.

I suppose you know that Roxie [Roxanna Johnson] is back in her apartment and Scotty back at Riverdale. At least, I think they are. Christie writes that her baby spoke for the first time last week. He said Hermione Gingold.

What about you? And Nan? I read somewhere that she was coming here to do that play you wrote me about. Is that true?

Oh yes. Merry Christmas, God damn it.

TO ALISTAIR COOKE

March 21, 1966

Dear A:

I think I've hit on a new way of making quite a tidy living with almost no effort. My negotiations with David Merrick reached an anagnorisis* in an offer to me of a royalty to withdraw from his *Breakfast at Tiffany's* and keep the hell out. Now if Merrick, widely known as a very smart hombre, is willing to pay me money simply to keep the hell out, why shouldn't other producers be prepared to consider similar protective arrangements?

My present plan is to begin cautiously with a solid little nucleus of four or five carefully selected producers who know a good thing when they see it. Meanwhile, my agents will spread the whisper around that Johnson is moving in and from now on it will be a matter of playing ball with me or else. I'm not going to be a pig though. My scale of terms will be flexible: one or two percent on the big Broadway musicals, half the gross and the leading lady in off-Broadway shambles. But no quibbling, haggling or under the counter deals. Either lay it on the line or Johnson will be in there writing on your play before you even know what hit you.

But my belief is that it can all be done very quickly and quietly. Once these hustlers begin to realize the value in actual dollars and cents of keeping me the hell out, I'm convinced it'll be another *Cimarron.* They'll be coming through the windows. And the beautiful part of it is that it'll be all mine, mine alone, for where else are you going to find a writer who can practically write his own ticket simply for keeping the hell out? Honestly, I could kick myself when I think of how cunctatious I've been about this idea.

Yrs.

* I imagine this is the word you were groping for—not anagnorosis.

Shana Alexander, a *Life* columnist, was the daughter of long-time friends of the Johnsons', the Agers. Cecelia Ager was film critic for *PM*, and Milton Ager, a songwriter, wrote "Happy Days Are Here Again," "Ain't She Sweet?" and "Hard-Hearted Hannah."

TO SHANA ALEXANDER

September 7, 1966

Shana dear,

First, I am shocked and saddened by the news that you are getting a divorce. It came so unexpectedly. I had assumed that yours was the right kind of marriage. It makes me unhappy to hear that a friend has reached such a breaking point.

Second, I didn't understand your inclusion of Milton among the losers. I take it that he was married once before, but that must have been so long ago, for God's sake, that I'm surprised that anybody remembers it. However, if he can document his qualification, we will let him in on the conference. With two sets of papers, I will still be the Dean of the group.

My defense of Ronnie Reagan (if I made one) was less out of an affection for actors than a sense of fair play, a quality which I like to think has governed my whole life. I resent a prejudice against minorities. It's all very well for you to dismiss actors as second-class citizens but the day may come when the streets will be red with blood as they rise up and demand ACTOR POWER! You can suppress a section of society only for so long. After all, they're paying taxes, some of them have developed qualities comparable even to those of writers, and it is only a question of time before the Screen Actors Guild springs to arms and will seize by force what they feel they are entitled to. This in fact may be the only hope of stopping Ronnie, for there are those who claim that he is not really an actor but only passing. That's the worst sort, you know.

I rejoiced at your letter, but I beg you not to answer this one promptly. One of the worst evils of our time is the prompt letter answerer. Once or twice I've been caught up with one of these cats (unhappily, I fall into the habit of answering promptly every now and then) and my life has become a pure hell, with both of us seeing which can answer the more promptly. Once I simply had to give up making a living and devote myself entirely to answering letters that arrived two or three times a day.

On the other hand, correspondence can be carried to the other extreme, as with your mother, who never answers either promptly or unpromptly. When that woman gave up writing she really gave it up all over. So far as I can remember, in the many years of our friendship she has written to me but once. It was a letter asking me to write a column for *PM* for nothing.

My suggestion is that you drop me a line about every four or five months. I will answer promptly, for I am occasionally compulsive about that. Between times I will have the pleasure of reading your page and being able to keep abreast of your activities. And when I come to California yours will be the first number I shall call. Yours and your mother's.

Bless you.

1967–1976

In 1968 Dorris and Nunnally returned to California. His last produced screenplay, *The Dirty Dozen*, written for producer Ken Hyman and directed by Robert Aldrich, had been released by MGM the year before. Much to Johnson's dismay, Aldrich brought in his own writer, Lukas Heller, during the filming, and the question of appropriate screen credit had to be arbitrated by the Screen Writers Guild. It was decided that both Johnson's and Heller's names should appear in the credits.

Although Johnson worked on three other screenplays, *Fortunes of War*, *The Frontiersmen*, and *Scuba Duba*, none was produced. His failing health made working difficult, and he officially retired in 1969.

Johnson's interest in the movies continued, and his correspondence with old friends and his grown children retained its importance. As one of the most respected screenwriters in Hollywood history, Johnson was a warm, interested advisor to young writers and film buffs.

He died in March 1977.

Robert Merrill wrote the score for *Henry, Sweet Henry*. Johnson wrote, "*Henry, Sweet Henry* . . . died slowly but gracefully, adding little either to the theatre's credit or mine. But since the story, *The World of Henry Orient*, had already been a novel by my daughter Nora and a picture under the same title, I suppose I had little to complain about. It was a nice story, a beautiful novel, an amusing picture, and you couldn't ask for much more mileage."

T O   R O B E R T   M E R R I L L

December 23, 1967

Dear Bob:

You ought to do very well with the libretto. Ideally, that's the way it should always be, because nobody knows better than the lyric writer how a scene should be constructed to prepare for the song, and that's really how a musical comedy should be arranged, each scene leading into a song. And you have a gift that is very very rare, the gift of true poetry in so many of your songs. Like "People." And the song about Boston in *Henry, Sweet Henry* was as delicate and as sensitive an appeal as any I can think of.

On the other hand, if you knock something out of the park when I, an old pro at dramaturgy, went o for 3 only a few years ago, I take all of this back. Moreover, do not try to get in touch with me again. Friendship can be stretched just so far.

But Merry Christmas and love to Dolores from the Grand Old Man of the Silent Screen and his sainted wife.

At this time John Crosby was the television columnist for the London *Observer*.

T O   J O H N   C R O S B Y

January 2, 1968

Dear John:

If Cooke has a fault, it is exaggeration. The pool is no larger than Rhode Island if you exclude Providence.

I have rejoined the Hollywood Establishment, probably for the remainder of time. It's just too much trouble to move again. But things have changed a bit. It's no use calling MGM and asking for Mr. L. B. Mayer, or Warner Bros. and asking for Colonel Warner, or 20th Century–Fox for Mr. Zanuck. You ask for people with names like Kenny and Dickie and Junior and Bobby. This takes getting used to. Dorris and I send you and Kate love and best wishes for the New Year.

June 23, 1968

Dear Miss Kael:

Ben Hecht didn't write *Roxie Hart*. I did. I take it as a compliment, of course, that you attribute it to Hecht, but if you had let me know you were going to be sloppy about it I could have named you a score of other pictures I've written that you would have been welcome to attribute to somebody else, anybody else, in fact.

This mistake shakes me. I was coming to take what you wrote as gospel. Now I don't know. It's like discovering that the *Encyclopedia Britannica* had blown one.

Very truly yours,

June 29, 1968

Dear Miss Kael:

My children (adult) read Pauline Kael too. So when Roxie (see?) brought in the letter with your name on it they were consumed with curiosity. Did I really know you? What in God's name would you be writing to me about? I hope you won't mind that I confessed to them that this was a romance that had been going on for some years now. You usually wrote me, I explained, in care of a cigar store mail drop in Burbank, and why you should have been so rash as to write me at home was completely beyond my understanding. I asked them not to tell their mother, who would either break into tears or laughter, I couldn't guess which. It's not often that an aging father finds an opportunity to bring a ray of sinful sunshine into his children's lives.

In any case, thank you for your nice letter. I was half prepared to hear that you had looked it up and discovered that Hecht did write *Roxie Hart*. That's the way things look some mornings.

My best to you.

Otis L. Guernsey, Jr., was the editor of the *Dramatists Guild Quarterly*. This letter was written in response to a questionnaire.

TO OTIS L. GUERNSEY, JR.

October 14, 1968

Dear Otis:

I find it impossible to answer this questionnaire in any way that would be fair or even truthful. My experiences in the theatre during the past couple of years do not permit such categorical answers or statements. I was a part of three projects, *Breakfast at Tiffany's*, *Henry, Sweet Henry*, and *Darling of the Day* [1968, based on Johnson's screenplay *Holy Matrimony*], all of which failed and for different reasons. But I don't think it would be of any use to particularize. As a generality, all human beings make mistakes, and this includes producers.

But I would like to make one emphatic point. The theatre is going to continue to wobble and sag until its economics in respect to the writers are thoroughly revised. As I see it now, only writers who are independently wealthy can afford to write for the theatre. To take my own case, I devoted two years to the three musicals I worked on and my total income for the two years was something like $12,000. I daresay others have fared even worse. This is an impossible arrangement, and it's no wonder that writers turn to the movies or even TV, where in any case a living can be made.

When I told Groucho Marx that I was going to work on a play in New York I was startled, in fact shocked, when he commented, "You must be out of your mind. The stage is where writers go when they have failed in Hollywood." The last half of the statement may or may not be true, but clearly there is a case to be made for the first half.

With little question, it is the writer who makes the greatest investment of time and effort in the creation of a play, and is the least protected. Even when the play has a modest run, he is persuaded to waive his royalties. Short of a smash hit, he is out of pocket from beginning to end. I don't pretend to know how this can be corrected, but until someone finds the answer the theatre will continue to lose the efforts of all writers with a weakness for eating three meals a day.

With best wishes,

In 1967 Johnson wrote in a biographical sketch a more complex version of his experiences in the New York theater.

My experience in the New York theatre, spotted over 20-odd years, is flawless: unsuccessful from the rising of the first curtain to the fall of the final. It would be a waste of time to describe my first opportunity to wander around backstage and mingle with the players; this was in 1927 or '28, when I contributed to a ragbag of a revue which was called *Shoot the Works* and produced by Heywood Broun for the benefit of out-of-work actors during the Depression. In a way it also benefited me: I gathered this waste of time into an article called "Stagestruck" which I sold to the *Saturday Evening Post*.

My first actual serious participation in a production was in the early '40s, when Jed Harris, a long-time friend, called on me for a curious collaboration. How the project was born I didn't know then and I don't know now. But three aging Russian actresses were engaged in writing a play for the clear purpose of providing themselves roles and employment. One of these authors was Eugenie Leontovich, wife of the late Gregory Ratoff and herself an actress of great effectiveness when her English was intelligible, which was not always. But in comparison with the English of her collaborators her speech was pure Dame Edith Evans. More to the point, when it came to the creation of a play, they not only couldn't write English, they couldn't even read it. Nevertheless, they were engaged in a noisy united effort to produce three acts in English about three broken-down Russian actresses visiting in the home of a wealthy tycoon on the north shore of Long Island.

As Harris explained it to me, their story, if ever it reached readable form, had a good deal of gentle charm and humor. But since the script he showed me had been concocted with the aid of a Russian-English dictionary and Roget's Thesaurus, these qualities were a bit murky. It had taken a good deal of persuasion and argument, all hysterical, to convince them that a fourth collaborator should be brought in to untangle their syntax.

In the end they agreed, but only on condition that this interloper's name should in no way be connected with their work. They readily agreed to allot one-third of the royalties and other usufructs, but otherwise I must remain a phantom.

The name of the play was *Dark Eyes*, and it received generally a favorable press, and ran six months and a day. I remember the length of this run with such accuracy because two years ago when I was asked to write a musical version of *Breakfast at Tiffany's* Truman Capote's contract with David Merrick prohibited the engagement of any writer who had not had a play that ran at least six months on Broadway. I made it, unfortunately, by 24 hours.

As I was to learn subsequently, the first thing a Broadway producer does after the curtain rises the first night is to ask the writer to waive his royalties until matters are more stable, and since matters are rarely stable on Broadway I drew very little money from the play in the form of royalties. But toward the end of this run, Harris exhibited one of the aspects of his genius as a producer. Just when he was getting ready to put up a closing notice, a Hollywood producer, who must have had very little to do that day, called and made a casual inquiry about the play. What this Warner Bros. representative actually had in mind may never be known, for Harris curtly interrupted him with the statement that the price was $250,000 and he had only until noon to make his decision. It was then ten minutes to twelve. This was a play that had been running for six months without a nibble from a moving picture company, and $250,000 was at that time a pretty stiff price even for a successful play. At five minutes to twelve the startled producer called back to say that it was a deal, which netted me $50,000.

I wrote another play that Harris produced with little success. It was called *The World's Full of Girls* and was adapted from a book called *All Brides Are Beautiful.** My only recollection of it is that it was about a soldier returning home after the war. I never saw it. I was busy in Hollywood when it opened and I received a phone call from a friend who attended the opening night. He told me simply to forget it, and it closed after a week or two. I remember scolding Harris for bringing it into New York when apparently it was hopeless even from its opening in Philadelphia. Harris explained that he knew it was hopeless but that he felt I might not accept this judgment without its being confirmed in New York. Perhaps. Even as sharp an intelligence as Harris's is susceptible to a hope that he may be wrong.

My next struggle with the stage came about when George Kaufman asked me to collaborate with him on a play based vaguely on a satirical article I had done for the *Saturday Evening Post*. The article was called "Holy Matrimony" and it was an effort to un-

---

* The play was actually based on Thomas Bell's novel *Till I Come Back to You*.

tangle a fictional engagement of two Hollywood personalities. It was suggested by a little story in *Variety* about the engagement of Douglas Fairbanks, Jr., I believe, and one of his wives. *Variety* had gone to the trouble of explaining the family backgrounds of the two principals and it was a study in complicated relationships. Kaufman thought that the general idea was as applicable to a certain New York social set as it was to Hollywood's aristocracy. He was disappointed that I had already disposed of the title to a picture I had written and produced, but wanted to go ahead with it anyway. Its title on Broadway was *Park Avenue*.

There were few writers in this country who wouldn't have leapt at an opportunity to work with George Kaufman, who was as near a god as there was on Broadway. It was not only his long record of successes but the man himself that made such an invitation irresistible. I promptly withdrew from my picture work and gave myself entirely to the Master.* . . .

Elaine Steinbeck is the widow of John Steinbeck.

TO ELAINE STEINBECK

December 30, 1968

Elaine dear:

If I hadn't been ill I would have been there to pay my last affectionate respects to John. In addition to all the other reasons for my devotion to him, even when we didn't see each other for long stretches of time, he played an important part in my life, both personal and professional. For one thing, he provided me with the opportunity for an accomplishment that heightened my reputation forever after [the screenplay for *The Grapes of Wrath*]. For another, in this same accomplishment he brought me nearer to Dorris. I can't think of anybody else who did anywhere near as much for my life. And finally, he brought us our friendship with you, which has been important to us too. . . . All too often, widows withdraw from contact with friends they have shared with their husbands. Please don't let that happen with us. Both Dorris and I didn't just accept you as John's wife. Our fondness for you grew to be as warm and genuine as it was for John.

* *Park Avenue*, a musical comedy with lyrics by Ira Gershwin and music by Arthur Schwartz, opened on Broadway in November 1946 and ran for nine weeks.

A friendship not just for the Steinbecks, but a friendship for John and a friendship for Elaine.

I know that you will have many readjustments to make during the coming months but when you have time and the convenience, do drop us a line.

Our love to you.

July 16, 1969

Roxie dear:

I don't know how welcome the enclosed letter will be but it was forwarded here from Barbados. Dorris also got a letter from me, forwarded from same. For fast communication there is nothing like the United States mail.

I am also enclosing an account of the hair-raising life of an English lady of title in darkest Hollywood. It appeared in an Irish newspaper and was sent to Bobby Dolan, who forwarded it to me. But perhaps it's not too far off after all. There was a story in the paper the other day that burglars had ransacked the house on De Longpre while it was unoccupied, Peter Lawford being in London. The only other event worthy of your attention is that on my way home the other afternoon three kids about seven or eight years old with some weeds in their hands asked me if I'd like to buy some marijuana. Since the weeds were obviously weeds, not marijuana, I do not hesitate to describe them as dirty little crooks. I may report them to J. Edgar Hoover.

We are anxiously waiting for the news of your arrival in London and how you found things there. Our household here has been increased, if not particularly benefited, by the visit of a young man named Stephen Daitsch, from South Africa and Brandeis. An odd chap even for South Africa and Brandeis. He talks like Peter Lorre, with some kind of mysterious accent that I can't place. This doesn't matter too much, for he has said nothing yet that I thought worth listening to. His wardrobe consists of about 2½ bikinis, and the rest of us, what with our pants and shirts and shoes, feel quite overdressed. He is a practitioner of Yoga, which means much meditation and yogurt, and no meat, with the result that sometimes Dorris has to cook two separate meals to accommodate his nuttiness. Privately we refer to him as the Guru. He has threatened to leave a couple of times but has managed to quell these rash impulses, and God only knows when he will resume his hegira to Mecca.

Nan has replaced Constance Cummings as Nicol Williamson's mum in *Hamlet* and it is opening here tonight. I managed to get three tickets which will have to be allotted to the four of us, Dorris and me and Scott and Christie. We will simply have to leave the Guru alone in his lotus position. . . .

Lots of love, we miss you, and please write.

TO SCOTT JOHNSON

November 20, 1969

Dear Scotty:

I shouldn't have written you about the present state of the theatre in the gloomy mood that was on me. Thinking it over since we talked last night, I think I can offer a more hopeful view of the situation. What I had in mind, I can see now, was my theatre, not yours. I failed to remember, or to acknowledge, that it is my theatre, the theatre that I have known and understood in a way, that is fading out, while your theatre has never been more lively.

My theatre is the kind that your generation more or less scorns. What we might call the standard theatre, the theatre of Rodgers and Hammerstein, Tennessee Williams, Howard Lindsay and Russel Crouse, that kind of story telling. It flourished for a long time, and it is the only one I can claim to understand at all. There is little doubt but that this kind of theatre is very low. I don't think it will disappear completely, but such plays may for a long time be the exception rather than the rule. Whether this is good or bad I have no idea, but for the time being the practitioners of that sort of theatre production are out of season, like oysters in August.

Your theatre is the Off-Broadway and the Off-off-Broadway, experimental. Also, out of necessity it will be less costly, and because it is not as affluent, its practitioners must be more ingenious and resourceful. Just as the kind of David Belasco set, with a complete automat on stage and real steam out of a teakettle, lost its appeal when designers came along with their brilliant three-dimensional sets with scrims that permitted a half a dozen sets to appear according to the ingenious lighting, so will other concepts come into favor. The concept of suggestion, of non-reality, of multi-usefulness. Or even of no sets per se, as Kazan used in Arthur Miller's *After the Fall*, a collection of different altitudes, actually solid blocks, that were perfectly satisfactory, cheaper, and a credit to whoever thought of it. This will probably be the settings of the future—until a few years from now some neo-David Belasco stuns an audience with a complete automat on the stage and real steam coming out of a kettle.

In other words, my theatre is shrinking and yours is expanding. My guess is that for every orthodox production in the future there will be four or five Off-Broadway and Off-off-Broadway productions, with their own new ideas, new concepts of what is dramatic, new kinds of stories, new everything. This is the theatre that will be open to you, a theatre in which I would be lost and hopeless. It's hard for an old-timer to recognize, much less accept, these revolutionary changes. But the fact is, this new theatre, your theatre, is wide open for you. It will give you the opportunities that would be impossible in the old theatre, my theatre.

I don't mean that it will be a breeze for you, nor do you assume so. Breaking into any kind of theatre, like breaking into writing or acting or painting or any other art form, is always tough and unless you are exceptionally lucky it will take time and you will have to go through many disappointments. But as I say, that is standard operating procedure in any art or craft. But as I might have stupidly implied in my last letter, you are not already doomed even before you get out of the starting gate. The effort will be in competition with other young men no better prepared or more experienced than yourself, so it'll be an even race. Once you take the plunge, it will all be up to you. And as the old saying goes, what could be fairer than that?

However, I must admonish you again about your attitude toward the individual project. You can't set yourself up as either the producer or a critic. The play may not be to your literary or esthetic taste but that's not the pertinent point for a designer. I remember Bobby Dolan once being somewhat apologetic about the eccentric shape of his lot in Bel-Air when he talked to [Richard] Neutra about building him a house. Neutra's reply, in effect, was that this awkwardness of the shape was all that appealed to him about the proposal. Any jerk, he said, could build a house on a square lot; to design one to fit this eccentricity was what made him eager to do it. It was a challenge, whereas the square lot was a bore. Ibsen may not be to your taste, nor Tennessee Williams, but they were what created the challenge, to create a design never heard of before to accommodate and possibly bring up to date these olden plays. George S. Kaufman once said to me that if he did a play about divorce, his aim was a play so complete and overwhelming that there would never again be any need for another play about divorce. This was of course extravagance, and George, being a sensible man, knew that it was hardly likely that he would be able to achieve such a production. Along the same lines, when Roxie was a little girl she asked me why I didn't write a picture that would win an Oscar. I told her that I had never written Fade In without hoping that this one would win an Oscar. What I mean to say is that you keep your eye on the problem directly in front of you, and yours not to reason why, yours but to try to make it the very best that was ever done. . . .

I would have written a shorter letter if I had had time.

All our love to both of you.

TO ROXIE JOHNSON
AND SCOTT JOHNSON

November 24, 1969

Dear Roxie and Scotty:

We went out another evening last week, to a whacking big dinner honoring Jack Warner, now that they've got his studio. It was really a big-time affair, and my guess is that it was the last of such things. The gentry of the town was there. . . .

Cocktails were served on the *Camelot* set, a beautiful and overwhelming arrangement, and the entrance to Stage 1 was a duplicate of the first nickelodeon that the Warner Brothers opened when they were young men in some little town in Pennsylvania. And that dreary old stage was completely draped in plush, and the highlight of the evening was a showing of clips from the important pictures that Warner Bros. had made, all the way from Rin-Tin-Tin to *Camelot*. The new regime is nearly all bearded, like General Grant's staff at Appomattox, and the studio is now known to some as The House of David. The new prez, Ashley, reported the New Order to date: one picture costing only a million and a half and another that came in under budget. It may have made him happy but I can't see how it's going to have much effect on the stock market. But I'll say this, he had guts to make this report after looking at those clips of the old Warner pictures. It was a nice evening and it may have ended our social season.

We are anxious to hear about you and the Milicis at the Yale-Harvard game. I spent most of the day taking care of Alex [Christie's son]. At one time he said, "My mommie told me," and then after thinking it over for a while, "Oh, I can't remember what she told me." In other words, one hell of a conversationalist.

Lots of love.

Robert Parrish, a child actor in films of the 1940s, later became a film editor and a director. He is also the author of the book *Growing Up in Hollywood*.

TO ROBERT PARRISH

April 9, 1969

Dear Bob:

. . . B. G. Six [Bob Goldstein] is flying to London today, so you can get all the news from him, such as it is. There's no reason why he shouldn't fly to London or even Singapore, because neither he nor anybody else is doing anything here. The biggest excitement of the last few months was the introduction of tamales for lunch in the commissary, courtesy of Mr. Goldstein. This kept us at fever pitch excitement for hours on end.

I am working on another World War II script and I'm trying to make it very au courant, but let me tell you it isn't easy to get a naked woman in a World War II battle. The homosexuality is no problem. I'm just bunking the first platoon in with the second. This project will probably join *The Frontiersmen* and *Scuba Duba* on the shelf. You wouldn't believe the amount of money they are throwing in to build up their backlog.

I may as well tell you that in my conflict with the studio B.G. Six has been a tower of jello. I can't get any help at all from him. To paraphrase the old Senator Joe McCarthy line, his policy is employment by association, which is why he is accompanying Kenny Hyman to London. My understanding is that Kenny is only going to find a house to live in when he departs the studio sometime this summer, but I daresay Bob will be of help in counting the rooms and turning on the water in the sink. My own belief is that this trip is an error of judgment, unless he knows something we don't. The new man in charge will be Ted Ashley, whom I don't know, but if I did you could bet your life his is the cigarette I'd be lighting, not Kenny's. Now that I think of it, I may send him some flowers or a box of Whitman's Sampler this afternoon. A little touch like that might just mean the difference. . . .

My family is as ever. My wife is a compulsive worker and was horrified the other day when her doctor gave her a physical check-up and reported that she was in fine shape. This chap may not know it but his days are numbered as her personal physician. We all send you and yours our love.

TO MARVIN JOSEPHSON

December 10, 1969

Dear Marvin:

Tighten your seat belt, please. . . .

I am finally packing it in. I was 72 last week and have begun to feel every minute of it. After about fifteen years as a newspaperman and short story writer, I have been at it in Hollywood since 1933, thirty-six years, and hardly a man is still alive, etc. Not a screenwriter, anyway. And now I'm running out of gas. I simply don't feel up to doing a job anymore, not a good job anyway, and when you begin to feel like that, that's the time to cut out.

So this is to ask you to strike my name from your list, and not to propose it to anyone, and if some misguided soul should bring it up, I suggest that you simply drop your eyes and leave the room in silence.

I'm sure I don't have to tell you how much our association has meant to me both professionally and as friends. I've never had a pleasanter or more profitable relationship professionally and I'm sure our personal relationship will continue. You will always be able to find me sitting beside the fireplace staring into space. Or at a centre-spread in *Playboy*. Memories, memories, memories!

Written firmly and bravely but with the suspicion of a tear in the eye.

TO ROBERT GOLDSTEIN

October 21, 1970

Dear Robert:

You wouldn't know the place [Hollywood]. I don't know one-third of the people mentioned in Joyce Haber's column. And things move very fast here too. There is some fellow who produced one successful picture, *Goodbye, Columbus,* and some studio was so staggered by this overwhelming success that they made him the head of the studio. Do you remember when Zanuck used to produce two pictures before eleven a.m.? As for the other head of Paramount, named [Robert] Evans, in two years he has lost almost as much money as Vietnam has cost us. So it's not surprising that they're going to give him a raise.

Harry Brand had a kind of an old boys luncheon at Hillcrest the other day—Frank McCarthy, Nat Dyches, David Brown and a couple of other veterans. David was surprised that I wasn't drawing a pension from Fox. He said he was going to look into it. I know already that I would have failed to qualify by about three days. It's like the time George Kaufman told me about the list of 100 deductible items in the income tax law, at the end of which it said, "except George S. Kaufman." Incidentally, Dorothy Manners told me the other night that Louella is not much more than half alive in the Motion Picture Relief Home and is drawing $500 a week pension from the Hearst Organization. You may also like to know that Dorothy is 68 years old. You don't get that kind of information from anybody else who writes to you.

Harry was as brisk and funny as ever and told a lot of very good inside stories about Joe Schenck and his dames. If enough of these people die Harry will be free to write one helluva book.

Thank you for the pictures of the Elizabeth Taylor wedding and so on. I don't know if things are going on around here like that or not. All I ever do is go to Schwab's Drugstore for a tube of Colgate's toothpaste, an uneventful errand.

We send you our best.

Gary Corbett Davis was the dean of Boston University's School of Public Communication.

TO GARY CORBETT DAVIS

March 5, 1971

Dear Mr. Davis:

All of my scripts, including those of *The Grapes of Wrath* and *The Moon Is Down*, are in Boston University's Mugar Memorial Library, as well as any correspondence connected with those two projects.

Even if we sat down face to face I doubt if I could answer many of the questions you ask. That was a long time ago and the details have long left my memory. I recall only that *The Grapes of Wrath* was bought by 20th Century–Fox Studio before the book was published or I had read it. I asked for the assignment and it was given to me. I met Steinbeck, talked to him a great deal, and began a friendship which lasted for the rest of his life, but I can't recall ever discussing any part of the script with him. My recollection is that he saw no part of it until it was finished.

As for *The Moon Is Down*, which I had seen as a play in New York, when I asked him if he had any suggestions about it he simply replied, "Tamper with it." And that was the only discussion we ever had about it.

This was not indifference on Steinbeck's part. He always hoped for the best but took the position that the book remained his statement, unaltered, whether the picture should turn out well or badly.

It is true that I had a good deal more respect for the Steinbeck material than much that I had worked on previously but this did not affect my way of converting it into screenplays. My custom was always the same, I looked for the skeleton of the story and set about fleshing it out as well as I could within the limits of a moving picture. . . . Once the first draft was finished, several people discussed it with me, mainly Darryl Zanuck, the head of the studio. I can't remember that John Ford the director, or Irving Pichel, the director of *The Moon Is Down*, took any part in these discussions. I am sure that both were invited to discuss the scripts, for both were experienced and intelligent men, and it may be that they made their contributions to the scripts although I'm afraid I can't remember that they did so. Trying to remember such details after thirty years is like walking around in fly paper.

I don't think there is anything I can add to this short account but perhaps you will be able to find something in my papers. I wish you the best of luck.

Mike Fowler was the son of Johnson's daughter Marjorie.

TO MIKE FOWLER

March 10, 1971

Dear Mike:

The quality that seems to me good for young people is cynicism's cousin, skepticism. (Is this really true? Is this guy really on the level?

Does this girl really mean what she says?) Skepticism is a step toward mature sophistication. The cynic condemns, the skeptic simply wants to know a little more about it. Cynicism is unhealthy, skepticism is a very healthy quality. . . .

A certain amount of cynicism is absolutely necessary. Without it you are pretty much of a chump. But there's a limit to it. There are people in this world who don't deserve to be suspected of larceny, and my guess is that you are finding that out on this trip. You seem to be meeting people with a new look, a less suspicious look. This is very good. By the time you finish the tour you will probably have an entirely new view of the world around you.

Actually, you are in the oldest tradition of show business, the theatre, or whatever you might want to call it. You are literally a strolling player, the troubadour who dates back hundreds of years, before there was any such thing as a theatre. You even have generally the same instrument, a stringed harp, and since you compose and create your own songs, you are following precisely in the footsteps of these historic strollers. . . .

You must remember that for a storyteller, either in words or music, everything that he sees or hears at this age is material that he may be using a thousand times in the future. What somebody looks like, the way he talks or sings, the way he grins or frowns, how he reacts to good news or bad, what makes you like him or dislike him and the same about her, all this is stuff that enriches you. It's better than a college education. You will be studying people. Which is the most important study of all. . . .

And now the sermon is over. Write again when you can.

Love from all of us.

In 1962 Darryl Zanuck had returned as president of 20th Century–Fox. His independent production *The Longest Day* (made before he rejoined the company, but distributed by it) and *The Sound of Music* brought in higher profits than 20th Century–Fox had realized in many years. Unfortunately, the next several "spectaculars" were hardly that, and by 1969 20th Century–Fox had a deficit of $36.8 million. Richard Zanuck, Darryl's son and head of production at the studio, and David Brown, a story editor, tried to take power from Zanuck senior. The board forced their resignations, but Darryl Zanuck himself withdrew from the corporation in 1971.

That year David Brown became an executive vice-president and member of the Board of Directors at Warner Bros. The following year he and Richard

Zanuck formed an independent production company; among the movies they produced were *Jaws* and *The Sting*. In 1979 both returned to 20th Century-Fox as producers.

TO DAVID BROWN

March 19, 1971

Dear David:

Now that you're in charge in Burbank I wonder if I could call your attention to a couple of scripts I left at Warner Bros.–Seven Arts a year or so ago. One is called *The Frontiersmen* and was written for Jack Warner, who simply handed me the book and asked me to turn it into a two-a-day Western. It turned largely into a life of Tecumseh.

But when I delivered the script to Warner he said he would have nothing to do with that son-of-a-bitch Kenny Hyman, who by an odd coincidence didn't want to have anything further to do with that son-of-a-bitch Jack Warner. In other words, they laid the script down in the middle of the road and walked away. I believe that Calley* said he wasn't interested in Westerns of any kind but I really know nothing about that. Do you think that Dick would be interested in a two-a-day Western?

You would be more familiar with *Scuba Duba*, for I imagine you saw the play. Bruce Jay Friedman's comedy was much too wonderful to be trifled with, so the picture script is largely the playscript. I was present when Walter Matthau turned down a million dollars to do the lead. (Those were the days!) He had been persuaded by Abe Lastfogel that such a picture would be controversial and Abe didn't think Walter should be in a controversial picture. Abe was so firm about this that he wouldn't even let Jack Lemmon read the script. He said that not only was the script controversial but that Jack was not available.

I don't think *Scuba Duba* would be controversial today. In fact, I think the climate could not be better for its startling racial comedy. In any case, I would appreciate it if you would take a look at it.

My interest in these pictures is only incidentally financial. I was paid in full for *Scuba Duba* and there is some sort of percentage of the profits codicil, but I have a feeling that Warner Bros.' book-

---

* John Calley was executive vice-president for worldwide production at Warner Bros. In 1975 he became president.

keeping, like Twentieth Century–Fox's, is quite capable of taking care of that. I was paid $200,000 for the *Frontiersmen* script with a contract for another $100,000 when and if it should go into production. There may be a percentage of the profits on this one too but I'm not sure about that. If ever I get my mitts on that other $100,000 we can skip the percentage.

My best to you.

In this letter to Lauren Bacall, Johnson reports on his son Scott's marriage to Amy Cohen.

TO LAUREN BACALL

August 19, 1971

Betty darling:

Your wire arrived and was read with that dazed look that falls on young people who suddenly realize that this is it. As you can imagine, I was not greatly moved by any of it. I've seen almost as many of these weddings as I have participated in.

But all in all, it was a gala affair. Once the ceremony had been performed and the guests had knocked down enough champagne, the younger element stripped off all their revolting garments and went skinny-dipping in the pool. It was the first time I have ever been present at what is generally thought of as a Hollywood party. Misled by understandings I once jumped into a pool starkers with Harold Ross's fiancee, likewise buck nekkid, but this orgy was over so quickly that it's hardly worth mentioning. Scott's festival was nearer to the mythology of such affairs.

I think everyone enjoyed it, even the members of Scotty's and Amy's set. One boy was 6 feet 7 inches tall with an Afro on top of that, a white Afro, for God's sake. He wore flowers in his hair and had an oil painting on his chest. His girl friend had the misfortune to look a good deal like Tiny Tim and so she could hardly have tempted me if she had stripped in my bedroom for me alone. One young man, apparently unaccustomed to champagne, awoke the next morning in our guest room. With him was his girl friend, who reported that he was deathly ill and would very likely need the combined services of Dr. Marcus Welby and the Mayo frères. It looked to me like a good old-fashioned hangover but I hesitated to say so, knowing how much better informed all young people are these days. . . .

I wish I could promise that we might see you in New York soon but I'm afraid there're no grounds for any such optimism. I can't say that my English is any worse but the fact is I am certainly not getting any stronger. When all those young girls leaped in the pool the other night I was compelled to call on friends to lift my chair a bit closer.

We send our love to you.

TO ROBERT GOLDSTEIN

September 17, 1971

Dear Robert:

. . . To my astonishment people are calling me with offers of jobs. One offer was from a couple of fellows at Fox. Another came yesterday from a couple of fellows at Warner's, who want me to do Harold Robbins' book *The Betsy*. This book is all about the automobile industry in Detroit and on page 3 the hero was in the kip with a girl named Cindy whose talents were breathtaking, though what this has to do with the automotive industry is not yet clear to me. My guess is that no matter what industry Robbins turns his attention to, steel, vacuum cleaners, freeze-dried coffee, or anything else, on page 3 the hero will be in the kip with a girl such as one rarely meets in real life. As Herman Mankiewicz used to say, why don't you ever hear of a fellow who is married to a nymphomaniac?

Scotty and Amy are still married and Christie is working on the Los Angeles *Free Press*, an underground paper. When you work on an underground newspaper you nearly always have a big laundry bill. When she comes over here we insist on her taking a shower before joining us in the drawing room.

We wish you the same.

TO ROBERT EMMETT DOLAN

November 26, 1971

Dear Bobby:

I hope you haven't too heavy a hang-up on the pure mechanics of writing. I understand your concern with sentences and paragraphs, I suppose all writers have that concern, but there is a way to cope with it. There ought to be no question in your mind about your ability to write, I mean to convey thoughts in a graceful and intelligent form, for your letters are ample proof of that. No one who writes the letters you write needs to doubt his gift of communication. Myself, I rewrite and rewrite and rewrite. And so, I'm sure, do you.

So why don't you forget the esthetics of sentences and paragraph structure in your first draft, giving all your concern to the narration, and do all your rephrasing and your restructuring in a second draft? After all, the grace of writing should come second. The first concern is the story telling.

The odd thing about this suggestion, which I know is good, is that I never follow it myself. Like you, I become concerned with the shape of the sentences and the structure of the paragraph. So instead of finishing a day's stint and then examining it the next morning for whatever improvement I can make in it, I do the rewriting then and there, slowing everything down and holding up the progress of the work. Pure stupidity. Nearly all writers that I know anything about do it the way I have suggested. It's obviously the most sensible way of handling it, and I swear to you that in my next incarnation that's the way I'm going to do it from the very beginning. . . .

Love to you and yours.

TO FRANK SULLIVAN

July 28, 1972

Dear Frank:

As usual I enjoyed your letter. I also enjoyed that piece from *Punch* about Thurber. Dorris and I have had nights like that with Jim. They are more amusing in retrospect than at the time. Not widely known is the fact that Jim carried on an old romance up to the time of his death, often with Helen's help. Helen is my source of information about this. Every now and then when Jim got quite tight and managed to hold Helen responsible for this situation he would inform her that he was going to reunite with a sweetheart of his youth. In the course of time that sweetheart had married, had children, and then grandchildren, and of late years was living in Bermuda. So one night at my house in London when Jim felt a yearning for this old sweetheart he put in a call and got her on the phone in Bermuda, where, surrounded by her husband and children and grandchildren, she assured Jim that she was still faithful to him and was prepared to receive him as soon as he could fly to her side. After such a call, reassured in the love of his life, Jim would go to sleep, and that's the last that lady would hear from him until months or years later when such a call would come again. Helen said it gave him great comfort and did her no harm. . . .

Love and all that.

TO HELEN HAYES

September 17, 1972

Helen dear:

There is no question about it. In the course of time you are going to have more honorary degrees than Herbert Hoover, and with far more right to them. We are particularly glad that the University of Michigan is going to honor you. Michigan has a very good team this year and has an excellent chance of playing in the Rose Bowl and we have no doubt that you'll be there smack on the 50 yard line, unless you decide to join the cheer leaders on the side lines.

We had dinner with Natalie Schafer the other night. She said the only way you could get a job out here these days is to be either black or naked or a bug.

Love from the kind of family that has made this country what it is today.

TO ROBERT GOLDSTEIN

November 26, 1972

Dear Robert:

Thank you for helping me keep track of my friends in your quaint little country. I saw Carl Foreman the other afternoon and he demanded a message for you the way young interviewers always ask an old writer (or actor or baseball player) for a word of advice for the youth of America. But I was unable to do anything for him because, for one thing, you are not the youth of America, and for another, I didn't have a word of wisdom for anybody, not even for myself.

This town is having what is called Filmex, a film festival, which means that a lot of pictures in Polish are being run at Grauman's Chinese. Not only in Polish but in Japanese, Czechoslovakian, French and Abyssinian. The interesting thing is that all of these pictures have been reviewed by Charles Champlin and those fellows at *Variety* and the *Hollywood Reporter* just as easily as if they were in plain old everyday English. I think *Young Winston* is the only English language picture in the whole festival. But Roxie, who takes a hack at these things, tells me that there is standing room only at these performances. (Roxie also goes to see things like *Henry IV*, Part 1. Part 2 is expected next year.)

An odd moment at a cocktail party that I attended was when I realized that the two old friends who had drawn up chairs to sit with me were Carl [Foreman] and John Lee Mahin.* For a minute or two I could hardly believe it. And yet here they were, bitter enemies, exchanging pleasantries again. The world has turned upside down.

Love and all that to all of you.

TO JOSEPH BRYAN III

February 13, 1973

Dear Joe:

We might as well get this understood right away, I don't want you or anybody else to try to explain to me what they mean by the devaluation of the dollar. I don't *want* to know what happened. Not that I'm doing anything else that that would interfere with. I simply don't want to look any stupider than I am. Stupider about finance, that is. In other fields I am a certified whiz kid. I mean like ask me who was the last man batted over 400 in the National League.

Do you read or have you read Peter De Vries? I can't remember your ever mentioning him but he is a very funny man, the only man aside from Wodehouse who can sustain first-rate humor in a book-length story. I just read a collection of his short stuff called *Without a Stitch in Time* and here was old Johnson laughing out loud again. And if anybody had ever told me that I would get a good ha-ha out of puns I would have taken him to court. And yet what are you going to do when a man writes that he has just bought a pick-up truck, nothing pretentious, just a van ordinaire?

Otherwise, I wade through detective stories. Agatha Christie's Belgian detective is about as revolting a character as I have ever encountered, and I have been unable to decide whether she does this intentionally or has rather a stupid idea that he is cute. But among such horrors he has long since passed Nero Wolfe, who held the title for so many years. And now as to writers, it's going to be a hot race between Rex Stout and Ellery Queen for the booby prize. In comparison, Agatha Christie, an acknowledged anti-wizard with words, begins to look like Walter Pater. (You had no idea I could be so nasty, did you? But that's because you never heard me on the subject of detective story detectives.) Right now I am rereading the Lord Peter Wimsey series, which I read so long ago that they are

---

* John Lee Mahin, a screenwriter whose credits include *Captains Courageous*, *Boom Town*, *Quo Vadis*, *The Bad Seed*, and *No Time for Sergeants*, had been involved in right-wing politics during the McCarthy period.

now like new to me. Dorothy Sayers was a first-rate detective story writer until her friends began telling her that she was worthy of better stuff. Apparently she thought better meant longer winded. She was like this fellow Ross MacDonald, who was told that he was worthy of better stuff and is now writing interminable books that I can't finish. I don't see why these California fellows can't keep writing the same story that I like so much. That is, this lady from Oxnard, California, comes to see this half-crocked private eye and reports to him that her niece has disappeared and would he please find her and bring her back. Clear so far? From then on all the characters begin shooting at each other and whoever is left at the end of 200 pages pays off the private eye and marry each other. That's the kind of story that sticks to your ribs.

Well, so much for that sordid subject. We are tolerably well and trust that you and Jackie are better than that. As well you should be, by God, living off the fat of the land. Strawberries and cream, fresh tuna, everything quick frozen. On second thought, to hell with you!

T O   L A U R E N   B A C A L L

June 12, 1973

Betty darling:

Lord Cooke is here to address a convention of book dealers. Also on the platform with him will be a brilliant young actress named Miss Linda Lovelace, star of a heartbreaking drama called *Deep Throat*. He does get in with the damndest people. Miss Lovelace was on television last night to tell about the book that she is writing. She said she had no sexual hang-ups and admitted that she loved sex especially if it was being photographed. I'm sure they'll make a pretty pair in front of that convention: Lord Cooke and No-lady Linda.

I offer you an odd footnote about this young Duse. I somehow suspect that Linda Lovelace is not really her name. It sounds a bit too romantic. On the other hand, next door to us when we lived on Mountain Drive was a young friend of Christie's whose true name was nothing less than Linda Lovelace. But this young artist that we saw on television was not our little neighbor, who probably has sexual hang-ups like everybody else but can't sell them to the movies.

I got a letter from Nat Benchley about Bogey's biography and if I can't remember anything about him Nat and I will cook up something just as good. But I won't be available for a couple of weeks. I am going into Good Samaritan Hospital not for anything dramatic but for some tests and treatments for my emphysema, which is a nuisance. As I scarcely have to tell you, I'd much rather have a sexual hang-up.

We booed our TV set when they failed to give you the Emmy that you deserved. It's awfully hard to get the full support of this town when you are so far removed from it. It's as if you had defected. But we did have one triumph that evening. Both Marjie and Gene won Emmys for their editing of *The Waltons* series. This didn't altogether make up for their injustice to you, but it helped.

I send you all [the family's] love and mine too, and I pray that I will hear from you before long.

TO FRANK SULLIVAN
September 11, 1973

Dear Frank:

. . . Everybody's writing the lives of everybody else around here. Nat Benchley dropped in to see me the other day about Bogart, whose biography he is writing. I don't think I was of much help to him for he seemed to know a good deal more about Bogey than I did. The next day a fellow came in to talk about Ava Gardner, whose life he was writing. What may turn out to be the most futile of all these efforts is the biography that a fellow is doing of me. Not being employed, I took the time off last week to figure out just how many people in the two hemispheres would be interested in a biography of old Nunnally Johnson, and it was a cool 71, not counting an uncle of mine who would be interested but can't read. Now of course you are going to say this is simply downright modesty and that millions of people in all three hemispheres are waiting for this work to come out, but I assure you that it is not. Only a few people are interested in writers. And usually it's only the writers who have some other reputation that attracts attention, like Hemingway or Mailer. The other day I read a very high-toned piece about the ablest writers practicing in this country today and in the list of about seven or eight there were three names that, honest to God, I had never even heard of. So it's no use arguing with me about this. You are wasting your time and mine. Nobody's interested in an old ex-screenwriter and that's all there is to that. I don't want to hear any more about it. . . .

TO NATHANIEL BENCHLEY

November 6, 1973

Dear Nat:

The other day I reread Robert Sherwood's *The Petrified Forest* and I believe I have made an important discovery about Bogey. If I'm not mistaken, Duke Mantee was Bogey's first tough character part. And more than that, it became the part that Bogey continued to play thereafter. In other words, the Bogey image was Sherwood's creation. I don't think I've ever seen a clear and indisputable source for such a reflection.

This is of course taking nothing away from anybody. It was a brilliant creation of Sherwood's, this hopelessly beset hero, and one can only speculate as to whether Bogey consciously or unconsciously decided to wear the character with one little variation or another from then on.

As a matter of fact, this itself is pure speculation, but I thought it might be of interest to you. Perhaps you should reread the play and see if you find it there too.

My best to you.

Walter Mirisch was president of the Academy of Motion Picture Arts and Sciences.

TO WALTER MIRISCH

February 1, 1974

Dear Mr. Mirisch,

A part of what makes the Academy such a superior professional body is its flexibility. While it has rules and regulations that must be properly observed it has never failed to give its attention to a member that it felt was entitled to exceptional recognition regardless of the polls. More than once, obviously, our Academy has paused and said, see here, we can't let an artist like so-and-so be continually overlooked simply because the eccentricities of circumstance have failed him. An actor or actress of distinction has not come in first because he has not been well served by either script or director or both. A director of unquestioned superiority never won, because chance robbed him of a script or cast that would have enabled him to exhibit his great talents. It is the same with more than one writer. A script that might have won him a triumph never found the proper artists to bring out its true value. In a business or art of so much complexity we all know that many laurels are lost through the vicissitudes that we all run.

But more times than I can remember the Academy has stepped in to bring about a correction of such a mischance. We all remember a director, or an actor, or an actress who was in time presented with the award that they had been deprived of by the electoral mathematics. And, never has the Academy shown itself in a more admirable and becoming light than when it has risen above the rigidity of rules, and honored this artist who deserved it. I daresay the culmination of this generous and understanding practice was the brilliant awards made so deservedly to our great artists Charlie Chaplin and Edward G. Robinson. These were salutes that also added stature to our Academy.

In this same spirit I hereby propose such an award that I believe would maintain the same high standard of its precedents. Obviously these extraordinary awards can never be made to any but the truly greatest of our company of players. Any lessening of the very highest standards would utterly destroy their value. My proposal now is an award for the Marx Brothers.

It would be possible, of course, to support this proposal with an account of their achievements, but I don't believe I can think of anything less called for. Everyone already knows them. Their maniacal comedy has trespassed all geographical divisions and made all races laugh at the same thing at the same time. The very mention of their name would be enough to brighten the entire membership of the United Nations General Assembly with smiles and chuckles. Indeed it may be that there is no other name in the noble business of making people enjoy themselves that is so widely known in the whole world. Originally there were four of them. Then Zeppo retired, and the great Harpo and the incorrigible Chico succumbed to time and are now angels. But the greatest of them is still with us, Groucho, the last of those important clowns, the Marx Brothers.

Respectfully yours,

TO LAUREN BACALL

March 11, 1974

Betty love:

That's the most staggering cast I ever heard of, the *Orient Express* cast. Very fast company indeed. But I do object to Finney as

Poirot. He's a beautiful actor but he no more belongs in that part than I do. As a matter of fact, now that I think of it, what would you think of suggesting me to the producer? But it's hard to believe that it's been seven years since you were in a picture.

Dorris went to Tallahassee, Florida, to see the *Stag at Bay* production, and while nobody seemed to have been very enthusiastic about it, they certainly had a great time. A veritable festival, with overwhelming VIP treatment for Dorris and Scott and Helen Hayes and Jim MacArthur representing the absent playwrights. Along the way Dorris picked up John MacArthur, Charlie's brother, who is one of the richest men in the world. Over two billion dollars. Okay, say one billion and it's still a comfortable sum. So no sooner had she got home than he telephoned to invite her to his birthday party in Chicago last week. Again nothing but limousines and other such VIP stuff. It was a two-day bash and I hope she remembered what I told her, that money isn't everything, only about 95%.

And all this time where do you think I was? Sitting right here thinking about you. The house is a nice and comfortable one, with a rather large living room in the middle and bedrooms around one side and kitchen, dining room and den around the other. No pool this time, but a pleasant little lawn with a nice view. It's all on one level, so I can stroll about occasionally without too much discomfort.

Dorris, when not consorting with billionaires, is busy getting this house in order. In the past four months we have managed to sell all our heavy property with the result that we are well fixed for the remainder of our time on this earth. No more financial burdens. Just children, that's all now. Dorris looks ten years younger. But one bit of sad news, we lost Harry Ruby. There was no one like him. This reduced the Senior Citizens Club to three, Sheekman, Grouch and me, and I don't give either Grouch or Sheeky much of a chance. However, the three of us are going to make one final appearance. There is a new college fad around here these days, streaking, a wild naked dash through a populated area, and Grouch and Arthur and I, with the aid of three walking sticks, are going to strip and streak just as soon as the weather gets a little more moderate.

We both send you our love.

TO H. L. KRAFT

Dear Hy:

I should tell you and Reata about my last conversation with Harry [Ruby]. I called to ask him if it was true that he was going to get married, as Grouch had told me. He said he was, and that the lady was sweet and charming, of an appropriate age, and had some dough. He was going to marry her, he said, in a couple of months. I protested. Why the delay?

Well, he said, you know rabbis. Especially Jewish rabbis. This guy wants a hundred and fifty bucks, he said. But if I stall around for a couple of months I'm sure he'll make it for fifty and that's really all it's worth.

He asked me if he'd ever told me what happened to his first wife. No, what? She was kidnapped, he said. Fellow called up and said he was holding her and wanted $2500 to let her go. Twenty-five hundred dollars! I told him I didn't have any kind of money like that. The fellow said, what about on time? Harry said he asked him how much. The fellow said could you go for a hundred a week? Harry said he felt he could handle that. And that's the way the deal was made. Harry said he paid the fellow $100 a week for 25 weeks and then he sent his wife back and everything turned out just fine for everybody.

Dick Meryman had written a biography of Louis Armstrong.

TO DICK MERYMAN

Dear Dick:

The other night I reread a book by Ben Hecht about Charlie MacArthur. It contained one of Mank's [Herman Mankiewicz] fancies that I wouldn't want you to miss. To illustrate the kind of charisma that Charlie had, Mank said just suppose that he and Charlie got loaded together and went to *Earl Carroll's Vanities* and sat in a stage box. If, Mank said, Charlie became so enthusiastic that he tumbled out of the box onto the stage and staggered around disrupting the show and taking grand bows in the wrong directions before stumbling off into the wings, the next day's report would differ a bit from what might be expected. "If I'd done that," Mank said, "everybody next day would be saying, 'Did you hear how Mank got loaded and made a fool of himself in the theatre last night?' But for MacArthur, the word that went around town would be, 'Did you hear how Charlie leaped onto the stage at Earl Carroll's last night and played d'Artagnan?'" This is as good an example of Mank's perceptiveness about people that I can think of.

With best wishes.

T O   H E L E N   H A Y E S

August 23, 1974

Helen darling:

To judge from your stationery, Burnham Beeches Hotel is a pretty impressive establishment and I don't see how Thomas Gray or any other poet could have afforded to shack up there. It looks more to me like the setting for at least a score of Maugham's short stories. Every now and then Dorris and I mutter about making a trip to England as our last hurrah. We love nearly everything about it. I'm sure the food in the Burnham Beeches is pretty ordinary but a worldly observer remarked that you could eat very well in England if you didn't mind three breakfasts a day. How right he was! The eggs we ate in England still tasted like eggs, and the bacon is ambrosial. And while kippers are not for everybody, they are strictly my dish.

But I suspect that I will never get out of this area again. Fortunately, there is nothing left of Richard Harding Davis in me. I mean, when Greece and Turkey joined battle I hadn't the slightest impulse to leap into my correspondent's uniform and fly off to send dispatches back through shot and shell. Neither do I long to return to the rive gauche and sit around a table with Djuna Barnes and Ezra Pound. And it doesn't matter a goddam to me if the chestnuts are in bloom in the Bois or not. Nor if the catfish are jumping in the Sewanee River. I never went to no college and so I'm not drawn to reunions to anything like Southeast Arkansas Methodist College. Or SAM as the old grads probably call it. I would like to have lunch again, not dinner, at 21, and I read about a magician's show on Broadway that I'm sure I would enjoy, but that's far from enough to induce me to visit New York again. Even for 24 hours. I have no interest in Taiwan or Baffin Bay or Melbourne or Nairobi or Bismarck, N.D., assuming that's where Bismarck is. If I could be magically transported to the homes of a few friends, just one drink, that's all, I would be quite content to drop all other thought of travel. But as long as I am attached to this pressure breathing therapy unit I doubt that even these little trips would be as much fun as I would like. . . .

If this letter is too long, tear it in half. I got started and couldn't stop. Incidentally, speaking of Cooke, don't fail to listen to his Letter from America on the wireless Sunday evening or Monday morning.

We all send you love.

TO HELEN HAYES

October 14, 1974

Helen darling:

I won't send this to England because I haven't enough faith in the mails. You'd be up and away before it got there. And besides, it will contain nothing of importance.

I take your criticism of English weather with mixed feelings. I remember those slate-gray days through many winters and they were indeed hard to take, but I'm not sure that it is worse than the weather here, where every day is more beautiful than the last. To put it bluntly, I am fed up with beautiful days. I have lived a long time (I am now 76 and 11/12) and I have seen more of them than I like. But now that it's October we should expect our annual showers. I can already see the headlines after the first drizzle: STORM LASHES CITY— TRAFFIC SNARLED. The head writers are clearly convinced that at the first drop of rain in this area everybody runs out and jumps in his car and drives into each other.

Dorris is in Las Vegas for a week or two with Mary Healy, and Roxie is in charge of our modest spread, Three Oaks. And she has really taken charge. I'm getting better care than Dorris gives me. I'm not sure that this can last but it's very nice for the time being.

And now in conclusion I will give you a sample of the kind of thing that makes me laugh. A man came out of his house one morning and found a chimpanzee on the lawn. Just then a cop car drove up. What do you do with a thing like this? he asked the cop. The cop said, Why don't you take it to the zoo? The fellow said, That's a very good idea. But that afternoon the cop, prowling through the same neighborhood, saw the fellow walking down the street hand-in-hand with the chimp. The cop said, I thought you were going to take him out to the zoo. The man said, I did, and he liked it so much I thought I'd take him down to the beach this afternoon.

We send you love.

Tom Dardis, author of *A Time in The Sun*, a book about the Hollywood years of Faulkner, Fitzgerald, Aldous Huxley, and Nathanael West, wrote to Johnson for information.

TO TOM DARDIS

November 8, 1974

Dear Mr. Dardis:

About Fitzgerald, my view of the way he fared in Hollywood is nearer yours than the Schulberg-Mizener notion. As *The Last Tycoon* proved, he was obviously not burned out. The explanation for his continual failure as a screenwriter is that he was simply unable to understand or turn out dramatic work. Long before Hollywood he wrote a play which was about as awkward and inept as a play could be. But nobody said then that the stage corrupted him. And he wasn't the first novelist who was unable to master the technique of dramatic writing. But Scott didn't think of that. He saw dozens of inferior writers being paid fat sums out here and although I don't think he ever had any genuine interest in screenwriting he could see no reason why he shouldn't get in on it and help himself out of his financial slump.

I knew Scott only during his last few years and whenever he was not drinking he seemed to me to be as thoroughly alive and alert as anybody I ever knew. His biggest misfortune, which I doubt he ever realized, was that they paid him fat money at the very beginning. And even though he blew his chances with inadequate work he believed that he should continue to draw such salaries or even larger ones. But I'm afraid he simply couldn't hack it. He probably couldn't have played first class chess either. It was nothing against him. He had simply wandered away from the field where he was a master and was sludging around in an area for which he had no training or instinct. And this is not pure hearsay. I read some of the work he did alone and unaided by a collaborator and it was downright bad. Worst of all, it was shamelessly imitative. Realizing that he could not cut the mustard on his own, he echoed some pretty shoddy stuff.

I'm afraid I'm not prepared to pass any judgment on Scott's personal life either out here or anywhere else. I had a feeling that Sheilah [Graham] was good for him and that she was largely responsible for his getting down to work on *The Last Tycoon*.

As for Faulkner, he worked on a script for me once but I never thought for a moment that he had the slightest interest in either that script or anything else in Hollywood. A director named Howard Hawks kept bringing him out here for reasons that I can only guess at. It may be that he simply wanted his name attached to Faulkner's. Or since Hawks liked to write, it was easy enough for him to do it with Faulkner, for Bill didn't care much one way or the other. You surprise me when you say he spent four years out here, I would never have guessed it. Admittedly Bill needed the money and if Hawks wanted to give it to him, why not? Hawks even enlisted Faulkner to work on a script about the building of the Pyramids or some such nonsense, and they engaged the late Harry Kurnitz to work with him on it. (Faulkner always had to have a collaborator, or it was unlikely that he would have written anything at all.) That was a real saga, Faulkner and his bourbon and Harry Kurnitz and Egypt, but apparently Bill wrote no more in the Land of the Pharaohs than he did in Zanuckland. But if he hated Hollywood he never mentioned it to me. Which was not very surprising. As you probably know, he had very little to say to anybody about anything.

I hope that this is what you had in mind, or at least somewhere near it.

With best regards.

TO AVA GARDNER

June 16, 1975

Ava Jean sugar,

I think that you should give me a little warning when you are going to telephone me. I need a little time to round up some witnesses. Of course, if it's hot stuff you've got on your mind, any old time will do day or night. But for casual gossip I'd like to be able to muster up some support.

The way it is, when I report that I have just had a little ding-a-ling from you some people were inclined to say, poor old Johnson's cracking up faster than we thought. Now he's talking about getting a phone call from Ava Gardner. The next thing you know, he'll be claiming that Queen Elizabeth gives him an occasional buzz. The fact is, I wouldn't accept a call from Q.E. My instinct tells me that we wouldn't be really congenial.

And besides, there's a language barrier. When I was a young reporter in New York, about 20 years of age, I was sent to interview an English lady who was very celebrated at the time, Margot Asquith, wife of the Prime Minister. At the end of about 10 minutes it was perfectly clear that we were getting nowhere. She spoke a sort of strangulated English that I had never heard before and I was equally incomprehensible to her. So she rang for her secretary, a young American not long down from Oxford or Cambridge, and he translated her discourse. When I left Georgia I never dreamed I'd run into things like that.

I called your ever loving sister to tell her about your call and we had a very merry little chat. She's a dear. But then so are you. Everybody in the Gardner family, I suppose.

My eternal love.

P.S. I hear things are still terribly expensive over there [London]. A friend of mine was in Fortnum & Mason's and said he heard an American lady say to the clerk, Two pounds for a cucumber! Well, you know what you can do with that cucumber! The clerk replied, as politely as ever in Fortnum & Mason's, I'm sorry, madam, but that's impossible. There's one already there.

TO ALISTAIR COOKE

June 23, 1975

Dear Alistair:

Did you realize that you have an imposter who is using the mails for God knows what? It was by the purest accident that I nailed him only last week. I had received a letter on your stationery, beginning Dear Donnelly, and everything looked absolutely comme il bloody faut, when all of a sudden I was shaken to my very heels. It never fails. The fellow does all of his research perfectly, he's almost home with the perfect crime, when that one fatal mistake betrays him. At first I could hardly believe what I read. Could this be the Alistair Cooke that I've known man and boy since we were at Rugby together? Watching *baseball* on television? Impossible. He not only mentioned it, he pressed on with it, describing night after night after night of TV baseball. How much more evidence did I need?

At any rate, knowing that the real Alistair Cooke wouldn't be caught dead in front of a TV baseball game, I lost no time in notifying the authorities. As might have been expected, the FBI had already steamed the letter open and was familiar with its contents. They promised to cooperate in every way they could. The same was true at the CIA and the IRS. You have no idea how many readers a privately written letter has in this country these days. In any case,

I'm sure they'll have the fellow under lock and key before many more days have passed. In some ways this is quite a pity. The bloke had handled the communication quite skillfully otherwise.

By the purest chance your son Johnny was here for dinner that evening. You can imagine the laugh we shared at the thought of Alistair Cooke watching a baseball game every night.

As ever.

TO WALTER KERR

November 10, 1975

Dear Walter:

I read the chapter on *The General* and *The Gold Rush* this afternoon and assuming that all of the rest will be as enjoyable I don't think I need to wait any longer to thank you from the bottom of my heart for *The Silent Clowns*. But you're not dealing with one of your trendy buffs, you know. I grew up with all these people. I discovered Charlie Chaplin in the Bonita Theatre; 5¢ in the afternoon. You may not be able to believe this but I sat through this first exposure, called *Behind the Scenes*, something like 15 times in one afternoon. I was so hypnotized by it that I failed to notice that it was dark when I got out of the theatre. I was still thinking of all this funny stuff when I reached my home and found a dozen or more people gathered around the front steps. The center of this group was an older boy, high school age, strapping a raincoat on his bicycle, clearly preparing to set out on a mission of some importance. Puzzled by this scene, I asked him where he was going. For an answer, he hit me square in the middle of the forehead with an expletive.

He was preparing to lead a countrywide search for me. The only movie my mother had ever seen was one about some gypsies who had evidently kidnapped somebody and were hurrying him across a field in a bag in a wagon. The good people and the police were chasing them. In the end the gypsies abandoned their wagon and contents and escaped into the woods, and when the bags were opened they were found to be full of geese. This early masterpiece left an indelible mark on my mother. She suspected the gypsies of kidnapping me about once a month, or whenever I was late for supper. In other words, I am no Johnny-come-lately to this world that you have just described.

In addition to which, I am probably your ideal customer. All I can do now is sit, and with a table in front of me I can manage a book of this size. And on top of everything else, I love all these old folks and will be happy to be with them again. I thank you and send you my best; you and that lady you live with. My love to her.

Sylvia Dudley was a former editor at McGraw-Hill and an old family friend of the Johnsons'.

TO SYLVIA DUDLEY

May 17, 1976

Sylvia darling:

That little comic who loped about the stage (not Groucho) in other years was one of the great clowns of all time, Bobby Clark. It was he, for one thing, who taught Nora, among a million others, what laughter could be. One night when she was about 15 or 16 I took her to see Bobby at a revival of *Naughty Marietta* (or one of those old-time musicals) and I could tell with what polite indulgence she was accommodating her aging father. But she put on a brave front and we went to the Shubert Theatre, this was in New York, to endure 2 or 3 hours of old cornpone comedy.

When we came out at intermission she looked at me as if she were seeing me for the first time, as if she had never known this man who called himself her father. She had laughed so continuously that her eyes were wet with tears. She, like all that generation, thought laughter was a series of little cackles, the kind of laughter you hear when Bob Hope is on. One-liner laughter. Nothing wrong with it. In fact it can be very wonderful at times. But there are no more clowns who keep you laughing until you hurt. Ed Wynn, Bobby Clark, the Marx Brothers at the Palace, Frank Tinney. And during the same years those marvelous movie funny men, Buster Keaton, Chaplin, Laurel and Hardy, a dozen others. Did you realize that there is no more such laughter as they brought? My God, how I wish I could hear Joe Cook explaining why he couldn't imitate 4 Hawaiians or playing the Skaters' Waltz with Dave Chasen sitting in the middle of that gigantic jungle gym that filled the whole stage, his sole contribution being a tap on the triangle that ended the piece. It's really extraordinary how such things could happen, this change of style in the art of making people laugh. So the next time you think of that little man whose spectacles were not steel but painted on his face, pause and send a short prayer of thanks to God for all of the pleasure.

Appendix

Published and Produced Works

Published Short Stories

THE SMART SET

Ashes to Ashes   May 1923
Scarehead   May 1923
I Owe It All to My Wife   July 1923
Doing Right by Nell   November 1923
Futility   November 1923

The Ad Section   January 1924
The Happy Ending   March 1924
Where Is Thy Sting?   March 1924
Twins   June 1924

SATURDAY EVENING POST

Rollicking God   October 11, 1924
Hero   March 14, 1925
Lovelorn   March 28, 1925
Hearse Horse   April 11, 1925
Laughing Death   April 25, 1925
Death of an Infinitive Splitter   September 5, 1925
Love of a Moron   February 27, 1926
His Name in the Papers   March 13, 1926
Fame Is a Bubble   April 3, 1926
Rough House Rosie   June 12, 1926
It Probably Never Happened   July 10, 1926
Portrait of the Writer   October 16, 1926
Straight from New York   October 30, 1926

Lady of Broadway   July 9, 1927
Good Little Man   October 8, 1927
An Artist Has His Pride   December 3, 1927
Belting Bookworm   January 7, 1928
Anti-New York   February 11, 1928
Comedy   March 17, 1928
Young Poison   April 7, 1928
Divine Afflatus   April 28, 1928
The Actor   May 26, 1928
Private Life of the Dixie Flash   June 2, 1928
New York—My Mammy   September 8, 1928
Who's Who, and Why   September 29, 1928

World's Shortest Love Affair   October 27, 1928
Simple Honors   December 22, 1928
Pain in the Neck   April 20, 1929
Not If You Gave It to Me   May 11, 1929
Pagliacci Blues   June 22, 1929
Mlle. Irene the Great   October 5, 1929
One Meets Such Interesting People November 30, 1929
Victim of the War   December 27, 1929
Faunthorpe's Folly   February 8, 1930
Away from It All   February 15, 1930
Sugar in Corn Bread!   March 1, 1930
Burgler's Bride   April 12, 1930
France on Two Words   April 26, 1930
Those Old Pals of Hers   May 3, 1930
Twenty Horses   May 17, 1930
There Ought to Be a Law   July 26, 1930
Artist Relaxed   July 19, 1930
How to Treat Reporters   August 2, 1930
It's in the Blood   August 30, 1930
Women Have No Sense of Humor September 13, 1930
Here We Go A-Nutting   September 27, 1930
Perfect Crime Case   October 11, 1930
Back to Barrie   November 15, 1930

Woman at the Wheel   December 27, 1930
Lowest Form of Humor   January 1931
Dixie Bell   February 28, 1931
Woman's Touch   March 21, 1931
Nightmare   April 4, 1931
Angler's Prayer   April 25, 1931
Lion of the Bronx   June 6, 1931
Author! Author!   July 4, 1931
Man on Horseback   July 11, 1931
Submachine-Gun School of Literature October 3, 1931
Pillar of Strength   October 17, 1931
Josie   October 24, 1931
Stage-Struck   November 14, 1931
No Hits, No Runs, One Error   December 19, 1931
Will You Please Stop That?   April 9, 1932
Man Who Made a Speech   July 9, 1932
Krazy   July 30, 1932
Blood from the Moon   November 12, 1932
They Laughed!   December 1932
Once a Sucker   January 14, 1933
Wizard   June 3, 1933
Twelfth Baronet   August 26, 1933
Clothes Make the Man   October 21, 1939

A M E R I C A N   M E R C U R Y

Nathalia from Brooklyn   September 1926
Shocking Care of Gregory Ellwood April 1930

Lulabel the Lulu   September 1933

C O L L I E R S

Noise Off-Stage   October 3, 1925

Produced Staged Plays

S H O O T   T H E   W O R K S
George M. Cohan Theatre, New York City, July 21, 1931

CONTRIBUTORS Heywood Broun, H. I. Phillips, Peter Arno, Sig Herzig, Edward J. McNamara, Michael H. Cleary, Philip Chagrig, Jay Gorney, Dorothy Fields, Ira

Gershwin, Alexander Williams, Robert Stolz, A. Robinson, Dorothy Parker, Nunnally Johnson, E. B. White, Jack Hazzard, Irving Berlin, Max Lieb, Nathaniel Lieb, E. Y. Harburg, Jimmie MacHugh, Vernon Duke, Herbert Goode, Walter Reisch. PRINCIPAL PERFORMERS Heywood Broun, William O'Neal, Johnny Boyle, George Murphy, Jack Hazzard, Edward J. McNamara, Al Gold, Percy Helton, Edgar Nilson, Julie Johnson, Imogene Coca, Frances Dewey, Margot Riley, Francis Nevins, Virginia Smith, Lee Brody, Lela Manor, Lila Manor.

(Johnson wrote some of the between-scenes dialogue for this review assembled by Heywood Broun and Milton Raison.)

DARK EYES
Belasco Theatre, New York City, January 14, 1943

PLAY Elena Miramova and Eugenie Leontovich. PRODUCER Jed Harris. CAST *Larry Field* Carl Gose. *Willoughby* Oscar Polk. *Grandmother Field* Minnie Dupree. *Pearl* Maude Russell. *Helen Field* Anne Burr. *Prince Nicolai Toradje* Geza Korvin. *Natasha Rapakovitch* Eugenie Leontovich. *Tonia Karpova* Elena Miramova. *Olga Schmilevskaya* Ludmilla Toretzka. *John Field* Jay Fassett.

(Johnson's friend, producer Jed Harris, asked Johnson to put this play, which had been written by its two stars, "into English." He received no writing credit on it.)

THE WORLD'S FULL OF GIRLS
Royal Theatre, New York City, December 6, 1943

COMEDY IN THREE ACTS Nunnally Johnson, based on the novel *Till I Come Back to You* by Thomas Bell. PRODUCED AND STAGED by Jed Harris. SETTING Stewart Chaney. CAST *Mr. Bridges* Thomas W. Ross. *Mrs. Bridges* Eva Condon. *Dave* Thomas Hume. *Hannah* Julie Stevens. *Florrie* Gloria Hallward. *Adele* Francis Heflin. *Nick* Walter Burke. *Edward* Charles Lang. *Miley* Berry Kroeger. *Sally* Virginia Gilmore. *Sergeant Synder* Harry Bellaver. *Mel Fletcher* John Conway. *Mrs. Fletcher* Cora Smith.

PARK AVENUE
Shubert Theatre, New York City, November 4, 1946.

MUSICAL COMEDY IN TWO ACTS Nunnally Johnson, George S. Kaufman. PRODUCER Max Gordon. MUSIC Arthur Schwartz. LYRICS Ira Gershwin. ORCHESTRATION Don Walker. CAST *Carton* Byron Russell. *Ned Scott* Ray McDonald. *Madge Bennett* Martha Stewart. *Ogden Bennett* Arthur Margetson. *Mrs. Sybil Bennett* Leonora Corbett. *Charles Crowell* Robert Chisholm. *Mrs. Elsa Crowell* Mata Errolle. *Reggie Fox* Charles Purcell. *Mrs. Myra Fox* Ruth Matteson. *Richard Nelson* Raymond Walburn. *Mrs. Betty Nelson* Mary Wickes. *Ted Woods* Harold Mattox. *Mrs. Laura Woods* Dorothy Bird. *James Meredith* William Skipper. *Mrs. Beverly Meredith* Joan Mann. *Mr. Meacham* David Wayne. *Freddie Coleman* Wilson Smith. *Carole Benswanger* Virginia Gordon.

HENRY, SWEET HENRY
Palace Theatre, New York City, October 23, 1967

MUSICAL based on the novel *The World of Henry Orient* by Nora Johnson. BOOK Nunnally Johnson. MUSIC AND LYRICS Bob Merrill. PRODUCERS Edward Specter Productions and Norman Twain. DIRECTOR George Roy Hill. CHOREOGRAPHY Michael Bennett. MUSICAL DIRECTION AND VOCAL ARRANGEMENTS Shephard Coleman. SCENERY AND LIGHTING Robert Randolph. COSTUMES Alvin Colt. ORCHESTRATION Eddie Sauter. DANCE MUSIC William Goldenberg, Marvin Hamlisch. PRODUCTION STAGE MANAGER William Dodds. STAGE MANAGER Henry Clark. CAST *Kafritz* Alice Playten. *Valerie Boyd* Robin Wilson. *Miss Cooney* Barbara Beck. *Marian Gilbert* Neva Small. *Henry Orient* Don Ameche. *Stella* Louise Lasser. *Mrs. Gilbert* Trudy Wallace. *Usherette* Julie Sargant. *Mrs. Boyd* Carol Bruce. *Russ* John Mineo. *Captain Kenneth* George McJames. *Hal* Robert Iscove. *Policeman* Gerard Brentte. *Mr. Boyd* Milo Boulton. *Policeman* Charles Rule. *Big Val* K. C. Townsend.

(This was a musical adaptation of the same novel Johnson had adapted into a film three years before.)

DARLING OF THE DAY
George Abbott Theatre, New York City, January 27, 1968

MUSICAL based on the novel *Buried Alive* by Arnold Bennett. MUSIC Jule Styne. LYRICS E. Y. Harburg. PRODUCER The Theatre Guild and Joel Schenker. DIRECTOR Noel Willman. CHOREOGRAPHY Lee Theodore. MUSICAL DIRECTOR AND VOCAL ARRANGEMENTS Buster Davis. SCENERY Oliver Smith. COSTUMES Paoul Pene du Bois. LIGHTING Peggy Clark. DANCE MUSIC Trude Rittman. ORCHESTRATION Ralph Burns. PRODUCTION MANAGER Phil Friedman. STAGE MANAGERS Michael Sinclair, Phil King. CAST *Oxford* Peter Woodthorpe. *Priam Farll* Vincent Price. *Henry Leek* Charles Welch. *Old Gentleman* Carl Nicholas. *Lady Vale* Brenda Forbes. *Cabby* Ross Miles. *Doctor, Judge* Leo Lyden. *Alice Challice* Patricia Routledge. *Daphne* Joy Nichols. *Alf* Teddy Green. *Bert* Marc Jordan. *Rosalind* Beth Howland. *Sidney* Reid Klein. *Attendant* Larry Brucker. *Frame Maker* Paul Eichel. *Duncan* Mitchell Jason. *Equerry, Constable* John Aman. *The King* Charles Gerald. *Mrs. Leek* Camila Ashland. *Curates* Herb Wilson, Fred Siretta. *Pennington* Michael Lewis.

(This was a musical adaptation of the same novel Johnson had adapted into the film *Holy Matrimony*. Johnson requested his name be taken off the credits.)

Filmography

ROUGH HOUSE ROSIE
Paramount, May 1927

WRITTEN BY Nunnally Johnson. TITLES George Marion, Jr. DIRECTOR Frank Streyer. CAST Clara Bow, Reed Howes, Arthur Houseman, Doris Hill, Douglas Gilmore, John Miljan, Henry Kolker.

(Although the film is based—very loosely—on a Johnson story, he had nothing to do with the writing of the film.)

FOR THE LOVE OF MIKE
First National, August 1927

WRITTEN BY John Moroso. DIRECTOR Frank Capra. CAST Ben Lyon, George Sidney, Ford Sterling, Claudette Colbert, Rudolph Cameron, Hugh Cameron, Mabel Swor, Richard Skeets Gallagher.

(Although uncredited, Johnson worked on the script for this film.)

A BEDTIME STORY
Paramount, 87 minutes, April 1933

SCREENPLAY Waldemar Young, Nunnally Johnson, adaptation by Benjamin Glazer, Waldemar Young, Nunnally Johnson, from the novel by Roy Horniman. DIRECTOR Norman Taurog. CINEMATOGRAPHY Charles Lang. MUSIC Ralph Rainger, Lee Robin. CAST *Rene* Maurice Chevalier. *Sally* Helen Twelvetrees. *Victor* Edward Everett Horton. *Paulette* Adrienne Ames. *"Monsieur"* Baby Leroy. *Max* Earle Foxe. ALSO Gertrude Michael, Ernest Wood, Reginald Mason, Henry Kolker, George MacQuarrie, Paul Panzer.

MAMA LOVES PAPA
Paramount, 70 minutes, July 1933

SCREENPLAY Nunnally Johnson, Arthur Kober, from the story by Douglas MacLean, Keene Thompson. ADDITIONAL DIALOGUE Eddie Welch. DIRECTOR Norman McLeod. CINEMATOGRAPHY Gilbert Warrenton. FILM EDITOR Richard Currier. RECORDING ENGINEER John A. Goodrich. CAST *Wilbur Todd* Charles Ruggles. *Jessie Todd* Mary Boland. *Mrs. McIntosh* Lilyan Tashman. *Mr. Kirkwood* George Barbier. *Tom Walker* Morgan Wallace. *Sara Walker* Ruth Warren. *Basil Pew* Andre Beranger. *Mr. Pierrepont* Tom Ricketts. *"The Radical"* Warner Richmond. *The Mayor* Frank Sheridan. *O'Leary* Tom McGuire.

MOULIN ROUGE
Twentieth Century Pictures, United Artists, 70 minutes, January 1934

SCREENPLAY Nunnally Johnson, Henry Lehrman. DIRECTOR Sidney Lanfield. CINEMATOGRAPHY Charles Rosher. FILM EDITOR Floyd Nesler. CAST *Helen Hall* Constance Bennett. *Douglas Hall* Franchot Tone. *Victor LeMaire* Tullio Carminati. *Mrs. Morris* Helen Westley. *McBride* Andrew Tombes. *Joe* Russ Brown. *Frenchman* Georges Renevant. *Eddie* Fuzzy Knight. *Ramon* Ivan Lebedeff. *Drunk* Hobart Cavanaugh.

THE HOUSE OF ROTHSCHILD
Twentieth Century Pictures, United Artists, 88 minutes, March 1934

SCREENPLAY Nunnally Johnson, from an unproduced play by George Hembert Westley. DIRECTOR Alfred Werker. CINEMATOGRAPHY Peverell Marley. ASSOCIATE DIRECTOR Maude Howell. MUSICAL SCORE Alfred Newman. CAST *Mayer Rothschild* and *Nathan Rothschild* George Arliss. *Ledrantz* Boris Karloff. *Julie Rothschild* Loretta Young. *Captain Fitzroy* Robert Young. *Duke of Wellington* C. Aubrey Smith. *Hannah Rothschild* Mrs. George Arliss. *Baring* Arthur Byron. *Gudula* Helen Westley. *Herries* Reginald Owen. *Metternich* Alan Mowbray. *Rowerth* Holmes Herbert. *Solomon* Paul Harvey. *Amschel* Ivan Simpson. *Carl* Noel Madison. *James* Murray Kinnell. *Talleyrand* Georges Renavant. *Prussian Officer* Oscar Apfel. *Prince Regent* Lumsden Hare.

BULLDOG DRUMMOND STRIKES BACK
Twentieth Century Pictures, United Artists, 80 minutes, May 1934

SCREENPLAY Nunnally Johnson, from a novel by H. C. McNeile. DIRECTOR Roy Del Ruth. PRODUCER Darryl F. Zanuck. ASSOCIATE PRODUCERS William Goetz, Raymond Griffith. CINEMATOGRAPHY Peverell Marley. ART DIRECTOR Richard Day. FILM EDITOR Allen McNeil. MUSIC Alfred Newman. COSTUMES Gwen Wakeling. CAST *Hugh Drummond* Ronald Colman. *Lola Field* Loretta Young. *Prince Achmed* Warner Oland. *Algy* Charles Butterworth. *Gwen* Una Merkel. *Inspector Nielson* C. Aubrey Smith. *Dr. Owen Sothern* Arthur Hoke. *Singh* George Regas. *Lola's Aunt* Ethel Griffies. *Hassan* Mischa Auer. *Parker* Douglas Gerrard.

KID MILLIONS
United Artists, 90 minutes, October 1934

SCREENPLAY Arthur Sheekman, Nat Perrin, Nunnally Johnson. DIRECTOR Roy Del Ruth. PRODUCER Samuel Goldwyn. CINEMATOGRAPHY Ray Rennahan. COLOR DIRECTION Willy Pogany. CHOREOGRAPHY Seymour Felix. SONGS Walter Donaldson, Gus Kahn, Burton Lane, Harold Adamson, Irving Berlin. CAST *Eddie Wilson Jr.* Eddie Cantor. *Dot* Ethel Merman. *Joan* Ann Sothern. *Louie* Warren Hymer. *Gerald Lane* George Murphy. *Colonel Larrabee* Berton Churchill. *Mulhulla* Paul Harvey. *Ben Ali* Jesse Block. *Tanya* Eve Sully. *Khoot* Otto Hoffman. *Toots* Doris Davenport. *Pop* Jack Kennedy. *Herman* Edgar Kennedy. *Oscar* Stanley Fields. *Adolph* John Kelly.

CARDINAL RICHELIEU
Twentieth Century Pictures, United Artists, 83 minutes, March 1935

SCREENPLAY Maude Howell, Cameron Rogers, W. P. Lipscomb, adapted from the play by Edward Bulwer-Lytton. DIRECTOR Rowland V. Lee. PRODUCERS William Goetz, Raymond Griffith. CINEMATOGRAPHY Peverell Marley. FILM EDITOR Sherman Todd. CAST *Cardinal Richelieu* George Arliss. *King Louis* Edward Arnold. *Father Joseph* Halliwell Hobbes. *Lenore* Maureen O'Sullivan. *Andre de Pons* Cesar Romero. *Baradas* Douglas Dumbrille. *Queen Marie* Violet Kimble-Cooper. *Queen Anne* Katherine Alexander. *Gaston* Francis Lister. *Fontrailles* Robert Harrigan. *Duke of Brittany*

Herbert Bunston. *Duke of Lorraine* Murray Kinnell. *Duke of Normandy* Gilbert Emery. *D'Esperron* Keith Kenneth. *DeBussey* Joseph R. Tozer. *Le Moyne* Russell Hicks.

(Johnson wrote the screenplay with Cameron Rogers but requested that his name be removed when George Arliss made changes in the script.)

BABY FACE HARRINGTON
Metro-Goldwyn-Mayer, 65 minutes, June 1935

SCREENPLAY Harry Segall, Barry Ravers, dialogue by Charles Lederer, adaptation by Nunnally Johnson, Edwin Knopf, from the play *Something to Brag About* by Edgar Selwyn, William LeBaron. DIRECTOR Raoul Walsh. PRODUCER Edgar Selwyn. CINEMATOGRAPHY Oliver T. Marsh. FILM EDITOR William S. Gray. CAST *Willie* Charles Butterworth. *Millicent* Una Merkel. *Ronald* Harvey Stephens. *Uncle Henry* Eugene Pallette. *Rocky* Nat Pendleton. *Dorothy* Ruth Selwyn. *Skinner* Donald Mack. *Edith* Dorothy Libaire. *Albert* Edward Nugent. *Judge Forbes* Richard Carle. *Hank* G. Pat Collins. *Colton* Claude Gillingwater.

THANKS A MILLION
Twentieth Century-Fox, 87 minutes, October 1935

SCREENPLAY Nunnally Johnson, from the story by Melville Crossman (Darryl F. Zanuck). DIRECTOR Roy Del Ruth. PRODUCER Darryl F. Zanuck. MUSIC AND LYRICS Gus Kahn, Arthur Johnston, Bert Kalmar, Harry Ruby. CAST *Eric Land* Dick Powell. *Ned Allen* Fred Allen. *Sally Mason* Ann Dvorak. *Phoebe Mason* Patsy Kelly. *Orchestra Leader* David Rubinoff. *Band* Paul Whiteman and his Orchestra. *Yacht Club Boys* Charles Adler, James V. Kern, Billy Mann, George Kelly. *Tammany* Benny Baker. *Governor* Charles Richman. *Mrs. Kruger* Margaret Irving. *Mr. Kruger* Alan Dinehart. *Mr. Grass* Andrew Rombes. *Judge Culliman* Raymond Walburn. *Maxwell* Paul Harvey. *Casey* Edwin Maxwell. *Mr. Bradley* Russell Hicks.

THE MAN WHO BROKE THE BANK
AT MONTE CARLO
Twentieth Century-Fox, 70 minutes, October 1935

SCREENPLAY Nunnally Johnson, Howard Ellis Smith, from the play by Ilia Surgutchoff, Frederick Swann. DIRECTOR Stephen Roberts. PRODUCER Darryl F. Zanuck. ASSOCIATE PRODUCER Nunnally Johnson. CINEMATOGRAPHY Ernest Palmer. MUSICAL DIRECTION Oscar Bradley. CAST *M. Gallard* Ronald Colman. *Helen Berkeley* Joan Bennett. *Ivan* Nigel Bruce. *Bertrand* Colin Clive. *Director* Montagu Love. *Office Man* Ferdinand Gottschalk. *Second Assistant Director* Frank Reicher. *Third Assistant Director* Lionel Pape. *Croupier* Charles Fallon. *Chief* Leonid Inegoff. *Check Room Girl* Georgette Rhodes. *Taxi Driver* Alphonse Du Bois.

THE PRISONER OF SHARK ISLAND
Twentieth Century-Fox, 95 minutes, February 1936

SCREENPLAY Nunnally Johnson. DIRECTOR John Ford. EXECUTIVE PRODUCER Darryl F. Zanuck. ASSOCIATE PRODUCER Nunnally Johnson. CINEMATOGRAPHY Bery Glennon. FILM EDITOR Jack Murray. CAST *Dr. Samuel Mudd* Warner Baxter. *Mrs. Peggy Mudd* Gloria Stuart. *Martha Mudd* Joyce Kay. *Colonel Dyer* Claude Gillingwater. *General Ewing* Douglas Wood. *Sergeant Cooper* Fred Kohler Jr. *Commandant* Harry Carey. *David Herold* Paul Fix. *Sergeant Rankin* John Carradine. *John Wilkes Booth* Francis McDonald. *Erickson* Arthur Byron. *Dr. McIntire* O. P. Heggie. *Lovett* John McGuire. *Hunter* Paul McVey. *O'Toole* Francis Ford. *Buck* Ernest Whitman. *Abraham Lincoln* Frank McGlynn Sr.

THE COUNTRY DOCTOR
Twentieth Century-Fox, 110 minutes, March 1936

SCREENPLAY Sonya Levien, based on newspaper stories by Charles E. Blake. DIRECTOR Henry King. EXECUTIVE PRODUCER Darryl F. Zanuck. PRODUCER Nunnally Johnson. CINEMATOGRAPHY John Seitz, Daniel B. Clark. FILM DIRECTOR Barbara McLean. TECHNICAL SUPERVISOR Dr. Allan Defoe. CAST *Quintuplets* The Dionne Quintuplets. *Dr. Roy Luke* Jean Hersholt. *Nurse Andrews* Dorothy Peterson. *Mary* June Lang. *Odgen* Slim Summerville. *Tony* Michael Whalen. *MacKenzie* Robert Barrat. *Mike* J. Anthony Hughes. *Asa Wyatt* John Qualen. *Greasy* George Chandler. *Sir Basil* Montagu Love. *Dr. Paul Luke* Frank Reicher. *Dr. Wilson* George Meeker. *Nurse* Jane Darwell. *Governor General* David Torrence.

THE ROAD TO GLORY
Twentieth Century-Fox, 95 minutes, June 1936

SCREENPLAY Joel Sayre, William Faulkner. DIRECTOR Howard Hawks. EXECUTIVE PRODUCER Darryl F. Zanuck. ASSOCIATE PRODUCER Nunnally Johnson. CINEMATOGRAPHY Gregg Toland. FILM EDITOR Edward Curtis. ART DIRECTION Hans Peters. SET DECORATION Thomas Little. MUSIC Louis Silvers. CAST *Michel Denet* Fredric March. *Paul LaRoche* Warner Baxter. *Papa LaRoche* Lionel Barrymore. *Monique* June Lang. *Bouffion* Gregory Ratoff. *Regnier* Victor Kilian. *Relief Captain* Paul Stanton. *Duflous* John Qualen. *Lieutenant Tannen* Julius Tannen. *Major* Theodore von Eltz. *Rigaud* Paul Fix. *Ledoux* Leonid Kinskey. *Courier* Jacques Lory. *Doctor* Jacques Vanaire. *Nurse* Edythe Raynore. *Old Soldier* George Warrington.

(The story was adapted from a French film, *Croix de Bois*, and several of the battle scenes from that picture were used in *The Road to Glory*.)

DIMPLES
Twentieth Century-Fox, 78 minutes, September 1936

SCREENPLAY Arthur Sheekman, Nat Perrin, from an idea by Nunnally Johnson. DIRECTOR William Seiter. EXECUTIVE PRODUCER Darryl F. Zanuck. ASSOCIATE PRODUCER Nunnally Johnson. CINEMATOGRAPHY Bert Glennon. FILM EDITOR Herbert Levy. SOUND Gene Grossman. ART DIRECTION William Darling. SET DECORATION Thomas Little. MUSIC AND

LYRICS Jimmy McHugh, Ted Koehler. DANCES STAGED Bill Robinson. MUSICAL DIRECTION Louis Silvers. CAST *Dimples* Shirley Temple. *Professor* Frank Morgan. *Mrs. Drew* Helen Westley. *Colonel Loring* Berton Churchill. *Allen Drew* Robert Kent. *Betty Loring* Delma Byron. *Cleo March* Astrid Allwyn. *Hawkins* Julius Tannen. *Mr. St. Clair* Paul Stanton. *Cicero* Stepin Fechit. *Rufus* Billy McClain. *Policeman* Robert Murphy. *Uncle Tom* Jack Clifford. *Topsy* Betty Jean Hainey.

B A N J O   O N   M Y   K N E E
Twentieth Century-Fox, 80 minutes, December 1936

SCREENPLAY Nunnally Johnson, from the novel by Harry Hamilton. DIRECTOR John Cromwell. EXECUTIVE PRODUCER Darryl F. Zanuck. ASSOCIATE PRODUCER Nunnally Johnson. CINEMATOGRAPHY Ernest Palmer. FILM EDITOR Hanson Fritch. SONGS Jimmy McHugh, Harold Adamson. CAST *Pearl* Barbara Stanwyck. *Ernie* Joel McCrea. *Grandma* Helen Westley. *Buddy* Buddy Ebsen. *Newt* Walter Brennan. *Leota* Katherine De Mille. *Chick Bean* Anthony Martin. *Ruby* Minnie Gombell. *Jules* George Humbert. *Warfield Scott* Walter Catlett. *Lope* Spencer Charters. *Hattie* Cecil Weston. *Eph* Louis Mason. *Gertha* Hilda Vaughn. *Slade* Victor Kilian.

N A N C Y   S T E E L E   I S   M I S S I N G
Twentieth Century-Fox, 85 minutes, March 1937

SCREENPLAY Hal Long, Gene Fowler, from the short story "Ransom" by Charles Francis Coe. DIRECTOR George Marshall. EXECUTIVE PRODUCER Darryl F. Zanuck. ASSOCIATE PRODUCER Nunnally Johnson. CINEMATOGRAPHY Edward Cronjager. FILM EDITOR Jack Murray. CAST *Dannie O'Neill* Victor McLaglen. *Michael Steele* Walter Connolly. *Sheila O'Neill* June Lang. *Jimmy Wilson* Robert Kent. *Professor Sturm* Peter Lorre. *Dan Mallon* Frank Conroy. *Wilkins* John Carradine. *Doctor on Farm* DeWitt Jennings. *Nancy* Shirley Deane. *Crowder* George Taylor. *Miss Hunt* Margaret Fielding. *Mrs. Flaherty* Jane Darwell. *Mr. Flaherty* Granville Bates. *Giuseppi* George Humbert.

C A F E   M E T R O P O L E
Twentieth Century-Fox, 84 minutes, April 1937

SCREENPLAY Jacques Deval. STORY Gregory Ratoff. DIRECTOR Edward Griffith. PRODUCER Nunnally Johnson. EXECUTIVE PRODUCER Darryl F. Zanuck. CINEMATOGRAPHY Lucien Andriot. FILM EDITOR Irene Morra. MUSICAL DIRECTION Louis Silvers. CAST *Laura Ridgeway* Loretta Young. *Alexis* Tyrone Power. *Victor* Adolphe Menjou. *Paul* Gregory Ratoff. *Ridgeway* Charles Winninger. *Margaret* Helen Westley. *Leroy* Christian Rub. *Monnett* Ferdinand Gottschalk. *Maitre d'Hotel* Georges Renavant. *Artist* Leonid Kinskey. *Thorndyke* Hal K. Dawson.

S L A V E   S H I P
Twentieth Century-Fox, 92 minutes, August 1937

SCREENPLAY Sam Hellman, Lamar Trotti, Gladys Lehman, William Faulkner. STORY William Faulkner, from the novel *The Last Slaver* by Dr. George S. King. DIRECTOR Tay Garnett. EXECUTIVE PRODUCER Darryl F. Zanuck. ASSOCIATE PRODUCER Nunnally Johnson. CINEMATOGRAPHY Ernest Palmer. FILM EDITOR Lloyd Nosler. MUSIC Alfred

Newman. SOUND Al Bruzlin. ART DIRECTION Hans Peters. CAST *Jim Lovett* Warner Baxter. *Jack Thompson* Wallace Beery. *Nancy Marlowe* Elizabeth Allen. *Swifty* Mickey Rooney. *Lefty* George Sanders. *Mrs. Marlowe* Jane Darwell. *Danilo* Joseph Schildkraut. *Grimes* Arthur Hohl. *Mabel* Minna Gombell. *Atkins* Billy Bevan. *Scraps* Francis Ford. *Proprietor* J. Farrell MacDonald.

L O V E   U N D E R   F I R E
Twentieth Century-Fox, 75 minutes, August 1937

SCREENPLAY Gene Fowler, Allen Rivkin, Ernest Pascal, from the play *The Fugitives* by Walter Hackett. DIRECTOR George Marshall. PRODUCER Nunnally Johnson. EXECUTIVE PRODUCER Darryl F. Zanuck. CINEMATOGRAPHY Ernest Palmer. FILM EDITOR Barbara McLean. MUSICAL DIRECTION Arthur Lange. CAST *Tracy Egan* Don Ameche. *Myra Cooper* Loretta Young. *Pamela Beaumont* Frances Drake. *Tip Conway* Walter Catlett. *Delmar* John Carradine. *Borrah Minevitch and Gang* Themselves. *General Montero* Sig Rumann. *Lieutenant Chaves* Harold Huber. *Rosa* Katherine De-Mille. *Captain Bowden* E. E. Clive. *Cabana* Don Alvarado. *Bert* Clyde Cook. *DeVega* George Regas. *Porter* George Humbert.

J E S S E   J A M E S
Twentieth Century-Fox, 105 minutes, January 1939

SCREENPLAY Nunnally Johnson. DIRECTOR Henry King. EXECUTIVE PRODUCER Darryl F. Zanuck. ASSOCIATE PRODUCER Nunnally Johnson. CINEMATOGRAPHY George Barnes. TECHNICOLOR CAMERAMAN W. H. Green. FILM EDITOR Barbara McLean. MUSIC Louis Silvers. CAST *Jesse James* Tyrone Power. *Frank James* Henry Fonda. *Zee* Nancy Kelly. *Will Wright* Randolph Scott. *Major Cobb* Henry Hull. *Jailer* Slim Summerville. *Runyon* J. Edward Bromberg. *Barshee* Brian Donlevy. *Bob Ford* John Carradine. *McCoy* Donald Meek. *Jesse James, Jr.* John Russell. *Mrs. Samuels* Jane Darwell. *Charles Ford* Charles Tannen. *Mrs. Ford* Claire DuBrey. *Clark* Willard Robertson. *Lynch* Paul Sutton. *Pinky* Ernest Whitman. *Bill* Paul Burns. *Preacher* Spencer Charters. *Tom* Arthur Aylsworth. *Heywood* Charles Halton. *Roy* George Chandler. *Old Marshall* Erville Alderson.

W I F E ,   H U S B A N D   A N D   F R I E N D
Twentieth Century-Fox, 80 minutes, March 1939

SCREENPLAY Nunnally Johnson, from the novel *Career in C Major* by James M. Cain. DIRECTOR Gregory Ratoff. EXECUTIVE PRODUCER Darryl F. Zanuck. ASSOCIATE PRODUCER Nunnally Johnson. CINEMATOGRAPHY Ernest Palmer. FILM EDITOR Walter Thompson. ART DIRECTION Richard Day, Mark Lee Kirk. SET DECORATION Thomas Little. MUSICAL DIRECTION David Buttolph. MUSIC AND LYRICS Samuel Pokrass, Walter Bullock, Armando Hauser. CAST *Doris* Loretta Young. *Leonard* Warner Baxter. *Cecil Carver* Binnie Barnes. *Hugo* Cesar Romero. *Major Blair* George Barbier. *Rossi* J. Edward Bromberg. *Mike Craig* Eugene Pallette. *Carol* Ruth Terry. *Wilkins* Harry Rosenthal. *Mrs. Craig* Renie Riano. *Hertz* Lawrence Grant. *Jaffee* Charles Williams.

(Johnson remade the same story ten years later as *Everybody Does It*.)

R O S E   O F   W A S H I N G T O N   S Q U A R E
Twentieth Century-Fox, 80 minutes, May 1939

SCREENPLAY Nunnally Johnson, from an unpublished story by John Larkin and Jerry Horwin. DIRECTOR Gregory Ratoff. EXECUTIVE PRODUCER Darryl F. Zanuck. ASSOCIATE PRODUCER Nunnally Johnson. CINEMATOGRAPHY Karl Freund. FILM EDITOR Louis Loeffler. MUSIC Louis Silvers. CAST *Bart Clinton* Tyrone Power. *Rose* Alice Faye. *Ted Cotter* Al Jolson. *Harry Long* William Frawley. *Peggy* Joyce Compton. *Whitey Brown* Hobart Cavanaugh. *Russell* Moroni Olson. *Barouche Driver* E. E. Clive. *Louis Prima* himself. *Cavanaugh* Charles Wilson. *Chumps* Hal K. Dawson, Paul Burns. *Toby* Ben Weldon. *Irving* Horace MacMahon. *District Attorney* Paul Stanton. *Dexter* Harry Hayden. *Kress* Charles Lane. *Specialty Act* Igor and Tanya.

T H E   G R A P E S   O F   W R A T H
Twentieth Century-Fox, 129 minutes, January 1940

SCREENPLAY Nunnally Johnson, from the novel by John Steinbeck. DIRECTOR John Ford. EXECUTIVE PRODUCER Darryl F. Zanuck. ASSOCIATE PRODUCER Nunnally Johnson. CINEMATOGRAPHY Gregg Toland. FILM EDITOR Robert Simpson. SOUND George Leverett, Roger Heman. MUSIC Alfred Newman. ART DIRECTION Richard Day, Mark Lee Kirk. SET DECORATION Thomas Little. CAST *Tom Joad* Henry Fonda. *Ma Joad* Jane Darwell. *Casy* John Carradine. *Grandpa* Charley Grapewin. *Rosasharn* Dorris Bowdon. *Pa Joad* Russell Simpson. *Al* O. Z. Whitehead. *Muley* John Qualen. *Connie* Eddie Quillan. *Grandma* Zeffie Tilbury. *Noah* Frank Sully. *Uncle John* Frank Darien. *Winfield* Darryl Hickman. *Ruth Joad* Shirley Mills. *Thomas* Roger Imhof. *Caretaker* Grant Mitchell. *Wilkie* Charles D. Brown. *Davis* John Arledge. *Policeman* Ward Bond. *Bert* Harry Tyler. *Mae* Kitty McHugh. *Bill* William Pawley. *Joe* Charles Tannen. *Lloyd* Paul Guilfoyle. *Frank* David Hughes. *City Man* Cliff Clark. *Bookkeeper* Joseph Sawyer. *Tim* Frank Faylen. *Truck Driver* Irving Bacon. *Muley's Wife* Mae Marsh.

I   W A S   A N   A D V E N T U R E S S
Twentieth Century-Fox, 81 minutes, May 1940

SCREENPLAY Karl Tunberg, Don Ettlinger, John O'Hara, based on an original production by Gregor Rabinovitsch, written by Jacques Companeeg, Herbert Juttle, Hans Jacoby, Michael Duran. DIRECTOR Gregory Ratoff. ASSOCIATE PRODUCER Nunnally Johnson. CINEMATOGRAPHY Leon Shamroy, Edward Cronjager. FILM EDITOR Francis D. Lyon. SOUND W. D. Flick, Roger Heman. ART DIRECTION Richard Day, Joseph C. Wright. SET DECORATION Thomas Little. MUSIC DIRECTION David Buttolph. DANCES George Balanchine. CAST *Countess Tanya Vronsky* Vera Zorina. *Paul Vernay* Richard Greene. *Andre Desormeany* Erich Von Stroheim. *Polo* Peter Lorre. *Herr Protz* Sig Rumann. *Henry Gautier* Fritz Feld. *Aunt Cecile* Cora Witherspoon. *Cousin Emil* Anthony Kemble Cooper. *Fisherman* Paul Procasi. *Fisherman's Wife* Inez Palange. *Jacques Dubois* Egon Brecher. *Heinrich Von Kongen* Roger Imhof. *Orchestra Leader* Fortunio Bonanova.

CHAD HANNA
Twentieth Century-Fox, 86 minutes, December 1940

SCREENPLAY Nunnally Johnson, from the novel by Walter D. Edmonds. DIRECTOR Henry King. PRODUCER Nunnally Johnson. EXECUTIVE PRODUCER Darryl F. Zanuck. CINEMATOGRAPHY Ernest Palmer, Ray Rennahan. FILM EDITOR Barbara McLean. ART DIRECTION Richard Day. SOUND Arthur Von Kirbach, Roger Heman. MUSIC David Buttolph. CAST *Chad Hanna* Henry Fonda. *Albany Yates* Dorothy Lamour. *Caroline* Linda Darnell. *Huguenine* Guy Kibee. *Mrs. Huguenine* Jane Darwell. *Bisbee* John Carradine. *Fred Sheptey* Ted North. *Ike Wayfish* Roscoe Ates. *Bell Boy* Ben Carter. *Burke* Frank Thomas. *Ciscoe Tridd* Olin Howard. *Mr. Proudfoot* Frank Conlan. *Fiero* Edward Conrad. *Elias* Edward McWade. *Pete Bastock* George Davis. *Budlong* Paul Burns. *Mrs. Tridd* Sarah Padden. *Mr. Mott* Tully Marshall. *Joe Duddy* Edward Mundy. *Mr. Pamplon* Leonard St. Leo. *Mrs. Pamplon* Elizabeth Abbott. *Mrs. Mott* Almira Sessions.

TOBACCO ROAD
Twentieth Century-Fox, 84 minutes, February 1941

SCREENPLAY Nunnally Johnson, from the play *Tobacco Road* by Jack Kirkland, based on the novel by Erskine Caldwell. DIRECTOR John Ford. PRODUCER Darryl F. Zanuck. CINEMATOGRAPHY Arthur Miller. FILM EDITOR Barbara McLean. ART DIRECTION Richard Day, James Basevi. SET DECORATION Thomas Little. SOUND Eugene Grossman, Roger Heman. MUSICAL DIRECTION David Buttolph. CAST *Jeeter Lester* Charley Grapewin. *Sister Bessie* Marjorie Rambeau. *Ellie May* Gene Tierney. *Dude Lester* William Tracy. *Ada Lester* Elizabeth Patterson. *Captain Tim* Dana Andrews. *Peabody* Slim Summerville. *Lov* Ward Bond. *George Payne* Grant Mitchell. *Grandma* Zeffie Tilbury. *Chief of Police* Russell Simpson. *County Clerk* Spencer Charters. *Teller* Irving Bacon. *Auto Dealer* Harry Tyler. *Major* Charles Halton. *Clerk* George Chandler.

ROXIE HART
Twentieth Century-Fox, 75 minutes, February 1942

SCREENPLAY Nunnally Johnson, based on the play *Chicago* by Maurine Watkins. DIRECTOR William Wellman. PRODUCER Nunnally Johnson. CINEMATOGRAPHY Leon Shamroy. FILM EDITOR James B. Clark. ART DIRECTION Richard Day, Wiard B. Ihnen. SET DECORATION Thomas Little. MUSIC Alfred Newman. DANCES STAGED BY Hermes Pan. SOUND Alfred Bruzlin, Roger Heman. CAST *Roxie Hart* Ginger Rogers. *Billy Flynn* Adolphe Menjou. *Homer Howard* George Montgomery. *Jake Callahan* Lynn Overman. *E. Clay Benham* Nigel Bruce. *Babe* Phil Silvers. *Mrs. Morton* Sarah Allgood. *O'Malley* William Frawley. *Mary Sunshine* Spring Byington. *Stuart Chapman* Ted North. *Velma Wall* Helen Reynolds. *Amos Hart* George Chandler. *Charles E. Murdock* Charles D. Brown. *Martin S. Harrison* Morris Ankrum. *Judge* George Lessey. *Gertie* Iris Adrian. *Announcer* Milton Parsons.

MOONTIDE
Twentieth Century-Fox, 94 minutes, April 1942

SCREENPLAY John O'Hara, from the novel by Willard Robertson. DIRECTOR Archie Mayo. PRODUCER Mark Hellinger. EXECUTIVE PRODUCER Darryl F. Zanuck. CINEMATOGRAPHY Lucien Ballard, Charles G. Clarke. FILM EDITOR William Reynolds. ART DIRECTION James Basevi, Richard Day. SET DECORATION Thomas Little. SOUND Eugene Grossman, Roger Heman. MUSIC Cyril Mockridge, David Buttolph. CAST *Bobo* Jean Gabin. *Anna* Ida Lupino. *Tiny* Thomas Mitchell. *Nusty* Claude Rains. *Dr. Brothers* Jerome Cowan. *Woman on Boat* Helen Reynolds. *Reverend Price* Ralph Byrd. *Bartender* William Halligan. *Takeo* Sen Yung. *Hirota* Chester Gan. *Mildred* Robin Raymond. *Pop Kelly* Arthur Aylsworth.

(Johnson did the final draft of the screenplay but received no screen credit.)

THE PIED PIPER
Twentieth Century-Fox, 88 minutes, August 1942

SCREENPLAY Nunnally Johnson, from the novel by Nevil Shute. DIRECTOR Irving Pichel. PRODUCER Nunnally Johnson. EXECUTIVE PRODUCER Darryl F. Zanuck. CINEMATOGRAPHY Edward Cronjager. FILM EDITOR Allen McNeil. ART DIRECTION Richard Day, Maurice Ransford. SET DECORATION Thomas Little. MUSIC Alfred Newman. CAST *Howard* Monty Woolley. *Ronnie* Roddy McDowall. *Nicole* Ann Baxter. *Major Diessen* Otto Preminger. *Aristide* J. Carrol Nash. *Mr. Cavanaugh* Lester Matthews. *Mrs. Cavanaugh* Jill Esmond. *Madame* Ferike Boros. *Sheila* Peggy Ann Garner. *Willem* Merrill Rodin. *Pierre* Maurice Tauzin. *Rose* Fleurett Zama. *Frenchman* William Edmunds. *Foquet* Marcel Dalio. *Mme. Bonne* Marcelle Corday. *Mme. Rougeron* Odette Myrtil.

LIFE BEGINS AT EIGHT-THIRTY
Twentieth Century-Fox, 85 minutes, December 1942

SCREENPLAY Nunnally Johnson, from the play *The Light of Heart* by Emlyn Williams. DIRECTOR Irving Pichel. PRODUCER Nunnally Johnson. EXECUTIVE PRODUCER William Goetz. CINEMATOGRAPHY Edward Cronjager. FILM EDITOR Fred Allen. ART DIRECTION Richard Day, Boris Leven. SET DECORATION Thomas Little, Al Orenbach. SOUND George Leverett, Roger Heman. CAST *Madden Thomas* Monty Woolley. *Kathi Thomas* Ida Lupino. *Robert* Cornell Wilde. *Mrs. Lothian* Sara Allgood. *Barty* Melville Cooper. *Gordon* J. Edward Bromberg. *Officer* William Demarest. *Producer* Hal K. Dawson. *Sergeant McNamara* William Halligan. *Announcer* Milton Parsons. *Mrs. Spano* Inez Palange. *Mr. Spano* Charles LaTorre. *Ruthie* Fay Helm. *Floorwalker* Wheaton Chambers. *Policeman* James Flavin. *Cab Driver* Bud Geary.

THE MOON IS DOWN
Twentieth Century-Fox, 90 minutes, May 1943

SCREENPLAY Nunnally Johnson, from the novel by John Steinbeck. DIRECTOR Irving Pichel. PRODUCER Nunnally Johnson. EXECUTIVE PRODUCER William Goetz. CINEMA-

TOGRAPHY Arthur Miller. FILM EDITOR Louis Loeffler. ART DIRECTION James Basevi, Maurice Ransford. SET DECORATION Thomas Little, Walter M. Scott. SPECIAL PHOTO-GRAPHIC EFFECTS Fred Sersen. MUSIC Alfred Newman. SOUND Eugene Grossman, Roger Heman. CAST *Colonel Lanser* Sir Cedric Hardwicke. *Mayor Orden* Henry Travers. *Dr. Winter* Lee J. Cobb. *Molly Morden* Dorris Bowdon. *Madame Orden* Margaret Wycherly. *Lieutenant Tender* Peter Van Eyck. *Alex Morden* William Post. *Captain Loft* Henry Rowland. *George Corell* E. J. Ballantine. *Peder's Wife* Violette Wilson. *Captain Bentick* Hans Schumm. *Major Hunter* Ernest Dorian. *Lieutenant Prackle* John Banner. *Annie* Helene Himig. *Joseph* Ian Wolfe. *Orderly* Kurt Kreuger. *Albert* Jeff Corey. *Schumann* Louis Arco. *Ole* Charles McGraw. *Foreman* Trevor Bardette. *Mother* Dorothy Peterson.

HOLY MATRIMONY
Twentieth Century-Fox, 87 minutes, August 1943

SCREENPLAY Nunnally Johnson, from the novel *Buried Alive* by Arnold Bennett. DIRECTOR John Stahl. PRODUCER Nunnally Johnson. EXECUTIVE PRODUCER William Goetz. CINEMATOGRAPHY Lucien Ballard. FILM EDITOR James B. Clark. ART DIRECTION James Basevi, Russell Spencer. SET DECORATION Thomas Little, Paul S. Fox. MUSIC Cyril J. Mockridge. SOUND E. Clayton Ward, Roger Heman. CAST *Priam Farll* Monty Woolley. *Alice Challice* Gracie Fields. *Clive Oxford* Laird Cregar. *Mrs. Leek* Una O'Connor. *Mr. Pennington* Alan Mowbray. *Dr. Caswell* Melville Cooper. *Duncan Farll* Franklin Pangborn. *Lady Vale* Ethel Griffies. *Henry Leek* Eric Blore. *Mr. Crepitude* George Zucco. *Critics* Fritz Feld, William Austin. *Judge* Montagu Love. *John Leek* Richard Fraser. *Harry Leek* Whitner Bissell.

CASANOVA BROWN
RKO-Radio, 94 minutes, August 1944

SCREENPLAY Nunnally Johnson, from the play *The Little Accident* by Thomas Mitchell and Floyd Dell, based on the novel *Bachelor Father* by Floyd Dell. DIRECTOR Sam Wood. PRODUCER Nunnally Johnson. CINEMATOGRAPHY John Seitz. FILM EDITOR Paul Weatherwax. ART DIRECTION Perry Ferguson. SET DECORATION Julia Heron. MUSIC Arthur Lange. SOUND Ben Winkler. CAST *Casanova Q. Brown* Gary Cooper. *Isabel Drury* Teresa Wright. *Mr. Ferris* Frank Morgan. *Madge Ferris* Anita Louise. *Mrs. Drury* Patricia Collinge. *Mr. Drury* Edmund Breon. *Dr. Zerneke* Jill Esmond. *Monica* Mary Treen. *Mrs. Ferris* Isobel Elsom. *Butler* Halliwell Hobbes.

WOMAN IN THE WINDOW
RKO-Radio, 99 minutes, October 1944

SCREENPLAY Nunnally Johnson, from the novel *Once Off Guard* by J. H. Wallis. DIRECTOR Fritz Lang. PRODUCER Nunnally Johnson. CINEMATOGRAPHY Milton Krasner. FILM EDITORS Gene Fowler, Jr., Marjorie Fowler. ART DIRECTOR Duncan Cramer. SET DECORATION Julia Heron. CAST *Richard Wanley* Edward G. Robinson. *Alice Reed* Joan Bennett. *Frank Lalor* Raymond Massey. *Dr. Barkstane* Edmund Breon. *Heidt* Dan Duryea. *Inspector Jackson* Thomas E. Jackson. *Mazard* Arthur Loft. *Mrs.*

Wanley Dorothy Peterson. *Steward* Frank Dawson. *Elsie* Carol Cameron. *Dickie* Bobby Blake.

THE KEYS OF THE KINGDOM
Twentieth Century-Fox, 137 minutes, December 1944

SCREENPLAY Joseph L. Mankiewicz, Nunnally Johnson, from the novel by A. J. Cronin. DIRECTOR John M. Stahl. PRODUCER Joseph L. Mankiewicz. CINEMATOGRAPHY Arthur Miller. FILM EDITOR James B. Clark. ART DIRECTION James Basevi, William Darling. SET DECORATION Thomas Little, Frank E. Hughes. SPECIAL PHOTOGRAPHIC EFFECTS Fred Sersen. SOUND Eugene Grossman, Roger Heman. CAST *Father Francis Chisholm* Gregory Peck. *Dr. Willie Tulloch* Thomas Mitchell. *Rev. Angus Mealy* Vincent Price. *Mother Maria Veronica* Rosa Stander. *Francis* (as a child) Roddy McDowall. *Rev. Hamish MacNabb* Edmund Gwenn. *Monseignor Sleeth* Sir Cedric Hardwicke. *Nora* (as a child) Peggy Ann Garner. *Nora* Jane Ball. *Dr. Wilbur Fiske* James Gleason. *Agnes Fiske* Anne Revere. *Lisbeth Chisholm* Ruth Nelson. *Joseph* Benson Fong. *Mr. Chia* Leonard Strong. *Mr. Pao* Philip Ahn. *Father Tarrant* Arthur Shields. *Aunt Polly* Edith Barrett. *Sister Martha* Sara Allgood. *Lieutenant Shon* Richard Loo. *Sister Clotilde* Ruth Ford. *Father Craig* Kevin O'Shea.

(Johnson completed a first-draft screenplay in 1943 before leaving Fox. After he left, the project was taken up and considerably rewritten by Joseph Mankiewicz.)

ALONG CAME JONES
RKO-Radio, 90 minutes, June 1945

SCREENPLAY Nunnally Johnson, from the story "Useless Cowboy" by Alan LeMay. DIRECTOR Stuart Heisler. PRODUCER Gary Cooper. EXECUTIVE PRODUCER William Goetz. CINEMATOGRAPHY Milton Krasner. CAST *Melody Jones* Gary Cooper. *Cherrie* Loretta Young. *George Fury* William Demarest. *Monte Jarrad* Dan Duryea. *Avery de Longpre* Frank Sully. *Ira Waggoner* Walter Sande. *Leo Gledhill* Don Costello. *Luke Packard* William Robertson. *Pop de Longpre* Russell Simpson. *Sheriff* Arthur Loft. *Boone* Lane Chandler. *Kriendler* Ray Teal.

THE SOUTHERNER
United Artists, 91 minutes, August 1945

SCREENPLAY Jean Renoir and Hugo Butler, based on the novel *Hold Autumn in Your Hand* by George Perry Sessions. DIRECTOR Jean Renoir. PRODUCER David L. Loew, Robert Hakim. CINEMATOGRAPHY Lucien Andriot. MUSIC Werner Jansen. FILM EDITOR Gregg Tallas. CAST *Sam* Zachary Scott. *Nona* Betty Field. *Granny* Beulah Bondi. *Daisy* Bunny Sunshine. *Joe* Jay Gilpin. *Harmie* Percy Kilbride. *Ma* Blanche Yurka. *Tim* Charles Kemper. *Revers* J. Carrol Nash. *Finlay* Norman Lloyd. *Doctor* Jack Norworth. *Bartender* Nestor Paiva. *Lizzie* Estelle Taylor.

(Although he did not receive screen credit, Johnson wrote the first draft of the screenplay with Renoir, basing it on Hugo Butler's adaptation of the novel. William Faulkner subsequently worked on the screenplay, also without credit.)

THE DARK MIRROR
Universal-International, 85 minutes, October 1946

SCREENPLAY Nunnally Johnson, based on a story by Vladimir Pozner. DIRECTOR Robert Siodmak. PRODUCER Nunnally Johnson. CINEMATOGRAPHY Milton Krasner. FILM EDITOR Ernest Nims. SPECIAL PHOTOGRAPHIC EFFECTS J. Devereaux Jennings, Paul Lerpas. PRODUCTION DESIGN Duncan Cramer. COSTUME DESIGN Irene Sharaff. SOUND Fred Lau, Arthur Johns. SET DECORATION Hugh Hunt. DIALOGUE DIRECTOR Phyllis Loughton. MUSIC Dmitri Tiomkin. CAST *Terry Collins/Ruth Collins* Olivia de Havilland. *Dr. Scott Elliott* Lew Ayres. *Detective Stevenson* Thomas Mitchell. *Rusty* Richard Long. *District Attorney Girard* Charles Evans. *Franklin* Gary Owen. *George Benson* Lester Allen. *Mrs. Didrickson* Lela Bliss. *Miss Beade* Martha Mitrovich. *Photo-double* Amelita Ward.

THE SENATOR WAS INDISCREET
Universal-International, 81 minutes, December 1947

SCREENPLAY Charles MacArthur, from the story by Edwin Lanham. DIRECTOR George S. Kaufman. PRODUCER Nunnally Johnson. ASSOCIATE PRODUCER Gene Fowler, Jr. CINEMATOGRAPHY William Mellor. FILM EDITOR Sherman A. Rose. ART DIRECTION Bernard Herzbrun, Boris Leven. SET DECORATION Russell A. Gausman. SOUND Leslie I. Carey. MUSIC Daniele Amfitheatrof. CAST *Senator Melvin G. Ashton* William Powell. *Poppy McNaughton* Ella Raines. *Lew Gibson* Peter Lind Hayes. *Valerie Shepherd* Arleen Whelan. *Houlihan* Ray Collins. *Farrell* Allen Jenkins. *Dinty* Charles D. Brown. *Waiter* Hans Conried. *Oakes* Whit Bissell. *Woman at Banquet* Norma Varden. *"You Know Who"* Milton Parsons. *Frank* Francis Pierlot. *Helen* Cynthia Corley. *Indians* Oliver Blake, Chief Thunder Cloud, Chief Yowlachie, Iron Eyes Cody. *Politicos* Boyd Davis, Rodney Bell.

MR. PEABODY AND THE MERMAID
Universal-International, 89 minutes, August 1948

SCREENPLAY Nunnally Johnson, from the novel *Peabody's Mermaid* by Guy Jones and Constance Jones. DIRECTOR Irving Pichel. PRODUCER Nunnally Johnson. ASSOCIATE PRODUCER Gene Fowler, Jr. CINEMATOGRAPHY Russell Metty. FILM EDITOR Marjorie Fowler. UNDERWATER CINEMATOGRAPHY David S. Horlsey. ART DIRECTION Bernard Herzbrun, Boris Leven. SET DECORATION Russell A. Gausman, Rubey R. Levitt. SOUND Leslie Carey, Corson Jowett. MUSIC Robert Emmett Dolan. CAST *Mr. Peabody* William Powell. *Mermaid* Ann Blyth. *Mrs. Peabody* Irene Hervey. *Cathy Livingston* Andrea King. *Mike Fitzgerald* Clinton Sundberg. *Dr. Harvey* Art Smith. *Major Hadley* Hugh French. *Colonel Mandrake* Lumsden Hare. *Basil* Frederick N. Clark. *Lieutenant* James Logan. *Wee Shop Clerk* Mary Field. *Mother* Beatrice Roberts. *Nurse* Cynthia Corley. *Waiter* Tom Stevenson. *Lady Trebshaw* Mary Somerville. *Waiter* Richard Ryan. *Boy* Bobby Hyatt. *Sidney* Ivan H. Browning.

EVERYBODY DOES IT
Twentieth Century-Fox, 98 minutes, October 1949

SCREENPLAY Nunnally Johnson, from the novel *Career in C Major* by James M. Cain. DIRECTOR Edmund Goulding. PRODUCER Nunnally Johnson. CINEMATOGRAPHY Joseph LaShelle. FILM EDITOR Robert Fritch. ART DIRECTION Lyle Wheeler, Richard Irvine. SET DECORATION Thomas Little, Paul S. Fox. SOUND Eugene Grossman, Roger Heman. MUSICAL DIRECTION Alfred Newman. MUSIC AND ITALIAN LYRICS Mario Castelnuovo-Tedesco. CAST *Leonard Borland* Paul Douglas. *Cecil Carver* Linda Darnell. *Doris Borland* Celeste Holm. *Major Blair* Charles Coburn. *Mike Craig* Millard Mitchell. *Mrs. Blair* Lucille Watson. *Wilkins* John Hoyt. *Rossi* George Tobias. *Hugo* Leon Belasco. *Make-up Man* Tito Vuclo. *Carol* Geraldine Wall. *Mrs. Craig* Ruth Gillette. *Chamberlain* Gilbert Russell. *Grand Priest* John Ford. *Housekeeper* Mae Marsh.

(This film was a remake of Johnson's 1939 *Wife, Husband and Friend*.)

THREE CAME HOME
Twentieth Century-Fox, 106 minutes, February 1950

SCREENPLAY Nunnally Johnson, from the book by Agnes Keith. DIRECTOR Jane Negulesco. PRODUCER Nunnally Johnson. EXECUTIVE PRODUCER Darryl F. Zanuck. CINEMATOGRAPHY Milton Krasner. FILM EDITOR Dorothy Spencer. MUSIC Hugo Friedhofer. MUSICAL DIRECTION Lionel Newman. ART DIRECTION Lyle Wheeler, Leland Fuller. SET DECORATION Thomas Little, Fred J. Rode. SOUND Clayton Ward, Roger Heman. CAST *Agnes Keith* Claudette Colbert. *Harry Keith* Patric Knowles. *Betty Sommers* Florence Desmond. *Colonel Suga* Sessue Hayakawa. *Henrietta* Sylvia Andrew. *Sister Rose* Phyllis Morris. *George* Mark Keuning. *Lt. Nekata* Howard Chuman. *Woman Prisoners* Drue Mallory, Carol Savage, Virginia Keiley, Mimi Heyworth, Helen Westcott.

THE GUNFIGHTER
Twentieth Century-Fox, 84 minutes, July 1950

SCREENPLAY William Bowers, William Sellers. STORY William Bowers and Andre de Toth. DIRECTOR Henry King. PRODUCER Nunnally Johnson. CINEMATOGRAPHY Arthur Miller. FILM EDITOR Barbara McLean. ART DIRECTION Lyle Wheeler, Walter M. Scott. MUSIC Alfred Newman. SOUND Alfred Bruzlin, Roger Heman. CAST *Jimmy Ringo* Gregory Peck. *Peggy Walsh* Helen Westcott. *Sheriff Mark Strett* Millard Mitchell. *Molly* Jean Parker. *Mac* Karl Malden. *Hunt Bromley* Skip Homeier. *Charlie* Anthony Ross. *Mrs. Pennyfeather* Verna Felton. *Mrs. Devlin* Ellen Corby. *Eddie* Richard Jaeckel. *First Brother* Alan Hale, Jr. *Second Brother* David Clark. *Third Brother* John Pickard. *Jimmie* B. G. Norman. *Mac's Wife* Angela Clarke. *Jerry Marlowe* Cliff Clark. *Alice Marlowe* Jean Inness. *Archie* Eddie Ehrhart. *Pablo* Albert Morin. *Swede* Kenneth Tobey. *Johnny* Michael Brandon. *Barber* Eddie Parkes.

(Johnson did the final rewrite on this film.)

THE MUDLARK
Twentieth Century-Fox, 99 minutes, December 1950

SCREENPLAY Nunnally Johnson, from the novel by Theodore Bonnet. DIRECTOR Jean Negulesco. PRODUCER Nunnally Johnson. CINEMATOGRAPHY Georges Perinal. FILM EDITOR Thelma Myers. ART DIRECTION C. P. Norman. MUSIC William Alwyn. SPECIAL EFFECTS W. Percy Day. CAST *Queen Victoria* Irene Dunne. *Disraeli* Alec Guinness. *Wheeler* Andrew Ray. *Lady Emily Prior* Beatrice Campbell. *John Brown* Finlay Currie. *Lt. Charles McHatten* Anthony Steele. *Sgt. Footman Naseby* Raymond Lovell. *Lady Margaret Prior* Marjorie Field. *Kate Noonan* Constance Smith. *Slattery* Ronan O'Casey. *The Watchman* Edward Rigby. *Herbert* Robin Stevens. *Sparrow* William Strange. *General Sir Henry Ponsonby* Kynaston Reeves. *Tucker* Wilfred Hyde White. *Hammond* Ernest Clark. *Assistant Lt. of Police* Eric Messiter. *Princess Christian* Pamela Arliss.

THE LONG DARK HALL
Eagle Lion Classics-United Artists, 86 minutes, May 1951

SCREENPLAY Nunnally Johnson. ADDITIONAL SCENES AND DIALOGUE W. E. C. Fairchild, from the novel *A Case to Answer* by Edgar Lustgarden. DIRECTORS Anthony Bushell, Reginald Beck. PRODUCER Peter Cusick. CINEMATOGRAPHY Wilkie Cooper. FILM EDITOR Tom Simpson. ART DIRECTION George Patterson. MUSIC Benjamin Frankel. CAST *Arthur Groome* Rex Harrison. *Mary Groome* Lilli Palmer. *Sheila Groome* Tania Heald. *Rosemary Groome* Henrietta Barry. *Mary's Mother* Dora Sevening. *Mary's Father* Ronald Simpson. *Chief Inspector Sullivan* Raymond Huntley. *Sgt. Cochran* William Squires. *Supt. Maxey* Ballard Berkeley. *The Man* Anthony Dawson. *Sir Charles Morton* Denis O'Dea. *Clive Belford* Anthony Bushell. *Judge* Henry Longhurst. *Rose Mallory* Patricia Wayne. *Mrs. Rogers* Brenda De Banzie.

(Johnson wrote this script while at Universal, and the script was subsequently sold to Huntington Hartford, who produced the film in England.)

THE DESERT FOX
Twentieth Century-Fox, 88 minutes, October 1951

SCREENPLAY Nunnally Johnson, from the book by Desmond Young. DIRECTOR Henry Hathaway. PRODUCER Nunnally Johnson. CINEMATOGRAPHY Norbert Brodine. FILM EDITOR James B. Clark. ART DIRECTION Lyle Wheeler, Maurice Ransford. SET DECORATION Thomas Little, Stuart Reiss. SOUND Eugene Grossman, Roger Heman. SPECIAL EFFECTS Fred Sersen, Ray Kellogg. MUSIC Daniele Amfitheatrof. CAST *Erwin Rommel* James Mason. *Dr. Karl Strolin* Cedric Hardwicke. *Frau Rommel* Jessica Tandy. *Hitler* Luther Adler. *General Burgdorf* Everett Sloane. *Field Marshall von Rundstadt* Leo G. Carroll. *General Fritz Bayerlein* George Macready. *Aldinger* Richard Boone. *Col. Von Stauffenberg* Eduard Franz. *Desmond Young* Himself. *Manfred Rommel* William Reynolds. *General Schultz* Charles Evans. *Admiral Ruge* Walter Kingsford. *Keitel* John Hoyt. *General Maisel* Don de Leo.

PHONE CALL FROM A STRANGER
Twentieth Century-Fox, 96 minutes, February 1952

SCREENPLAY Nunnally Johnson, from the story by I. A. R. Wylie. DIRECTOR Jean Negulesco. PRODUCER Nunnally Johnson. CINEMATOGRAPHY Milton Krasner. FILM EDITOR Hugh Fowler. ART DIRECTION Lyle Wheeler, J. Russell Spencer. SET DECORATION Thomas Little, Bruce MacDonald. MUSIC Franz Waxman. SOUND Eugene Grossman, Roger Heman. SPECIAL EFFECTS Ray Kellogg. CAST *Binky Gay* Shelley Winters. *David Trask* Gary Merrill. *Dr. Fortness* Michael Rennie. *Eddie Hoke* Keenan Wynn. *Sally Carr* Evelyn Varden. *Marty Nelson* Warren Stevens. *Mrs. Fortness* Beatrice Straight. *Jerry Fortness* Ted Donaldson. *Mike Carr* Craig Stevens. *Jane Trask* Helen Westcott. *Marie Hoke* Bette Davis. *Stewardess* Sydney Perkins. *Dr. Brooks* Hugh Beaumont. *Mr. Sawyer* Thomas Jackson. *Dr. Fletcher* Harry Cheshire. *Dr. Fernwood* Tom Powers. *Thompson* Freeman Lusk. *Doctor* George Eldredge. *Headwaiter* Nestor Paiva. *Mrs. Brooks* Perdita Chandler.

WE'RE NOT MARRIED
Twentieth Century-Fox, 85 minutes, July 1952

SCREENPLAY Nunnally Johnson, from the story "If I Could Remarry" by Gina Kaus and Jay Dratler. ADAPTATION Dwight Taylor. DIRECTOR Edmund Goulding. PRODUCER Nunnally Johnson. CINEMATOGRAPHY Leo Tover. FILM EDITOR Louis Loeffler. SPECIAL MONTAGE William Cameron Menzies. ART DIRECTION Lyle Wheeler, Leland Fuller. SET DECORATION Thomas Little, Claude Carpenter. MUSIC Cyril Mockridge. SOUND W. D. Flick, Roger Heman. CAST *Ramona* Ginger Rogers. *Steve Gladwyn* Fred Allen. *Justice of the Peace* Victor Moore. *Annabel Norris* Marilyn Monroe. *Jeff Norris* David Wayne. *Katie Woodruff* Eve Arden. *Hector Woodruff* Paul Douglas. *Willie Fisher* Eddie Bracken. *Patsy Fisher* Mitzi Gaynor. *Frederic Melrose* Louis Calhern. *Eve Melrose* Zsa Zsa Gabor. *Duffy* James Gleason. *Attorney Stone* Paul Stewart. *Mrs. Bush* Jane Darwell. *Detective Magnus* Alan Bridge. *Radio Announcer* Harry Golder. *Governor Bush* Victor Sutherland. *Attorney General* Tom Powers.

O'HENRY'S FULL HOUSE
Twentieth Century-Fox, 117 minutes ("The Ransom of Red Chief" episode, 26 minutes), October 1952

DIRECTOR Howard Hawks. PRODUCER Andre Hakim. CINEMATOGRAPHY Milton Krasner. CAST *Sam* Fred Allen. *Bill* Oscar Levant. *J.B.* Lee Aaker. *Mr. Dorset* Irving Bacon. *Mrs. Dorset* Kathleen Freeman. *Ellie Mae* Gloria Gordon. *Storekeeper* Alfred Mizer. *Yokels* Robert Easton, Robert Cherry, Norman Leavitt.

(Johnson wrote the screenplay for "The Ransom of Red Chief" episode. He was so distressed at the changes made by Hawks in both the dialogue and the overall tone that he requested his name be taken off the credits.)

MY COUSIN RACHEL
Twentieth Century-Fox, 98 minutes, December 1952

SCREENPLAY Nunnally Johnson, from the novel by Daphne du Maurier. DIRECTOR Henry Koster. PRODUCER Nunnally Johnson. CINEMATOGRAPHY Joseph LaShelle. FILM EDITOR Louis Loeffler. ART DIRECTION Lyle Wheeler, John de Cuir. SET DECORATION Walter M. Scott. MUSIC Franz Waxman. SOUND Alfred Bruzlin, Roger Heman. SPECIAL PHOTOGRAPHIC EFFECTS Ray Kellogg. CAST *Rachel* Olivia de Havilland. *Philip Ashley* Richard Burton. *Louise* Audrey Dalton. *Nick Kendall* Ronald Squire. *Rainaldi* George Dolenz. *Ambrose Ashley* John Sutton. *Seecombe* Tudor Owen. *Reverend Pascoe* J. M. Kerrigan. *Mrs. Pascoe* Margaret Brewster. *Mary Pascoe* Alma Lawton. *Pascoe Daughters* Ola Lorraine, Kathleen Mason. *Signora* Argentina Brunetti. *Caretaker* Mario Siletti. *Tamblyn* Lumsden Hare. *Lewin* Trevor Ward. *Philip—Age 10* Nicholas Koster. *Philip—Age 15* Robin Camp. *Foreman* Victor Wood.

HOW TO MARRY A MILLIONAIRE
Twentieth Century-Fox, 95 minutes, November 1953

SCREENPLAY Nunnally Johnson, based on the play *The Greeks had a Word for It* by Zoë Akins, and the play *Loco* by Dale Eunson, Katherine Albert. DIRECTOR Jean Negulesco. PRODUCER Nunnally Johnson. CINEMATOGRAPHY Joe MacDonald. FILM EDITOR Louis Loeffler. ART DIRECTION Lyle Wheeler, Leland Fuller. MUSICAL DIRECTION Alfred Newman. INCIDENTAL MUSIC Cyril Mockridge. SOUND Alfred Bruzlin, Roger Heman. CAST *Loco* Betty Grable. *Pola* Marilyn Monroe. *Schatze Page* Lauren Bacall. *Freddie Denmark* David Wayne. *Eben* Rory Calhoun. *Tom Brookman* Cameron Mitchell. *J. Stewart Merrill* Alex D'Arcy. *Waldo Brewster* Fred Clark. *J. D. Hanley* William Powell. *Mr. Otis* Tudor Owen. *Man at Bridge* Emmett Vogan. *Model* Charlotte Austin.

NIGHT PEOPLE
Twentieth Century-Fox, 93 minutes, March 1954

SCREENPLAY Nunnally Johnson, from a story by Jed Harris, Thomas Reed. DIRECTOR Nunnally Johnson. PRODUCER Nunnally Johnson. CINEMATOGRAPHY Charles G. Clarke. FILM EDITOR Dorothy Spencer. ART DIRECTION Hanns Kuhnert, Theo Zwierski. MUSIC Cyril Mockridge. MUSICAL DIRECTION Alfred Newman. SOUND Hans Wunschel, Roger Heman. CAST *Van Dyke* Gregory Peck. *Leatherby* Broderick Crawford. *Hoffy* Anita Bjork. *Miss Cates* Rita Gam. *Foster* Walter Abel. *Sgt. McColloch* Buddy Ebsen. *Frederick S. Hobart* Casey Adams. *Frau Schindler* Jill Esmond. *Petrechine* Peter Van Eyck. *Kathy* Marianne Koch. *Johnny* Ted Avery. *Burns* Hugh McDermott. *Whitby* Paul Carpenter. *Stanways* John Horsley. *Lakeland* Lionel Murton.

BLACK WIDOW
Twentieth Century-Fox, 95 minutes, November 1954

SCREENPLAY Nunnally Johnson, from a novel by Patrick Quentin. DIRECTOR Nunnally Johnson. PRODUCER Nunnally Johnson. CINEMATOGRAPHY Charles G. Clarke. FILM EDI-

TOR Dorothy Spencer. ART DIRECTION Lyle Wheeler, Maurice Ransford. MUSIC Leigh Harline. SOUND Eugene Grossman, Roger Heman. CAST *Lottie* Ginger Rogers. *Peter* Van Heflin. *Iris* Gene Tierney. *Detective Brown* George Raft. *Nanny Ordway* Peggy Ann Garner. *Brian* Reginald Gardiner. *Claire Amberly* Virginia Leith. *Ling* Otto Kruger. *Lucia* Cathleen Nesbitt. *John* Skip Homeier.

H O W   T O   B E   V E R Y ,   V E R Y   P O P U L A R
Twentieth Century-Fox, 93 minutes, July 1955

SCREENPLAY Nunnally Johnson, from the novel *She Loves Me Not* by Edward Hope, and the play by Howard Lindsay, and the play *Sleep It Off* by Lyford Moore and Harlan Thompson. DIRECTOR Nunnally Johnson. PRODUCER Nunnally Johnson. CINEMATOGRAPHY Milton Krasner. FILM EDITOR Louis Loeffler. ART DIRECTION Lyle Wheeler, John De Cuir. SET DECORATION Walter M. Scott, Chester Bayhi. MUSIC Cyril J. Mockridge. SOUND E. Clayton Ward, Harry M. Leonard. CAST *Stormy* Betty Grable. *Curly* Sheree North. *Wedgewood* Bob Cummings. *Tweed* Charles Coburn. *Eddie* Tommy Noonan. *Toby* Orson Bean. *Mr. Marshall* Fred Clark. *Midge* Charlotte Austin. *Miss Syl* Alice Pearce. *Flagg* Rhys Williams. *Moon* Andrew Tombes. *Cherry Blossom Wang* Noel Toy. *Chief of Police* Emory Parnell.

T H E   M A N   I N   T H E   G R A Y   F L A N N E L   S U I T
Twentieth Century-Fox, 153 minutes, April 1956

SCREENPLAY Nunnally Johnson, from the novel by Sloan Wilson. DIRECTOR Nunnally Johnson. PRODUCER Darryl F. Zanuck. CINEMATOGRAPHY Charles G. Clarke. FILM EDITOR Dorothy Spencer. ART DIRECTION Lyle R. Wheeler, Jack Martin Smith. SET DECORATION Walter M. Scott, Stuart A. Reiss. MUSIC Bernard Herrmann. SOUND Alfred Bruzlin, Harry Leonard. CAST *Tom Rath* Gregory Peck. *Betsy* Jennifer Jones. *Hopkins* Fredric March. *Maria* Marisa Pavan. *Judge Bernstein* Lee J. Cobb. *Mrs. Hopkins* Ann Harding. *Caesar Gardella* Keenan Wynn. *Hawthorne* Gene Lockhart. *Susan Hopkins* Gigi Perreau. *Janie* Portland Mason. *Walker* Arthur O'Connell. *Bill Ogden* Henry Daniell. *Mrs. Manter* Connie Gilchrist. *Edward Schultz* Joseph Sweeney. *Barbara* Sandy Discher. *Pete* Mickey Maga. *Mahoney* Kenneth Tobey. *Florence* Ruth Clifford. *Miriam* Geraldine Wall. *Johnson* Alex Campbell. *Freddie* Jerry Hall.

O H   M E N !   O H   W O M E N !
Twentieth Century-Fox, 90 minutes, February 1957

SCREENPLAY Nunnally Johnson, from the play by Edward Chodorov, as produced on the stage by Cheryl Crawford. DIRECTOR Nunnally Johnson. PRODUCER Nunnally Johnson. CINEMATOGRAPHY Charles G. Clarke. FILM EDITOR Marjorie Fowler. ART DIRECTION Lyle Wheeler, Maurice Ransford. SET DECORATION Walter M. Scott, Stuart A. Reiss. MUSIC Cyril Mockridge. SOUND Alfred Bruzlin, Harold Root. CAST *Arthur Turner* Dan Dailey. *Mildred Turner* Ginger Rogers. *Dr. Alan Coles* David Niven. *Myra Hagerman* Barbara Rush. *Cobbler* Tony Randall. *Mrs. Day* Natalie Schafer. *Miss Tacher* Rachel Stephens. *Dr. Krauss* John Wengraf.

(Although the writing credits for the film are listed above, in fact they did not appear in the film. Because Chodorov had been blacklisted, his name was not allowed to appear on the screen. Johnson had his own name removed from the writing credits in protest.)

THE TRUE STORY OF JESSE JAMES

Twentieth Century-Fox, 93 minutes, March 1957

SCREENPLAY Walter Newman, based on a screenplay by Nunnally Johnson. DIRECTOR Nicholas Ray. PRODUCER Herbert B. Swope, Jr. CINEMATOGRAPHY Joe MacDonald. FILM EDITOR Robert Simpson. ART DIRECTION Lyle R. Wheeler, Addison Hehr. SET DECORATION Walter M. Scott, Stuart A. Reiss. MUSIC Leigh Harline. SOUND Eugene Grossman, Harry M. Leonard. CAST *Jesse James* Robert Wagner. *Frank James* Jeffrey Hunter. *Zee* Hope Lange. *Mrs. Samuels* Agnes Moorehead. *Cole Younger* Alan Hale. *Remington* Alan Baxter. *Rev. Jethro Bailey* John Carradine. *Ann* Rachel Stephens. *Dr. Samuels* Barney Phillips. *Jim Younger* Biff Elliot. *Major Cobb* Frank Overton. *Attorney Walker* Barry Atwater. *Rowena Cobb* Marion Seldes. *Askew* Chubby Johnson. *Charley* Frank Gorshin. *Robby* Carl Thayler. *Hollstron* John Doucette.

(Nominally, this was a remake of Johnson's screenplay for the 1939 film, but in fact it bears no resemblance to it.)

THE THREE FACES OF EVE

Twentieth Century-Fox, 95 minutes, September 1957

SCREENPLAY Nunnally Johnson, from the book by Corbett H. Thigpen, M.D., and Hervey M. Cleckley, M.D. DIRECTOR Nunnally Johnson. PRODUCER Nunnally Johnson. CINEMATOGRAPHY Stanley Cortez. FILM EDITOR Marjorie Fowler. ART DIRECTION Lyle Wheeler, Herman A. Blumenthal. SET DECORATION Walter M. Scott, Eli Benneche. MUSIC Robert Emmett Dolan. SOUND W. D. Flick, Frank Moran. NARRATION Alistair Cooke. CAST *Eve* Joanne Woodward. *Ralph White* David Wayne. *Dr. Luther* Lee J. Cobb. *Dr. Day* Edwin Jerome. *Secretary* Alena Murray. *Mrs. Black* Nancy Kulp. *Mr. Black* Douglas Spencer. *Bonnie* Terry Ann Ross. *Earl* Ken Scott. *Eve—Age 8* Mimi Gibson.

THE MAN WHO UNDERSTOOD WOMEN

Twentieth Century-Fox, 105 minutes, December 1959

SCREENPLAY Nunnally Johnson, from the novel *The Colors of the Day* by Romain Gary. DIRECTOR Nunnally Johnson. PRODUCER Nunnally Johnson. CINEMATOGRAPHY Milton Krasner. FILM EDITOR Marjorie Fowler. ART DIRECTION Lyle Wheeler, Maurice Ransford. SET DECORATION Walter M. Scott, Paul S. Fox. SOUND Charles Peck, Harry M. Leonard. MUSIC Robert Emmett Dolan. CAST *Willie Bauché* Henry Fonda. *Ann Garantier* Leslie Caron. *Marco Raniere* Cesare Danova. *Preacher* Myron McCormick. *LeMarne* Marcel Dalio. *G.K.* Conrad Nagel. *Baron* Edwin Jerome. *Kress* Harry Ellerbe. *Milstead* Frank Cady. *Soprano* Bern Roffman. *French Doctor* Ben Astar.

THE ANGEL WORE RED
Metro-Goldwyn-Mayer, 99 minutes, September 1960

SCREENPLAY Nunnally Johnson, from the novel *The Fair Bride* by Bruce Marshall. DIRECTOR Nunnally Johnson. PRODUCER Goffredo Lombardo for Titanus-Spectator Productions. CINEMATOGRAPHY Guiseppe Rotunno. FILM EDITOR Louis Loeffler. ART DIRECTION Pier Filippone. MUSIC Bronislau Kaper. CAST *Soledad* Ava Gardner. *Arturo Carrera* Dirk Bogarde. *Hawthorne* Joseph Cotten. *General Clave* Vittorio DeSica. *Cannon Rota* Aldo Fabrizi. *Insurgent Major* Arnoldo Foa. *The Bishop* Finlay Currie. *Mercedes* Rossana Rory. *Captain Botargas* Enrico Maria Salerno. *Father Idlefonso* Robert Bright. *Jose* Franco Castellani. *Mac* Bob Cunningham. *Major Garcia* Gustavo DeNardo. *Captain Trinidad* Nino Gastelneuvo.

FLAMING STAR
Twentieth Century-Fox, 92 minutes, December 1960

SCREENPLAY Clair Huffaker, Nunnally Johnson, from the novel by Clair Huffaker. DIRECTOR Don Siegel. PRODUCER David Weisbart. CINEMATOGRAPHY Charles G. Clarke. FILM EDITOR Hugh S. Fowler. ART DIRECTION Duncan Cramer, Walter M. Simonds. SET DECORATION Walter M. Scott, Gustav Bernsten. MUSIC Cyril Mockridge. SOUND E. Clayton Ward, Warren B. Delaplain. TECHNICAL ADVISOR Colonel Tom Parker. CAST *Pacer* Elvis Presley. *Clint* Steve Forrest. *Roslyn Pierce* Barbara Eden. *Neddy Burton* Delores Del Rio. *Pa Burton* John McIntire. *Buffalo Horn* Rudolph Acosta. *Dred Pierce* Karl Swenson. *Doc Phillips* Ford Rainey. *Angus Pierce* Richard Jaeckel. *Dorothy Howard* Ann Benton. *Tom Howard* L. Q. Jones. *Will Howard* Douglas Dick. *Jute* Tom Reese. *Ph'sha Knay* Marian Goldina. *Ben Ford* Monte Burkhart. *Hornsby* Ted Jacques. *Indian Brave* Rodd Redwing. *Two Moons* Perry Lopez.

(Johnson completed his draft of the script in 1958; it remained unproduced for two years.)

MR. HOBBS TAKES A VACATION
Twentieth Century-Fox, 116 minutes, July 1962

SCREENPLAY Nunnally Johnson, from the novel *Mr. Hobbs' Vacation* by Edward Streeter. DIRECTOR Henry Koster. PRODUCER Jerry Wald ASSOCIATE PRODUCER Marvin Gluck. CINEMATOGRAPHY William C. Mellor. FILM EDITOR Marjorie Fowler. ART DIRECTION Jack Martin Smith, Malcolm Brown. SET DECORATION Walter M. Scott, Stuart A. Reiss. MUSIC Henry Mancini. SOUND Alfred Bruzlin, Warren Delaplain. CAST *Mr. Hobbs* James Stewart. *Peggy* Maureen O'Hara. *Joe* Fabian. *Byron* John Saxon. *Mrs. Turner* Marie Wilson. *Reggie McHugh* Reginald Gardiner. *Katey* Lauri Peters. *Marika* Valerie Varda. *Janie* Lili Gentle. *Mr. Turner* John McGiver. *Susan* Natalie Trundy. *Stan* Josh Peine. *Brenda* Minerva Urecal. *Danny Hobbs* Michael Burns. *Plumber* Richard Collier.

TAKE HER, SHE'S MINE
Twentieth Century-Fox, 98 minutes, November 1963

SCREENPLAY Nunnally Johnson, from the play by Phoebe and Henry Ephron. DIRECTOR Henry Koster. PRODUCER Henry Koster. CINEMATOGRAPHY Lucien Ballard. FILM EDITOR Marjorie Fowler. ART DIRECTION Jack Martin Smith, Malcolm Brown. SET DECORATION Walter M. Scott, Stuart Reiss. SOUND W. D. Flick, Elmer R. Raguse. MUSIC Jerry Goldsmith. CAST *Frank Michaelson* James Stewart. *Mollie* Sandra Dee. *Anne* Audrey Meadows. *Pope-Jones* Robert Morley. *Henri* Philippe Forquet. *Mr. Ivor* John McGiver. *Alex* Robert Denver. *Linda* Monica Moran. *Adele* Cynthia Pepper. *Sarah* Jenny Maxwell. *M. Bonnet* Maurice Marsac. *Miss Wu* Irene Tsu. *Liz* Charla Doberty. *Policeman* Marcel Hillaire. *Stanley Bowdry* Charles Robinson.

THE WORLD OF HENRY ORIENT
United Artists, 106 minutes, May 1964

SCREENPLAY Nora Johnson, Nunnally Johnson, from the novel by Nora Johnson. DIRECTOR George Roy Hill. PRODUCER Jerome Hellman. CINEMATOGRAPHY Boris Kaufman, Arthur J. Ornitz. FILM EDITOR Stuart Gilmore. MUSIC Elmer Bernstein. CAST *Henry Orient* Peter Sellers. *Stella* Paula Prentiss. *Isabel Boyd* Angela Lansbury. *Frank Boyd* Tom Bosley. *Mrs. Gilbert* Phyllis Thaxter. *Valerie Boyd* Tippy Walker. *Marian "Gil" Gilbert* Merrie Spaeth. *Boothy* Bibi Osterwald. *Joe Byrd* Peter Duchin. *Sidney* John Fiedler. *Store Owner* Al Lewis. *Doctor* Fred Lewis. *Emma* Philippa Bevans. *Kafritz* Jane Buchanan.

DEAR BRIGITTE
Twentieth Century-Fox, 100 minutes, February 1965

SCREENPLAY Hal Kanter, from the novel *Erasmus with Freckles* by John Haase. DIRECTOR Henry Koster. PRODUCER Henry Koster. CINEMATOGRAPHY Lucien Ballard. FILM EDITOR Marjorie Fowler. ART DIRECTION Jack Martin Smith, Malcolm Brown. SET DECORATION Walter M. Scott, Steve Potter. MUSIC George Dunning. SOUND Alfred Bruzlin, Elmer Raguse. CAST *Professor Leaf* James Stewart. *Kenneth* Fabian. *Vina* Glynis Johns. *Pandora* Cindy Carol. *Erasmus* Billy Mumy. *Upjohn* John Williams. *Dr. Voker* Jack Kruschen. *The Captain* Ed Wynn. *George* Charles Robinson. *Dean Sawyer* Howard Frieman. *Terry* Jane Wald. *Brigitte Bardot* Herself.

(Johnson wrote the screenplay for the film, and Hal Kanter was brought on the project to write the final sequences and some revisions. Johnson asked to have his name taken off the credits.)

THE DIRTY DOZEN
Metro-Goldwyn-Mayer, 150 minutes, June 1967

SCREENPLAY Nunnally Johnson, Lukas Heller, from the novel by E. M. Nathanson. DIRECTOR Robert Aldrich. PRODUCER Kenneth Hyman. CINEMATOGRAPHY Edward Scaife. FILM EDITOR Michael Luciano. ART DIRECTION W. E. Hutchinson. SPECIAL EFFECTS Cliff

Richardson. MUSIC Frank de Vol. CAST *Major Reisman* Lee Marvin. *General Worden* Ernest Borgnine. *Joseph Wladislau* Charles Bronson. *Robert Jefferson* Jim Brown. *Victor Franko* John Cassavetes. *Sgt. Bowren* Richard Jaeckel. *Major Armbruster* George Kennedy. *Pedro Jiminez* Trini Lopez. *Capt. Stuart Kinder* Ralph Meeker. *Col. Dasher-Breed* Robert Ryan. *Archer Maggott* Telly Savalas. *Vernon Pinkley* Donald Sutherland. *Samson Posey* Clint Walker. *General Denton* Robert Webber. *Milo Vladek* Tom Busby. *Glenn Gilpin* Ben Carruthers. *Roscoe Lever* Stuart Cooper. *Corp. Morgan* Robert Phillips. *Seth Sawyer* Colin Maitland. *Tassos Bravos* Al Mancini. *Pvt. Gardner* George Ronbrick.

A NOTE ON THE TYPE

The text of this book was set on the Linotype in
Janson, a recutting made direct from type cast from
matrices long thought to have been made by the
Dutchman Anton Janson, who was a practicing type
founder in Leipzig during the years 1668–87. However, it has been conclusively demonstrated that these
types are actually the work of Nicholas Kis (1650–
1702), a Hungarian, who most probably learned his
trade from the master Dutch type founder Dirk
Voskens. The type is an excellent example of the
influential and sturdy Dutch types that prevailed in
England up to the time William Caslon developed his
own incomparable designs from them.

This book was composed by The Maryland Linotype
Composition Company, Inc., Baltimore, Maryland. It
was printed and bound by American Book–Stratford
Press, Inc., Saddle Brook, New Jersey.

Design by Judith Henry